*To Liliane, with love*

*John Haden*

# Oh Uganda

may God uphold thee

by

# John Haden
and
# John Ondoma

First published by Barny Books 2012
Reprinted with amendments 2012

All rights reserved
Copyright © John Haden and John Ondoma 2012

No part of this publication may be reproduced or transmitted in any way or by any means, including electonic storage and retrieval, without the prior permission of the publisher.

Scripture taken from the HOLY BIBLE, NEW INTERNATIONAL VERSION® NIV®. Copyright© 1973, 1978, 1984, 2011 by Biblica, Inc.TM. Used by permission of Biblica, Inc.TM. All rights reserved worldwide. "NIV" and "New International Vesion" are trademarks registered in the United States Patent and Trademark Office by Biblica, Inc.™

ISBN No: 978.1.906542.46.7

Publishers:  Barny Books, Hough on the Hill,
Grantham, Lincolnshire NG32 2BB

Tel: 01400 250246

Copies of this book may be purchased from the publishers at: www.barnybooks.biz/

Cover photograph: Rev. Lusania Kasamba and the Committee of the Mvara Senior Secondary School SU Group 1970

For

Ned, Hugh, Blake, Iris
and Letasi Esther

and

The Ushindi Schools,
Arua, Uganda

# Contents

**Foreword**  6
by the Bishop of Madi and West Nile

**Introduction**  8

**Part 1. Into West Nile**
    1.1 Going to Arua   12
    1.2 From Independence to 1968   21
    1.3 John Ondoma's story   37

**Part 2. Mission and School**
    2.1 Mvara   40
    2.2 Science and Uniforms   62
    2.3 Christmas and Easter   78

**Part 3. Living and Working in Arua**
    3.1 Impenetrable Hides   108
    3.2 Mountains and Moving to the Left   118
    3.3 Starting a 6$^{th}$ Form   132
    3.4 Rusting spears   151

**Part 4. Surviving Idi Amin**
    4.1 Things fall apart   165
    4.2 Picking up the pieces   184
    4.3 Amin's tyranny   203

**Part 5. Enduring Obote II and the coming of the NRM**
    5.1 Living with trouble in West Nile   214
    5.2 Taking over Mvara – again   233
    5.3 Uganda Link   248

**Part 6. God does not make blunders**
    6.1 Going back to West Nile   274
    6.2 May God uphold thee   300

Notes and Acknowledgements   311

**Foreword by the Rt. Rev Dr. Joel Obetia, Bishop of Madi and West Nile Diocese, Church of Uganda**

It is my joy to introduce to you the book of John Ondoma and John Haden. "Oh Uganda may God uphold thee" is the first line of the first stanza of the Uganda National anthem. The Anthem is a powerful prayer in itself and so is this book that sees God at work through the ups and downs of life of individuals, the nation and peoples.

I have known John Ondoma for the last 30 years and heard of John Haden before as a Teacher in Mvara and recently met him in my office in Mvara. My spirit was knit with his as I saw a passion for the Lord and his ministry in him. The two Johns have combined to take us on a journey to discover the faithfulness of God amidst the challenges of nation building, personal search for fulfillment and growth. This book mixes the work of God in two lives from two different countries: Uganda and England where the common denominator is God; God the Father who is Father of all peoples, His Son Jesus Christ the Saviour of all and the Holy Spirit the counselor to all.

The four decades from 1960s to 1990s were decades of cascading changes in Uganda and Africa at large. There were great expectations but also great anxieties and sufferings as a result of these changes. Our two friends John Ondoma and John Haden take us through these very expectations, anxieties and sufferings that God in his wisdom allowed to happen to prove that he is the God of all history and life and is faithful even when things turn our lives upside down. The Ondomas are true witnesses and testify to this assertively.

Indeed God never fails even when all things fail. As you read, I pray you will find the thin line of God's faithfulness that weaves through their lives' experiences and expectations holding everything together to present them, not perfect but whole.

May you walk that line too!

Joel Samson Obetia (PhD)

**Introduction**

The Republic of Uganda was born at midnight on Monday October 8th, 1962. The Duke of Kent, on behalf of Her Majesty the Queen, received the colours of the 4th Battalion, King's African Rifles and presented the same soldiers with their new colours as the Uganda Rifles. As the RAF flew past, traditional dancers performed and the Union Jack was lowered. Prime Minister Dr Milton Obote stood in the spotlight as the new Uganda flag was raised. The band played the new National Anthem and the people sang:

> Oh, Uganda! may God uphold thee,
> We lay our future in thy hand;
> United, free, for liberty,
> Together we'll always stand.

On October 9th 2012, His Exellency Yoweri Kaguta Museveni, President of Uganda, will stand and take the salute for the celebrations of Uganda's fiftieth anniversary. He will have been in power in Uganda for twenty-six years, just over half of the history of the country. In the twenty-four years that preceded Museveni's coming to power, Uganda saw more conflict, bloodshed and turmoil than at any other time in its history. Many African states went through a violent and bloody fight for independence. Uganda was spared this but few other countries have had such suffering after becoming a new nation.

The fiftieth anniversary is a good time to look back and take stock. We have tried to tell the story of those fifty years through two voices, one a *muzungu*, as Europeans are called in Uganda, and the second a Ugandan. For the *muzungu*, Uganda was first my home and then, when Jenny and I got married, our home. It was the place which gave us our best and worst times, rich experiences which we shared and the place to which we have returned many times since. For the Ugandan, this is the story of living through those fifty years, of finding faith and serving God as a teacher and a Headteacher, of finding a wife and establishing a family. It is also the story of suffering when sickness struck, of facing misunderstanding and violence and of making a new start.

The part of Uganda which we know best is in the extreme north-west, bordering both the Congo and the Sudan, a land separated from the rest of the country by the Albert Nile. For a time, the region was called West Nile District. Even before Idi Amin seized power in Uganda, this district was a place to be feared by most Ugandans. It was relatively poor and under-developed, populated by tall Sudanic and Nilotic peoples. If you came from the south of Uganda, you simply did not go to West Nile unless you had to. Before Uganda's independence, the Bantu kingdoms of Buganda and Bunyoro had centuries of sophisticated history. For much of this time, West Nile as an entity did not even exist. It was carved by the Colonial powers out of the homelands of five tribal groups, at first as part of the Belgian Congo, then in the Sudan and finally added to Uganda.

West Nile will always be associated with the name of Idi Amin, the nation's second president, whose murderous eight years in power resulted in the deaths of perhaps three hundred thousand Ugandans. West Nile was his home and West Nile has been blamed for much of what he did. Some places just have a bad name: the killing fields of Cambodia, Nanking, Auschwitz. Each carries terrible memories of human suffering. In Uganda, West Nile shares that infamy. To add to the horror, a new disease was found in the United States, West Nile Fever, caused by a virus first identified in West Nile in the 1930s. It came into the USA in 1999 and, within ten years, was carried by birds and mosquitoes across the North American continent. It became known as 'death from the Nile'. Like SARS, Bird 'Flu and other mysterious harbingers of death, West Nile fever and West Nile itself were to be feared.

One of us comes from West Nile and still lives there. The other chose to go to West Nile to join both a Christian Mission community and a government secondary school. We both know the people of the area to be amongst the friendliest and most welcoming of any you may meet anywhere. We have both struggled with the challenges of teaching students whose parents spoke no English and lived in grassed roofed mud huts. We have both tried to lead schools as Headteachers, to build them up to A level standard and to ensure high standards of teaching and learning. For a time, we were both the 'loyal servants' of Idi Amin. Then, for the *muzungu,* tensions within our school tore it apart, with a student strike and violent incidents for which the school itself became infamous. We chose to stay long enough to help to pick up the pieces and start all over again. Others then decided that we should leave West Nile and serve as teachers in Kampala until it was time to go home, leaving Uganda in the hands of a murderous dictator.

It is also the story of how, together, we started to build a link between one school in West Nile and one in England. That link broke down when jealousy and suspicion nearly destroyed the Ondomas. But the story ends in hope for the future, as John Ondoma found a new role and founded new schools, the Ushindi (Victory in Christ) Schools, Arua. We tell of how these schools now provide a high quality education within a Christian ethos for this most remote corner of Uganda.

We have each had to learn to forgive and start again when disaster strikes, how there can be a victory over adversity and how we can support the young people of Uganda as we leave their future in God's hand. From memories and diaries, published writings, letters, emails and many conversations, we have tried to piece together the story of this part of Uganda, its Christian Church and its schools, as our contribution to the celebration of Uganda's first fifty years.

| | |
|---|---|
| John Haden | John Ondoma |
| Oakham, England | Arua, Uganda |

October 2012

Map 1. Uganda in 1962 – roads, towns and places to visit

## Part 1: Into West Nile
## 1.1 Going to Arua

The East African Airways[1] VC10 was full of expensive British expertise. We were all on generous contracts which enhanced our salaries from the 'local' level, to be paid to us in Uganda or Kenya, to the UK level by an ODM allowance[2] paid from Britain. Old hands, cool in their well-worn tropical cotton, returning from leave to some secluded suburb of Entebbe or Nairobi, crammed in with new recruits like me, already sweating in English summer clothes. Harassed mothers vainly struggled to subdue their bored and noisy children while their babies screamed their fury at being confined to the 'sky-cots' swinging above our heads. I knew that somewhere on this flight were two other recruits for Mvara Secondary School, a Northern Irish couple who also had links with the Africa Inland Mission[3] but it was not until the first transit stop that I had a chance to identify them.

We spent four hours of bored wandering at Rome in the vast glass ostentation of the new Leonardo de Vinci Airport in the middle of the night. The shops were closed and the lavatories locked. We were told that the plane had 'engine trouble', so we waited while the children and the uninhibited did what they had to do among the potted plants of the transit hall. Trying to find a couple with Irish accents from overheard conversations proved not too difficult and I met up with Gordon and Grace McCullough and exchanged a few sentences before we were all herded back on the 'plane for what was left of the night.

We crossed the Libyan Desert with the flares of oil rigs flickering in the dying darkness and watched the grey east blush into dawn. The sand and even the sky itself was ablaze with all the explosive energy of an African day. Sand-dunes gave way to semi-desert and the burnt hills of the Southern Sudan as we followed the shining ribbon of the Nile south through the swamps to the Uganda border. We found a gap in the heavy thunder-clouds that veil the shores of Lake Victoria and came in low over flocks of egrets startled out of the dark green trees. White painted stones spelled out 'ENTEBBE' as the gentle lisping tones of our Ugandan stewardess purred a welcome to her home.

'Radies and gentlemen, welcome to Uganda. We hope that you have enjoyed your fright with East Africa Airways and look forward to meeting you again when you next fry with us.'

The airport buildings, when I arrived in Entebbe that wet August morning in 1968, were small, gloomy and full of lake-flies. Clouds of them drifted in through open doors of the customs hall, built when the Dakota was the largest thing that flew. Our luggage was set out on the floor, rows of labelled cases, push-chairs and crates. We had, it seemed, to find our belongings and stand behind them ready for 'customs clearance'. A young and very miserable customs officer wandered along the rows looking at the labels. He came to my old and battered case, stopped and cheered up immediately.

'Sir,' he beamed, shaking my hand as if it were a rattle. 'You are going to Mvara?'

'Yes, I am.'

'Then you are going to the school where I studied for my Cambridge. I must take you to the Headmaster.'

Somewhat to my embarrassment at this sudden preferential treatment, with a flourish of grey chalk, he accepted me and almost all my worldly goods into Uganda, duty free. Grasping my case in one hand and my hand in the other, he charged out of the crowd of increasingly angry expatriates. We paused briefly at Immigration for my passport to be stamped. 'He is my brother' confided my escort as we burst into the waiting area just ahead of a posse of porters all hoping to pick up my case should it be dropped along the way.

The front row of the reception party consisted of African officials from the various Ministries, well-dressed young men determined to welcome their new recruits and help them on their way. Behind them hovered several older Europeans, up-country Headmasters, equally determined to ensure that in the general *bonhomie* of the official welcome, their new teachers were actually provided with transport, somewhere to stay and clear instructions on how to get to their schools and to no other. Some were confident golfing types who looked as if they could run a boarding school between rounds and not get too worried about what went on while they relaxed over a beer or two at the Club. Others looked more anxious and diffident, thin and pale under a tropical tan.

'Excuse me, Mr Stephenson,' said the Customs Officer to one of the quieter men at the back of the group. 'I have a new teacher for you.'

Lewis Stephenson smiled and put out his hand in greeting. 'Welcome to Uganda', he said. 'You must be John Haden.' He thanked the Customs man and shook his hand too.

It seemed that Ugandans shake each others' hands all the time.

'So you found him for me, Anguyo. How are things with you?'

'Things are a bit all right. I hope that you will give my greetings to Mrs Stephenson. But excuse me. I have to see to the other teachers now.'

Before I could thank him for my rapid progress through the formalities of arrival, he saluted us both smartly and disappeared back into the Customs Hall.

'He's a Lugbara from Arua,' Lewis explained. 'He always tries to find our new staff for me and to whisk them through Arrivals. We had better get you to a Kampala hotel before the pack arrives. They've arranged a room for you at the Speke. I came down yesterday to do some shopping so I thought I would come out to meet you – we'll go up to Arua tomorrow.'

We found his long black Mercedes saloon in the car-park and headed up the Kampala road. It was a short drive along a tarmac road through the bananas and bright flowering shrubs around small concrete houses along the roadside. After the early morning rain, the red earth steamed gently and bright birds flew across the road. We reached the Kampala suburbs and were engulfed in a sea of traffic, mostly Japanese minibuses crammed with passengers and driven with lunatic determination. Kampala itself was like a hot and humid Milton Keynes with a broad street running through the centre planted with canna lilies and oleander trees. Rows of concrete shops selling drugs and clothes lined the main street with occasional taller hotels and government buildings at the far end.

We stopped at the Speke, an old-fashioned looking place with spacious bars, a dining room and two floors of rooms under a red tiled roof. It all seemed very 'colonial', comfortable and well-organised, just what I had imagined Nairobi must have been like before Independence.

'The Ministry have booked you here for tonight,' Lewis explained as I surrendered my passport to the clerk at Reception. 'They want you to go round to see them in the morning to complete the formalities and then I'll take you up to West Nile tomorrow.'

The hotel lobby was decorated with maps of Speke's Uganda journeys[4]. In 1857, he and Burton had set out from Zanzibar on the Indian Ocean coast, trying to find the great lake that was said to be in the heart of East Africa. Travelling west, they first found Lake Tanganyika but the Arab traders they met told them of another, even greater lake, to the north. Burton and Speke fell out, parted company and Speke went on alone to reach the southern shore of the lake he named, Victoria, in honour of his queen, before returning in 1858 to Zanzibar and home to London. The Royal Geographical Society of London then sent Speke back to Africa in 1860, this time with Grant. They set out again from Zanzibar, reached the great lake, travelled around its western shore and were the first Europeans to enter the Kingdom of Buganda. Travelling on eastwards round the Lake, Speke found the falls where the waters spill out to form the Victoria Nile, which he named the Ripon Falls. To bring the news back to London, Speke and Grant followed the Nile all the way downstream to Cairo. Overall, their journey took three years, from Zanzibar to the Mediterranean Sea. It was all there, on a hotel wall, to welcome me to Uganda.

Next morning, I found the Ministry of Education was housed about five minutes walk away in a modern tower block. After a good lunch at the Speke, I joined the other new teaching recruits there and we all went through the formalities of becoming 'loyal servants of the Government of Uganda'. It was all very efficient. An open plan office staffed by courteous Ugandan clerks dealt with everything from payment of salary to notifying next of kin. 'Hopefully, we won't need this,' smiled a young woman, receiving my form. 'But it is good to be prepared for everything!'

I signed the Uganda Official Secrets Act, took an oath swearing loyalty to the President of Uganda, His Excellency Dr Milton Obote, and joined my colleagues waiting to be introduced to the Under-Secretary for Education, Mr E Nyanzi, whose office occupied half the top floor of 'Crested Towers'. He was a short, jovial man who shook each of us by the hand and welcomed us warmly to Uganda.

'We are very pleased that you have all decided to join our schools,' he told us. 'We need teachers from UK still although there are now more Ugandan graduates coming into our schools. Over the last two years we have managed to push up the number of Senior Secondary Schools to over eighty and there will be further expansion over the next few years, so we shall still need your help.'

He spoke to each of us in turn and enquired where we were being sent. It seemed that I was the only one going to West Nile. Most of the other teachers seemed to be going to schools in the Kampala area or the south-west and we exchanged contact details and promised to keep in touch.

For the rest of that afternoon, I walked back past the Parliament Buildings and through the city. Old Kampala is wrapped around the central hill on which Captain Lugard[5] built Nakasero Fort in 1890 on behalf of the British East Africa Company. Flanking Nakasero to the east, the Golf Course ran up one valley. A plantation of blue flowered jacaranda trees filled the other valley to the west. The city centre seemed quite small, no larger than an English town. Residential roads were lined with more flowering trees, the homes of ex-pats and affluent Ugandans. On a ring of hills about a mile from the centre, each of the world faiths had set up a base, the Protestant Church of Uganda in their Cathedral on Namirembe Hill, the Catholics across the valley on Rubaga. On the other side of town, the Moslem Mosque at Kibuli had a less attractive view across the railway sidings and go-downs of the business area. There was a Hindu Temple, less ostentatiously placed in a side road, but the Indian community it served seemed to be running most of the businesses along Kampala Road. This wide dual carriageway linked the key services, the banks, the airline offices and government agencies. Between the Catholics and the Protestants, another cluster of buildings on yet another hill housed Makerere University, set in colourful gardens with many flowering trees. It all looked very tidy, very European, a city of brick and concrete with nothing older than 1900. There was nothing obviously African except for the flocks of brightly coloured birds calling between the trees.

But just below the air-condition cleanliness of Kampala Road, in the taxi park and Nakasero Market, African activity seethed like an over-boiling pot. Taxi drivers shouted for customers among the suicidal pedestrians surging across the roads. Blind beggars, pavement crawlers and the maimed jostled for space pleading for shillings from the Bwana. Men in loin cloths ran with their hand carts loaded with goods, plastic bowls and jerry-cans, stems of green bananas and sacks of sweet potatoes. The stream of carts ran from the market to the bus park to be piled on roof-racks and taken out of Kampala to the towns around.

Lewis came to pick me up the following morning in the big black Mercedes crammed full of school supplies, books and lab equipment, packs of paper and duplicating stencils.

'We could go up the main road towards Gulu, the way the buses go,' Lewis explained. 'That road runs across the great empty area around Luwero. I prefer to go up to Hoima and then through the Park.'

'Sounds fine to me,' I replied. I only knew that it was over three hundred miles to Arua whichever way we went.

So we set off for the north along the Bombo Road just as dawn was breaking. On both sides of the road, streams of workers were striding into the city. Above them, flocks of great black fruit bats came twittering back to roost in the trees along the valley. We joined the road to Hoima at the foot of Namirembe Hill where rusty shacks of panel beaters and paint-sprayers were already busy. Signs advertised *Speyas kwa Mota*, 'Aspro', and 'Pepsi' brightening up the clusters of hovels by the roadside. We passed the road to the great reed tomb-houses of the Ganda Kings at Kasubi[6].

'Those tombs are just about the only monuments to an African past you'll see anywhere in the Kampala area,' Lewis told me as we drove on into the fertile red hills and swamp filled valleys of the Lakeside region.

Bananas grew everywhere, the tall black stems of green *matoke* bananas, the staple diet of the people living around Lake Victoria, and the shorter green stems of the yellow sweet bananas by the mud-walled, iron roofed houses. Old men sat beside the road swathed in loose long white gowns, puffing the day away in tobacco smoke and conversation. Along the green strip of grass by the road, brown children with swollen bellies beat the bony rumps of wide-horned humped back cattle. Stately matrons sailed by in their brightly coloured voluminous dresses.

'*Busutis*, they're called,' explained Lewis. 'They were invented by the early missionaries to ensure the modesty of women and caught on as standard wear for the respectable!'

Baskets swayed on heads, loaded with oranges and sweet-potato roots, balanced on grass rings above a mattress of glistening hair. We passed small stalls with bunches of sweet bananas, neat pyramids of tomatoes and mangoes, piles of ground-nuts and small neat packages of coffee beans bound up with banana fibres. In each valley bottom, the tall papyrus reeds choked the swamps with the sheer vegetable vitality of Africa.

After about thirty five miles, the tarmac ended and Lewis eased the car over the step between the made-up surface and the red earth strip that ran on northwards.

'From here to home, it's *murram*[7] all the way, but the surface is quite good for the first hundred miles or so.'

We started slowly, rattling across the ridges which had built up on the surface of the earth road. As the car accelerated to thirty, then to forty and up to fifty, the violent rattling became a noisy drumming. At sixty, the drumming almost stopped. It seemed that we were now skimming across the corrugations in the road in comparative comfort with only the rattle of an ash-tray betraying the roughness of the road.

'It's fine provided you don't have to brake suddenly or change direction,' Lewis said with a grin. 'Then you discover that you're barely in contact with the road and it's easy to do a four-wheel drift into the nearest swamp.'

But the road was straight and we pushed on, leaving a cloud of red dust in our wake much to the discomfort of men on bicycles wobbling along in the loose gravel of the verge. They carried wives and milk-churns, tied up goats and calves and once even a bed, all lashed with old strips of inner tube to sagging carriers. All along the road, the well-dressed would-be taxi travellers with their cardboard suitcases and resigned expressions, stood up as we approached, tried to flag us down and disappeared in the choking cloud of dust.

Slowly the lush green hills and swamps faded into the dullness of Uganda's drier heartland. The soft blue jacaranda trees and bright yellow cassias were replaced with occasional scarlet flame trees. Much of the dusty land seemed uninhabited. Black scars left by grass-fires ran right up to the side of the road. Where the burnt scrub was still smouldering, black kites wheeled through the smoke snatching scorched insects. Thirsty herds of cattle lowed through the dull drab land. I was glad when we reached the neat lawns and the tarmac roads of the town of Hoima. We called in at the government rest house for a cup of good coffee and filled up with petrol, the last available for two hundred miles. Hoima was typical of hundreds of small towns set out by the British across East Africa, a neat grid of square plots bordered by beds of *canna* lilies and white painted stones. The hospital stood next to the Post Office. The Rest House looked over a clipped hedge across the Police parade ground. Barclays and Grindleys Banks competed at opposite ends of the main street. It was all spotless. The British had come to organise Uganda into efficiency, but behind the main street, Uganda was still flourishing in the messy chaos of the market and the bus park.

We ate our dry and dusty sandwiches under a mango tree watched by a ring of silent children with dark hungry eyes. Then it was back to the short strip of tarmac out of the town and onto the old stony road running westwards towards Lake Albert and some of the most dramatic scenery in Western Uganda. We drove through a deep forest and then, just before the Lake, the road started to drop down through a series of hairpins over the edge into the Western branch of the Great Rift Valley. In the far distance, the Blue Mountains of the Congo lined the far side of the Lake. They looked so far away - cloud covered peaks from another world. Lewis pulled over and we stopped to admire the view. He told me about those who had explored this area.

'This was the way Speke and Grant came in the 1860s and Sir Samuel Baker walked the other way, travelling up the Nile from Egypt and through the Sudan in the company of his Hungarian wife, Florence[8]. She apparently caught his eye as a slave for sale in a Turkish market. She must have been a very tough young woman as well as being strikingly beautiful. They struggled up through the swamps of the Sudan and eventually reached the place where the Nile flows out of the great lake which you can see down there. It was Baker who named it the 'Albert Nyanza' and it's still Lake Albert today. The bit of the Nile which flows out of the Lake is called the Albert Nile.'

Lewis explained that Baker and Florence then found another great river flowed into this Lake from the east, which is still called the Victoria Nile.

'It's really the same river,' he said. 'They followed it upstream to discover the waterfall which is still known as Murchison Falls because Baker named it after Sir Roderick Murchison, President of the Royal Geographical Society. All the land to the north of the river was occupied by the Acholi. They had suffered for generations from attacks by Arab slavers and Baker had been given the task of trying to stop the trade in slaves. He built a fort at Patiko in Acholi territory to use as his base. Baker's efforts are still remember by the Acholi. The best school in Gulu is named the Sir Samuel Baker Senior Secondary School in his honour.'

We set off down the hairpins to reach the foot of the escarpment and the single track road to the north which skirted the shore of Lake Albert. Signs warn that this was tsetse fly country. Endemic sleeping sickness has prevented settlement and there were no herds of cattle or fields of cotton, just a game reserve acting as a buffer zone for the Murchison Falls National Park. The heat hit us on the plain, the airless enervating heat that throbbed all along the Nile valley. There was little evidence of game, just a few baboons shuffling through the stunted trees in copulating companies. Bataleur eagles drifted tail-less across the brazen sky. We passed through the Park gate, paying our Uganda Residents rate fees for access to this modern Eden, the home of thousands of elephants and great herds of antelope. We joined the road from Masindi and the queue of safari vehicles full of camera-toting tourists waiting for the ferry across the Victoria Nile. Paraa Safari Lodge on the north bank of the river provided long cold drinks and a chance to wash off some of the dust of travel but we did not stay long. Lewis was worried about the black storm clouds building to the north.

'If we get caught in heavy rain on the Tangi Track,' he said, 'we'll never get out of the Park tonight.'

So we pushed on through the elephant grass on a muddy, winding track stopping only to allow three rhinoceros to cross at their own leisurely pace.

We reached the main road before the rain began to fall, great curtains of rain turning the culverts into rivers and the surface of the road into a slithery mud slide. But it was still passable. We reached the ferry at Pakwach and crossed the Albert Nile into West Nile as the clouds lifted. The bored policeman guarding the barrier across the road let us through. Lewis exchanged greetings with him, explained that we were on our way from Kampala to Arua. 'Welcome to West Nile, John. They're trying to catch car thieves taking cars through to the Congo without much success.'

From the Nile to Arua was about eighty miles of *murram* road. Lewis was tired after the long drive up from Kampala. To keep us both awake, we talked about West Nile and the school. He explained that the man at the barrier was, like most of the people living in the south of the District, Alur.

'Tall and very black, typical Nilotic[9] people, traditionally feared by the Baganda living around the Lake. Around Arua, most of the people are Lugbara, again tall and very black Sudanic people,' Lewis said with a grin. 'You'll learn to recognise the differences in time but I doubt if you'll learn their languages. Our students come from all five language groups, Alur, Lugbara, Okebu, Kakwa and Madi and the school rule states that, while at school, all must speak English.'

'But it is impossible to enforce,' said Lewis wryly. 'How can you punish a teenager who slips into his native tongue when he's not thinking? It would be like trying to enforce BBC English amongst a group of Cockneys, Geordies and West-countrymen. They would just laugh at you.'

He told me about *enya*, the local staple diet, a boiled mixture of cassava[10] and millet.

'It's a bit like eating nutty and gritty Plasticine. Not bad with a meat stew or a ground-nut sauce. You'll get to like it eventually.'

He explained that when the cassava roots are dug up, they are broken up and soaked in water. This reduces the soluble bitter-flavoured content which is poisonous. The cassava is then dried in the sun on a bare rock and ground up with a rock on a stone surface. This is children's work so the place where this is done is often called 'the place of the children'.

Just as the night was falling and the street lights at the outskirts of Arua town were coming on, we turned off the main road and down a side road.

'This goes to Mvara,' Lewis said as we passed an old church with a large rusting corrugated iron roof. 'Emanuel is the Anglican Cathedral for West Nile. Most of the Mission staff live just down here. Oh, and I forgot to tell you. Your house at the school is not yet ready so I've arranged for you to stay for a while with Peggy and Seton Maclure. They live next to Margaret Lloyd.'

He stopped the car by a low bungalow with a wide veranda festooned with flowering creepers and said, 'Welcome to Mvara, John. I'm glad you decided to join us.'

## 1.2 From Independence to 1968

When the Republic of Uganda was born, one of the Ugandan officers on parade that day in October 1962 was lucky to be there at all. Lt Idi Amin[11] had been in command of a platoon in C Company, 4$^{th}$ KAR, when they were tasked, earlier in 1962, to cross the Uganda border from Karamoja into the Turkana area of Kenya. Their mission was to raid Turkana villages in search of illegal arms. Amin's platoon came back to base empty handed. Angry and frustrated, he then decided to take his men back across the border later that night. They got their illegal arms. But the Turkana villagers complained to the Kenyan Police and an investigation revealed recent shallow graves. These held the bodies of Turkana men who had clearly been tortured before they were killed. Amin was held responsible and he should have been court-marshalled.

The British Deputy Governor of Kenya phoned the Governor of Uganda to request that the officer responsible be handed over to the Kenya Police. The Governor of Uganda, realising the sensitivity of the situation, consulted Dr Milton Obote. They discussed the acute embarrassment that would be caused if one of only two Ugandan commissioned officers was court-marshalled just before Independence Day. Obote advised the Governor that Amin should be dealt with in Uganda and given a 'severe reprimand'. This was done and Governor then warned Obote that Amin could cause him trouble in the future – a view that was to prove all too accurate. So on that day on 1962, Lieutenant Idi Amin was on parade with the Uganda Rifles as the excited crowd sang their new National Anthem.

Before Independence, Milton Obote's party, the Uganda People's Congress, had built its power base in the Protestant communities of the Uganda Protectorate, where the Church Missionary Society had for years been active in setting up Anglican churches, schools and hospitals. Uganda had, and continues to have, the highest percentage of professing Christians of any African country but with this strength came political divisions along religious lines. The UPC had strong Protestant links. The Catholic Church in Uganda had become closely linked to the Democratic Party (DP), with a strong commitment to opposing the Kabaka's involvement in Uganda politics. At the 1961 General Election, organised by the British to decide who would govern independent Uganda, the DP defeated the UPC across the Protectorate, with the elections boycotted in Buganda.

But at the talks in London between the parties, the UPC formed a strategic alliance with the Kabaka Yekka (KY)[12]. These 'Kabaka Alone' Buganda nationalists were committed to keeping the Kabaka as President of Uganda. It was clear that this UPC/KY alliance could defeat the DP nationally if the Baganda voted and in the 1962 re-run of the General Election the alliance achieved an overall majority. The KY won all but three seats out of sixty six in Buganda. Across the country, the UPC/DY alliance won fifty five seats to the DP's twenty four. As independent Uganda was born, Milton Obote, as the leader of the UPC/KY alliance, became Prime Minister. A year later, the Kabaka became President and Commander in Chief of the Armed Forces while the DP remained a very discontented 'loyal opposition'.

But the UPC/KY alliance did not last. KY leaders were accused of plotting against Obote. Allegations were made by the UPC that the Kabaka was arming the Baganda with heavy weapons. By early 1966, any chance of a stable government involving both parties had gone and Obote moved against the Kabaka. He announced the suspension of the 1962 constitution in February with the abolition of the posts of President and Vice-President. An interim constitution with Obote as President was passed by the UPC and Obote ordered Idi Amin, now

Colonel, to lead an Army attack on Kabaka Mutesa's palace at Lubiri, Kampala. Mutesa fled into the sanctuary of the Kampala Roman Catholic Cathedral and was allowed to slip out of Uganda for exile in London. In the following year, all kingdoms in Uganda were abolished and the whole country became a Republic. Idi Amin was promoted to Major General by a grateful Obote and the Army's status was enhanced as it grew in size, equipment and training opportunities. Baganda had been placed under a state of emergency in early 1966 and this was made permanent as Uganda moved to a one-party state. Leading politicians, including the leaders of the DP and close relatives of the Kabaka still in Uganda were arrested and detained as the country drifted into a dictatorship. Through 1967 and early 1968, Milton Obote consolidated his grip on Uganda, partly through the sinister operations of the notorious 'General Service Unit' headed by his cousin, Akena Adoko. Obote developed new Socialist policies for the country, published when fully formed as 'The Move to the Left', just as I was preparing to leave for Uganda. In the six years, from Independence to 1968, there had been dramatic change. Over the same six years, I too had been through very significant personal change.

*

When Uganda was born, two British students who ended up together at Mvara Secondary School were starting their second year on the Oxford Chemisty course. I was one of them, the other was Jenny Peck. Her father, Philip, was an engineer in Rugby with a keen interest in the work of overseas missions. This stemmed from his experience as a boy at a Crusader Class[13] run by 'Commie Williams'. 'Commie' had two sons, both of whom became Doctors working with AIM in Uganda. Jenny's mother, Mary, was also keenly interested in missionary work and hoped, and no doubt prayed, that her children would one day work as overseas missionaries. Another link was through the Rugby Anglican Church of St Matthew's whose member, Margaret Lloyd, had gone with AIM to teach in the same area of Uganda as the Williams brothers. Regular visits from missionaries at home on furlough and attendance at conferences run by AIM had maintained this link over many years.

Both of Jenny's parents were Methodist Local Preachers[14]. They brought up their two daughters and son to be fully involved in the local Methodist Church. Jenny also had the huge advantage of a strong Sunday School and a memorable RE teacher, whose wisdom she still quotes. It would be hard to imagine a more Christian family and she grew up with a strong personal faith and a desire to share it. School holidays were spent on the Norfolk Broads sailing with Christian groups and when she won a place at St Hilda's College, Oxford, she was soon fully involved in the Oxford Christian Union.

\*

If Jenny Peck had grown up well informed about the work of AIM, I knew nothing about Uganda until I met her. I was also born during the Second World War, and christened at Croxley Green, Hertfordshire, where my grandparents lived. My father had been called up from a career in teaching to a commission as an anti-tank gunner. His unit left England for Burma shortly after I was born and we did not see him again until 1946.

After the war, we lived in Bickley, Kent, and as a family went to the services at the relatively high local Anglican parish church. It offered little in the way of concession to children. In my early teens, I did, briefly, go to a Crusader Class for boys, but none of my friends went, so I soon stopped. We continued to go as a family to Church every Sunday, and were encouraged to think of ourselves as supporters of the Church of England, without getting too excited about it.

When I was thirteen, I was sent as a weekly boarder to St Paul's School, in West London. This highly selective London day school with a small minority of boarders gave me an excellent academic education and useful boarding survival strategies. When it was suggested to us at about the age of 14, that 'Confirmation'[15] was a good idea, my friends and I went along with the majority. After a brief preparation by the School Chaplain, we were confirmed in the crypt of St Paul's Cathedral by the Bishop of London. My memories of that day lack focus, literally, as I broke my glasses in the morning and made my way through the ceremony following the boy in front very closely, with a hand on his shoulder like a gas casualty of World War I.

Thanks to some excellent teaching I did well enough at St Paul's for my father and the school to decide that an attempt to get a place to read Chemistry at Oxford was not out of the question. A miserable and freezing two days and nights at my father's college, Wadham, produced a firm 'no thank-you'. I had resigned myself to going elsewhere when it was suggested that one final attempt could be made in the late season round-up operated by St Catherine's Society. At the time, this non-collegiate body offered places on Oxford courses without having a residential college building to house them in. Members of 'St Catz' all lived in 'digs', small rooms in private houses owned by fierce Oxford land-ladies. So I took the papers and spent a very happy hour discussing Georgian architecture (my best essay answer in the General Paper) with Freddie Brewer, the avuncular Chemistry Tutor. To my delight, I was offered a place.

Jenny Peck and I spent four years studying for Oxford Chemistry degrees although her commitment to Chemistry was far greater than mine and our paths seldom crossed. My interests were more on the river than in the laboratory and I slowly progressed from cox to bow, from beginner to Captain of Boats. My Chemistry Tutor's acerbic comment, when he heard the news of my election to this office, was that the administrative experience would probably prove useful. He clearly had little hope of my finding a future in Chemistry.

One evening, after a dinner to celebrate a minor rowing success, I and a group of friends were involved in a tragic accident on the bank of the River Cherwell. One of us ended up in the water. We dived in and fished him out but to our horror found that he had drowned. Although his parents, the College authorities and the Coroner were all supportive, it left us all with an overwhelming sense of guilt. Somehow, the 'comfortable words' of my Anglican background had nothing to offer in this situation. Not until months later, was I able to find any sort of peace.

A friend suggested that I should go with him to a talk given by John Stott as part of a Mission to the University. He set out in clear and demanding terms the claims of the Christian gospel. The idea that I should make some sort of response to this teaching was quite new. No-one before then had ever suggested to me that the way to find faith was by giving in, not by trying harder to earn the approval of God. When I did, and accepted that I had a need of God's forgiveness, it was as if a new world opened to me. I just knew that it was true, that the love of God could pour into me in a quite breath-taking way. I wanted to be with those who had this same experience. So I joined the Christian Union, and although rowing and to some extent chemistry, still took up some of my time, my life seemed now to have a new sense of purpose. There was no sudden blinding light, no gift of strange tongues and no voice from heaven. I just knew that what Jesus had said and did for me was true.

A friend who had travelled the same road to faith decided that my lack of Chemistry was going to be a serious problem in a few months time when Finals had to be faced. So he, probably the best Chemist of his year, and I, probably one of the worst, walked around the Parks together until I had absorbed enough for me to at least understand some of the questions in our Finals Examinations. He got a starred First. I got a Third, just enough to get me into the fourth year of the course. This involved a year's research project in the Inorganic Chemistry Laboratories where my Tutor had a team working on the Thermodynamics of Transition Metal Oxides. He found me a quiet corner in which to set up a small project. At first, this seemed to consist mainly of delicate glass-blowing as we built our vacuum lines and metal-work to construct furnaces for the heating of pellets of metal oxides. Four large male research chemists with sharp elbows and short tempers shared a very small space with a lot of very fragile glass.

Inevitably, there were frequent and acrimonious accidents as an elbow went through a vital vacuum line. Our collective safety valve was the coffee machine down the corridor and the chance to drink the foul liquid it produced in the neighbouring large laboratory. This was home to three St Hilda's chemists also doing their fourth year projects. They provided an essential source of sympathy and we got to know them well. Jenny Peck was one of the three and she was also a keen member and leader of the Oxford Christian Union.

After this year, and my decision to do a Post-graduate Diploma in Education[16], we met again as she too decided to go into teaching. We had both decided that we would start at schools which had a strong academic tradition. We wanted to learn how to teach in an environment where teaching and learning were valued. Our teaching practice experience of trying to teach in schools where crowd-control was the first and only priority led us to turn away from such challenging places, at least at first. She got a job at Nottingham Girls' High School and I joined the Chemistry Department of the King's School, Worcester.

King's was then a Direct Grant Grammar School, a boys' school which provided free places for Worcester's 11+ successes and fee-paying places, boarding and day, for affluent families. It also included the Cathedral Choir School and was a very gentlemanly place, occupying a cluster of attractive Georgian houses edging the peace of the Cathedral

Green and hiding a jumble of Victorian brick behind. The majority of the boys were intelligent and well-mannered, and relatively well-behaved. I found it professionally exciting. The Head of the Chemistry department was keen to take up the latest initiatives of the Nuffield Science Foundation and was also a deep thinker and published poet. Under this guidance I immersed myself with high expectation in all the chemistry teaching, colts rowing coaching, Scout Troop leadership and boarding house tutoring that I was asked to do.

But I soon discovered one thing that saddened me about the school, its spiritual torpor. The vast bulk of the Cathedral, the enduring, unchanging, faith of past generations, seemed to stifle the boys' slow groping towards a faith of their own. 'Christianity is old, cold and nearly dead' was the message of its grey stone and greying clergy. I longed for opportunities to say how wrong this was and to share my own experience of a new and vital faith with both my colleagues and the boys. There was already in the school a small Bible-study group which met almost furtively, well away from the Cathedral Green. Every Sunday evening a dozen or so boys would tiptoe past the Dean's front door to talk and to pray together in a private house about a mile away from the school. After a while, they invited me to join them. In the company of those young Christians, full of honest doubts and yet burning with a conviction that life had a meaning and a purpose, I found something of the warmth and joy I remembered from long coffee-drinking evenings with Christian Union friends.

In the middle of that first year of teaching, over an icy January weekend, I joined a conference run by AIM which I had heard about from Jenny Peck. On the face of it, it seemed impossibly old-fashioned. They took the code language of religion completely seriously, using phrases like 'being led', 'gaining a blessing' and 'the Lord will provide' as part of their conversation. Yet those AIM workers were anything but old-fashioned. They were professional teachers and doctors, water engineers and university lecturers as up to date as any in Worcester. They had no difficulty in joining hands across denominational boundaries to evangelise the bit of Africa that they each called home, to thank God for what He had done for them in the past and to trust their future to Him. I found them to be interesting lively people and left the conference with no clear idea how this might affect me but with a list of useful contacts and the address of the nearest place to Worcester where there was a regular AIM prayer group.

I never admitted to my colleagues at school just what I did on every first Thursday evening in the month from then onwards. If asked, I mumbled something about a meeting in Birmingham and it is doubtful if they would have believed me had I told them the truth. For I spent an hour on the bus and half an hour on foot simply to sit with a small prayer group led by an eighty year old widow and a young police-woman in a bedsit smelling of cats, praying for the work of AIM in Africa. They would have thought me mad. Yet I valued those Thursday evenings. They offered an escape from the spiritual frustration of the Cathedral. I went back again to the AIM conference in the following year, wondering about the future.

When I expressed interest in teaching abroad to the elderly clergyman who ran the AIM administration in England, I got the blunt rebuttal I deserved. I must have given the impression that I was not too sure that the Mission would be able to make good use of my considerable talents and experience as a teacher. He gently made it very clear that it was I who was under-qualified and ill-equipped. The Mission might find it hard to fit a teacher of A level Chemistry into its work.

'Can't you do anything else?' he enquired gently.

'Not that I know of, although I have taught Divinity as well.'

'Hm…..I see. Well missionary life may be many things, John, but you cannot tailor it to a career – even in a career as useful as teaching. You'll have to choose one thing or the other.'

He smiled at my abashed expression. 'But the Mission does have an interest in a secondary school in Northern Uganda. We started it and the Church is still very much involved although it is now a Government school. We do sometimes sponsor short-term teachers there but we don't really like to spend all that money flying you out there for a short stay in the sun. It depends how much they need your subject. Why don't you write to the Headmaster?

I left that conference depressed and confused, convinced that I did not have a 'call' to full-time service as a Missionary but doubtful of the value of a short-term visit to Uganda. In any case, even if there was an opening with this school in Uganda, I could not walk out on my present job after only eighteen months in Worcester. There was also the question of the future of the Bible-study group which had come to depend more on my leadership. But I did write to the Headmaster of Mvara Secondary School, Arua, and also to the

Government Department, the Ministry of Overseas Development (ODM), which arranged the recruitment of British teachers for East Africa. The letters posted, I tried to put the whole idea into the back of my mind.

It took three weeks to get the first reply, a sheaf of forms from Eland House, the home of ODM. I tucked them behind the pewter pots won by the Colts VIII which I proudly kept on the mantelpiece, and tried to ignore them. The letter from Mvara Secondary School took three more weeks to reach me. It was short and to the point. The Headmaster needed a chemist.

'Apply through the Government,' he wrote. 'I will ask the Ministry here to send you to us.'

This struck me as risky. When I had a look at the ODM forms, it was clear that I could specify which Country I wanted to go to, whether I preferred city or 'up-country', and 'boys or girls or mixed', but there was no space for an actual choice of school. If I was accepted by the Uganda Government, they could send me to any one of eighty secondary schools. But I really wanted to go to the one where I knew there was a need and already had some contact. When the boys' Bible study met that evening, I was even less sure that this was all a good idea.

'Will you lead us next week, Sir?' they asked hopefully. 'We can do it ourselves but it is better when you lead us.'

I really did not know what to do and put the forms back behind the pewter pots. In many ways I was happy at the school, enjoying learning to teach interesting chemistry courses to intelligent boys and getting a great deal of satisfaction from coaching eight boys to row a boat as fast as they could. I knew it was a narrow life. As a boarding-house tutor I had little spare time and many would have called me dull and un-enterprising, but I was getting as much out of the life as I could.

Every Sunday morning, the King's School boarders, tidied for the day into their dark suits and polished shoes, would crocodile across College Green into the great Cathedral nave for compulsory Matins. The Dean and Chapter, as the school's Governors, insisted that the boys attend the service but did little to make it interesting or even remotely relevant to their adolescent searching. As a House Tutor, I too was expected to be there in my pew behind the senior staff, caught in the vicious draught between the cloister and the choir. After my week of indecision, I sat swathed in coat, scarf, gloves, gown and hood like a black academic pumpkin decorated with rabbit fur.

The service, with all the musical beauty and remoteness of choral Anglicanism, washed around the boys like a mild disinfectant as they sat in blocks by Houses down one side of the nave. Eventually, the Right Revd Dean wheezed his way up into the Victorian pulpit, peered out into the semi-darkness and said in a one long exhalation,

'InthenameoftheFatherandoftheSonandoftheHolyGhost, Amen.'

'For my text this morning I have chosen that really rather delightful little book, the Song of Solomon, in the first chapter and the fifth verse: 'I am black but comely, O ye daughters of Jerusalem', or as we should render it in these days of improved race relations, and I quote from the New English Bible, 'I am dark but lovely'.'

He smiled, very slowly, like a yawning chameleon. Far below him in bored blocks, the boys tittered briefly at the thought that black is beautiful, and rapidly returned to their comics, paperbacks, pocket chess sets and penknives busy on the darker corners of their pews. The Dean, quite satisfied that he had made even the briefest contact with youth, rambled on in a deep droning voice that would have lulled even the most alert of us asleep if it had not been so cold. What he actually said, no-one remembered. No-one was listening. Race relations may have been a burning issue not far away in Birmingham but in the affluent community of Worcester, there were few immigrants, and not a black face in the school. As the boys grew more restless, the well-padded red faced worthies of the City, sitting opposite the school, were far too busy expressing their disapproval by impotent glares and whispered mutterings to listen to the sermon.

So the Dean preached and one half of his congregation fidgeted in fury while the other half behaved as any group of several hundred boys would, knowing that no-one could stop them. At last he finished and we all straightened our stiffened knees to sing the final hymn. The boys loved this moment of the service. It was almost the end of their internment and they had an opportunity to express themselves in a way that no-one could control. The Dean had chosen Isaac Watt's great hymn on the church universal, 'Jesus shall reign where're the sun', as the climax to his thoughts on racial harmony. The resonant nave soaked up the sound of the organ and the choir and rolled back an echo, rich and heavy.

The boys sang, for the first time in the service, as loudly as they could. We started more or less together but through the second and third verses, the boys at the furthest end of the nave began to ponder long and lovingly on the last lines of the verse. 'Dwell on his love with sweetest song and infant voices shall proclaim' they sang holding the echo and then pouring it back at the choir's brave attempt to move onwards. By the last verse, the farthest House were still completing 'and all the sons of want are blest' as the choir were singing 'let every creature rise and sing'. The Dean, trapped in a cacophony of sound, his colour rising at the growing choral chaos, quivered with rage from the altar steps. The boys sang on 'And earth prolong the joyful strain' with all the power and delight of a Welsh Rugby crowd. They ended, one House after another, down the length of the nave, in perfect order, before standing, silent at last and smirking at each other for the final blessing. To his eternal credit, the Dean did succeed in pronouncing a public benediction over them, through tight lips and closed eyes. Then he sailed out of the nave at the tail of the defeated choir. Compulsory matins was never quite the same again but that service helped me to make up my mind.

The staff met after the service, over the dry sherry that the Headmaster served as a de-icing agent. I tried to explain what I felt.

'There may be some who enjoy the music but the great majority think that Christianity is old-fashioned, boring and oppressive.'

'Drink up, John, they're absolutely right,' was the staffroom cynic's response when the Headmaster had left the room to carve the Sunday joint. So that afternoon I sent off the application form to the ODM and dared to make a pact with God. If the Government of Uganda agreed to send me to Mvara Secondary School, and if the Headmaster of King's found another member of staff to support the Bible Study group, I would go to Uganda. After a suitably bureaucratic delay, the ODM invited me for an interview in London. One sharp spring morning I took time off from school to catch the train to London and the ODM.

I was interviewed by a pair of ancient and very white civil servants behind an enormous empty desk.

'Come in, come in, Mr er Adden is it?'

'Haden,' I said.

'Ah yes, Mr Haden, and you want to go to Uganda.'

He looked at the slip of paper in his hand. 'Now, why do you want to go there?'

I wondered for a moment whether I should tell him the whole story, but decided to make no mention of the Almighty.

'I just want to use the teaching skills I've learnt over the last two years to help a developing nation and I know a little about Uganda.'

He looked at me as if I was the first applicant to suggest such a radical reason.

'Really? How nice to find some idealism! Do you think that you are the sort of person who adapts easily to new situations? Could you improvise at all?'

'Well, I could try,' I said hoping to look the type who could turn a banana leaf into something resembling a test tube.

'Good. I see that you want to go to the West Nile District – never been there myself, it's a bit up-country but I expect it's a decent sort of place. Most of the places we send our chaps to are decent enough places even though there are lots of Ugandans around in the schools now.'

I told them what I knew, describing the slides of the area which I had seen at Mission meetings and the impressions in letters I had read. I told them of the school and of their need of a science teacher. The old man nodded encouragingly. When I had finished, he said, 'That's very interesting. You certainly seem to have done your homework on the place. I'm sure that you'll find it very rewarding working there.' Then he remembered that this was supposed to be a selection interview, not a valedictory meeting.

'Any questions George?' The other man shook his head. Mr Harper wound up the proceedings. 'There are just one or two formalities to complete. I'm sure you'll be agreeable to Uganda but it is their country you know and they will make the final decision. When we hear from them, we'll let you know.'

I heard nothing from Eland House for several weeks and the deadline for resignation from my King's post was approaching fast. My impatient Headmaster, anxious to replace me if he had to, rang Eland House on the resignation deadline day.

'Yes', they said. 'Mr Haden will probably be appointed to a contract, and will probably be posted to West Nile.'

This was not good enough for the Head, who curtly told them that if that was the way they recruited teachers he was surprised that they got any at all. On the strength of this vague assurance from ODM, I gave him my letter of resignation. Next morning, an envelope arrived from 'your obedient servant, J Harper.' He informed me that 'subject to the approval of the Consultant Physician, I had been selected for appointment for one tour of two years in the service of the Government of Uganda as an Education Officer, posted to Mvara Senior Secondary School.' He added that the Minister of Overseas Development hoped that I would find this appointment interesting and sent his good wishes. Would I please send him the acceptance slip by return of post?

Very decent of the Minister, I thought, pushing the letter into my pocket on my way to teach A level Chemistry, but I'll take my time just as you did. I went up to London again to have my knees tapped and my lungs sounded by another friendly old man and a week or so later, a teacher was appointed to the staff of King's who had an interest in supporting the school Christian group. Having already resigned my post, I could send off the acceptance of the Uganda contract now that all parts of my private agreement seemed sealed.

Wanting to share my interest in the church in West Nile with colleagues and students, I invited Canon Seton Maclure of the Africa Inland Mission to talk to the school. Seton was in England on furlough from Uganda and his account of life and work with the Anglican Church in West Nile interested me and influenced several of the boys who heard him. Two later joined us at Mvara for gap-years at the school. Seton also explained some things which puzzled me, such as the role of a mission like AIM in a country which was otherwise served by the CMS. He showed us a map of the work of AIM in Central Africa.

'If you go back to 1917, the time of the first British District Commissioner in West Nile,' Seton explained. 'The CMS had already been in the Baganda area for decades, but there was no Christian church in West Nile. The DC asked the CMS to send missionaries so that the Native Anglican Church could be established but the CMS did not have people to send. Just over the border in what was the Belgian Congo, AIM missionaries were already working amongst the people of the north-east Congo. Some of these AIM workers were travelling through West Nile on their way to the Congo when one of them became seriously ill just before they reached the Uganda/Congo border.

The AIM group stayed in West Nile until she recovered. While waiting, they helped to distribute famine relief supplies. Realising that the people on the Uganda side of the border were the same tribes as those in the Congo, the AIM party asked the DC if they could plant churches in West Nile. They had to agree with the Church Missionary Society and the District Commissioner that they would work within the Anglican tradition and any church that grew from their work would be part of the Native Anglican Church in Uganda. That's why,' Seton said with a grin, 'we've still got a mixed bag of AIM workers, American and British, from the Anglican, Presbyterian, Methodist and Baptist churches serving in West Nile as if they were Anglicans. They founded an Anglican Diocese and it began to grow.

AIM mission stations in Central Africa in the 1960s

He explained that AIM work grew from a small mud house near the Congo border where a British AIM Missionary couple first lived and preached. Blackwater fever and Spanish flu nearly killed them and they had to move to Kenya's healthier climate. The work continued slowly at a new AIM Mission station at Mvara just outside Arua. By 1923, when Rev.

and Mrs Vollor arrived at Mvara, the first Gospel, Mark, had been translated into Lugbara. The Vollors spent forty years at Mvara. The story of the growth of the church in West Nile is largely the story of how God worked through them. Canon Vollor was both pastor and schoolmaster at Mvara, initially without a church or a school, but after two years, there was a small school and a church building. He encouraged Lugbara evangelists to go out into the villages to preach and lead worship. Soon there were hundreds of churches spread across the District.

The Vollors travelled all over West Nile, establishing churches and primary schools, often accompanied by their three children. At first on foot and then using bicycles, this intrepid couple journeyed through country where lions, leopards and buffalo could still be encountered, to the terror of their porters, but leaving them unscathed. Their unrelenting focus was on literacy and numeracy through a chain of church primary schools. Canon Vollor founded a teacher training college at Mvara which still trains teachers and uses the stone chapel which he built.

The Mission set up a Junior Secondary School to provide post-primary opportunities for the best students who completed their six year Primary course in the sixty Church Primary Schools in the Arua area, but it was started much later than the church secondary schools of the south of Uganda. The CMS and the Colonial Government had between them decided to set up schools for the sons and daughters of Kings and Chiefs, well before the Second World War. By the 1950s many of their students went on to Makerere University. In other districts of Uganda, in Ankole, Bunyoro, Busoga, and Teso, similar schools were set up, all following the boarding model of the British Public School. They had British Heads and mainly British teachers and they provided the growing middle class of Uganda with an educational ladder into the Civil Service.

In West Nile, the local people did not have kings and some did not even have chiefs, so there was no pressure to establish elite schools. The Lugbara, Madi and Kakwa churches were happy to go along with the AIM priority for literacy through primary schools. AIM had and still has a majority of American members, who had no interest in setting up replicas of British Public Schools. Eventually, AIM and the West Nile Church leaders realised that there was a real need for secondary opportunities for pupils leaving Primary School in West Nile and they set up Mvara Junior Secondary School.'

*

When my colleagues on the staff at the King's School heard what I was planning to do, they split into roughly equal halves, those who now knew what they had suspected all along, that I was mad, and those who rather wished that they were coming too. Leading the latter group was the chubby middle-aged Scout master who had spent his twenties working in India.

'Make sure you take plenty of pants,' he advised over lunch one day. 'Pure cotton's best. Terribly uncomfortable, damp pants in the Tropics, will wear you out in no time.'

The jeremiahs on the other hand were led by a colleague who took my arm one Break, and pinned me against the Staff-room pigeon-holes. With a look of horror in his big brown eyes, he warned me of the dangers to come.

'You do understand, don't you, that you will have to live amongst Africans.'

He clearly thought that no civilised human being would survive this experience. I assured him that I did understand and that I was looking forward to the experience. Not long afterwards he insisted on taking me to see a film which happened to be on at the local cinema. 'Africa Addio' it was called. It was appalling, a revolting catalogue of hideous violence and sickening racism. From the Mau-Mau rebels, hacking at the cattle of Kenya's white settlers, via white mercenaries slaughtering African villagers, through the Zanzibar massacre of Arabs being driven into the sea, past the swollen, fly-blown corpses of victims of Frelimo in Mozambique, the final section ended the orgy of violence with the rape of Italian nuns by the Simba of the Congo. On our way out, I read the film's promotional justification of this depiction of savagery:

'The old Africa has disappeared. Untouched jungles, huge herds of game, high adventure, the happy hunting ground - those are the dreams of the past. Today there is a new Africa - modern and ambitious. The old Africa died amidst the massacres and devastations we filmed. But revolutions, even for the better, are seldom pretty. America was built over the bones of thousands of pioneers and revolutionary soldiers, hundreds of thousands of Indians, and millions of bison. The new Africa emerges over the graves of thousands of whites and Arabs, and millions of blacks, and over the bleak boneyards that once were the game reserves.'

'Well, don't say that you weren't warned,' was my colleague's comment as we stumbled out into the glorious colours of an English sunset. 'Africa is bad.'

But I was not to be dissuaded. 'Anyway,' I pointed out rather primly. 'There was no mention of violence in Uganda in the film and some pretty nasty things happen here in England too.'

Up to this point, I realised that although I had found out a lot about Uganda I had not had a chance to meet a single black Ugandan. The ODM sent me on a weekend 'orientation' course in the unlikely setting of a Surrey castle and there I met Mr Kasigwa. He was a Musoga from Jinja and in England on a Barclays UK course for senior managers. He had been invited to talk to us about his country. After a good dinner we got into conversation.

'So you're going to teach. Where are they sending you?' he asked.

'Arua in West Nile,' I replied. 'I hope to teach at Mvara.'

His eyes bulged alarmingly as he tried to swallow a mouthful of his beer at the same time as suppressing a roar of laughter.

'You're going to Arua?' he spluttered. 'But that's miles away. No-one wants to go to Arua. It's where they send you if you do something really bad. Those men in the north, they are really fierce.'

When I explained that I knew a bit about the place and really did want to go there, he became concerned.

'I would arrange a transfer if I were you, somewhere safe and civilised, like Jinja. It's not too late to change your mind.'

White, brown and black, most now agreed that I was making a big mistake but there was no going back. Over the summer term, I had a chance to read all I could find about Uganda and particularly about West Nile. All that reading made me realise just how significant the District's geographical and ethnic position had been for at least a century, from the time that Burton and Speke set out from Zanzibar in 1856 to try to solve the mystery of the source of the Nile.

### 1.3 John Ondoma's story

In 1948, a grandson was born to a soldier from the 4th Battalion of the King's African Rifles (KAR) in the high country in the north west of West Nile. His village was typical of the

Lugbara, a cluster of grass-roofed mud-walled round huts with small thatched granaries on wooden poles to keep the stored food out of the rain and away from the rats. His extended family lived together, a community of people who had no chiefs and no kings, just a loyalty to their own kith and kin. The child was the son of Elisha Yobuta, a skilled carpenter or *fundi* and his wife Ana Oleru Yobuta.

As is the tradition amongst the Lugbara, when the time came to name the child a few days after he was born, they gave him a Lugbara name which reflected a difficulty which the family had experienced in the time before his birth. They called him '*Ondoma*', literally 'I am the one barren', as his parents had already been married for three years before the child was born, a long period of barrenness for a Lugbara couple. He was also given the name '*Yohana*' which he changed when he was baptised to 'John'.

John Ondoma, who became our friend and with whom we have shared a love of teaching and a desire to serve God, has written an account of his childhood in that Lugbara village:

*'I enjoyed a lot of love and care from my parents and other relatives such as my grandparents and my aunt. When I was able to walk up to our local church, my father always told me to walk in front of him. I carried his books tucked in a bag of cloth which I hung across my shoulder. I loved and respected my parents.*

*My father often encouraged me to go along with him to the fields where he went to dig, and to the forests where he went to take timber out of the woods. He was the carpenter for the entire village. Many people both within and without the village bought furniture, doors and windows from him. That is partly how he got money to meet some of the family needs. I was able to learn how to make furniture under his tutorship. This enabled me to earn my own pocket money I needed in school.*

*As I grew up and later joined school, I made sure I did not do anything that would disappoint my parents. They were actually to me my immediate gods. That respect and love for them helped to restrain me from joining other young people in some form of mischief or atrocious social misbehaviour.'*

John goes on to describe how he and his father would listen to the world news in Kiswahili on the radio, a language his father had learnt growing up in the KAR barracks in Nairobi. As a child and a young man, he always went to church on Sundays with his family, but John remained a nominal

Christian, afraid that a deeper commitment to Christ as his Saviour and Lord would stop him having fun.

*'My own assumption was that if I committed my life to Christ at a tender age, I would easily back-slide and not continue with the faith at all. At a more advanced age, pride and the pleasures of youth would go out of my head and I would remain saved till my life's end.'*

There were many in West Nile at that time with links to the KAR. The 4th Battalion had served in the Second World War in the Somaliland campaign against the Italians. With them on that campaign was a young West Nile Christian who had become a KAR Chaplain, Silvanus Wani[17] In 1943, the Battalion were sent to Burma to fight against the Japanese. The British and Indian units fighting alongside them by chance included the Royal Artillery battery commanded by my father.

After the Second World War, the 4th KAR served again outside Uganda when they were used in 1952 by the British in the suppression of the Mau Mau rebellion in Kenya. By that time, their former Chaplain, Silvanus Wani, had become a Canon of the Church of Uganda. He was then chosen in 1964 to be the first African Bishop of Northern Uganda. When that diocese was split and Janani Luwum became Bishop in Gulu, Wani became Bishop of West Nile and Madi. Finally, when Archbishop Janani Luwum was murdered in 1977 by order of a former KAR Sergeant, Idi Amin, Wani became the Archbishop of Uganda.

*

There is another KAR link in this Uganda story. The name of the current President, Yoweri Kaguta Museveni, shows that he comes from the *Abaseveni*, the Luganda word for the 'people of the 7th King's African Rifles'. 7th KAR were the troops from the West of Uganda who were recruited as a Territorial Battalion at the time of the Second World War. All over the north and the west of Uganda, families still remember those who went away to fight on behalf of the British.

**Part 2: Mission and School**
**2.1 Mvara**

Staying with Seton and Peggy for the first few weeks of my time in Arua, especially the week before the school term started, proved to be an ideal introduction. After an early breakfast on the first day, Seton went off to take an ordination class in an outlying village. I spent the morning exploring what was said to be the 'Mvara Mission'. As I wandered around, a posse of small children followed, all offering repeated 'howareyou?'s with broad grins as that was about the limit of their English and well beyond my Lugbara.

On the corner where the side road to Mvara Mission left the main road down to the Nile, Emmanuel Cathedral slumbered in the sun, a vast and rusting corrugated iron roofed building with low walls, no windows, just open spaces to catch any breeze. I wandered in to find no fans, no chairs, just rows of concrete benches built up from the concrete floor. It had a pulpit and a hymn board and a simple altar at the east end – little more than a worship barn big enough to welcome a thousand or more. It was empty and silent and I thought about the irony of moving from one great Cathedral to another – how very different they were!

A row of large detached houses ran down one side of the road, each almost buried in a riot of flowering shrubs and creepers, white, red and purple bougainvillea, scarlet hibiscus and orange flamboyant. Each roof was the same rusting corrugated iron, and each had a wide veranda with insect-excluding netting over the windows and doors. In front of each house, a neat lawn of short deep green grass had been planted and tended with a forest of banana, pawpaw, guava and avocado trees at the back. All the houses seemed to be occupied by European couples or families, with just one house, beyond the Maclures, allocated to the Bishop, the Rt Rev Silvanus Wani. It all seemed very 'colonial'.

The Diocesan Offices were across the narrow cambered hard-packed earth road. Deep gulleys on both sides carried away the rain water and the next compound housed a large primary school, Arua Demonstration School. Simple single-storied classrooms were built around an open court-yard. Next, the Teacher Training College had more substantial classroom blocks, each with the outside walls covered in blackboards on which students could hone their teaching skills. The stone Chapel that Canon Vollor had built complete with tower, high windows and rows of seats, still looked impressive, a statement in stone that the Mission and the Church were here to stay. Training students to spread primary education, and especially literacy, was still vital to the Church throughout the District and the old bungalow where the Vollors had lived was equally well preserved.

The next cluster of buildings looked tired and neglected. The faded painted sign said that this was the Mvara Senior Secondary School Old Site, a quadrangle of classrooms with one laboratory in the corner. They had once housed the Junior Secondary School but now the school had grown to the full four years of study to the equivalent of O level. This was the school to which I had so carefully arranged to be sent, to teach in bare classrooms and an even barer laboratory. There was a shed labelled 'Staff Room' and a small office labelled 'Head Teacher'.

By the time I had strolled back up to the Maclure's house, it was time for lunch and I spent the afternoon asking Peggy about the missionaries who lived at Mvara, while she made a huge saucepan of guava jelly.

'If we start from the top, by Emmanuel,' she said, 'the first house is Lewis and Angela. He's the Head of the Secondary School – you've met him already. They have lots of children. Some are at school down in Kigezi. They came to Mvara with the Mission but they are now with the Government, just like you. Next house is Stuart and May Cole from Belfast. He runs the Teacher Training College and she also teaches there. They're also ex-Mission, now on Government contracts. Stuart's father was with AIM in the Congo in the 1920s and moved to Goli in the south of the District to work there until just before WWII.

Then it's us and beyond us the Bishop's house and beyond him, Margaret Lloyd[1]. She came to Mvara in 1946 four years after we got to Arua. Margaret has always been keen on the Revival Movement – she'll tell you all about it when she asks you 'are you saved?' She ran the Junior Secondary School here and when that closed down, the Church asked her to open the Senior Secondary School, just before Independence. At that time, the government took over all the secondary schools and she became an Education Officer like most of the British staff. She stayed on as Head before Lewis took over.'

I asked Peggy where the African teachers were living as all the houses seemed to be allocated to people who had worked with the Mission.

'They're all over on the New Site,' she said as if I would know where that was. 'If you go down the path past Jericho and across the valley, you'll see the new buildings.'

So later that afternoon I did what she suggested, walking about half a mile across the valley on a narrow path through the ten foot high elephant grass. Along the way, women carrying water pots on their heads passed me with a cheery greeting. '*A zi mi ci*', they called in Lugbara and I smiled a 'hello' response which reduced them to helpless giggles. At the bottom a small stream with a low dam made a place for collecting water and washing clothes.

Where the path climbed up the other side of the valley, the first of the new buildings appeared, almost-finished houses standing in islands of cleared land surrounded by ten foot high grass. They were two semi-detached bungalows, small but each big enough for one or two, and beyond them larger houses and further blocks of semi-detached bungalows each in its cleared patch of land. At the top of the hill, near to the road which ran on into the town, a row of large dormitory buildings and a block of two new classrooms had been built. All the structures were of concrete blocks with plastered walls and roofs of aluminium sheets. This was the 'New Site' which Peggy had mentioned and, on the roadside, a large hoarding proclaimed 'World Bank Project: Mvara Senior Secondary School'. A boy in a ragged pair of shorts sat under the hoarding chewing a length of sugar-cane and keeping half an eye on his herd of thin humped-backed cows grazing across the school site. There was no fence, no boundary marker, just acres of high grass with new buildings dotted about in what looked like a random pattern, clearly a very new and very unfinished school.

When I got back to Mvara, Peggy reminded me that supper was at 6 pm and I spent an hour or two snoozing on the bed in the little guest house in their garden. Fortunately, I woke up in time and after a short wash in the bowl with a jug of water, I went up to their house. Seton, Peggy and Lewis were sitting round their large dining table with an elderly African hovering by the kitchen door resplendent in a long pink apron trimmed with lace. He brought in a dish which looked like a fish pie and put it in on the table.

'*A wa di fo*, Burua,' she thanked him. Then she explained who the Bwana *Muzungu* was, the new European, me. He bowed his head solemnly in my direction and then produced a string of unintelligible but obviously very respectful noises, before taking my right hand in his and clasping first the fingers  and then the thumb, in a curious switching hand shake.

'He says that he praises God for your coming and that he will pray for you so that when you teach the children, they may learn the things of God. You may think that you're here to teach Science or something, but to Burua, schools still have only one function, spreading the Gospel. Sometimes, I agree with him!' She invited me to help myself to fish pie.

'This is Nile Perch,' she explained. 'They catch it down at Rhino Camp, great big fish as long as a bicycle and then peddle all the way up to Arua to sell it in the market. It's like a giant fresh-water cod. You buy it in great chunks by the pound and it's very good if it's fresh. The green slurpy stuff is avocado straight from our garden so that should be even fresher!'

Peggy Maclure in 1968

I later learnt that Peggy's fish pie was famous throughout Northern Uganda. She seemed to give it an elastic quality so that no matter how many people turned up, mssionaries on their way to Sudan or the Congo, or Government officers visiting Mvara, there was always enough. It was excellent!

I walked back to my little guest house armed with a torch, through the frangipani bushes and moon-flowers with their heavy sweet scent on the evening breeze. Seton had showed me a pair of small brick-built huts behind their house. He explained that these were the 'long-drops', earth latrines.

He hoped that I would be comfortable! Back in my room, under the mosquito net and into bed, I watched the geckos chase flies across the ceiling in my torch beam and listen to the frogs calling from the drainage ditch outside. All around in the distant night, insistent drumming came from nearby villages. It all seemed very peaceful and I was glad that I had come.

Early the next morning, I made my way up to the Maclure's house. It seemed very quiet and looking through the window, I saw a ring of bowed heads. Seton was reading from his Bible. It was the Mvara early-morning prayer meeting. Should I join them? Just as I was about to tiptoe away, Peggy looked up and gestured to the empty seat beside her. I slipped into the meeting and listened to their conversation with God. An older dark-haired lady with a strong beaked nose was praying for a boy who had got into trouble.

'Lord, help him to find you,' she pleaded. 'Help him to find your peace and to know that he can be washed with the blood of Jesus.'

There was a pause, and a strong Belfast accent prayed for the coming school and college term.

'Thank you for our new staff. Help them to settle in soon and to be effective in their teaching,' he prayed.

He was a business-like, fit looking man with very smartly pressed white shorts and short-sleeved shirt. This must be Stuart, the TTC Principal, I thought.

The last 'Amen' ran round the room and by the strange telepathy that signals the end of prayer meetings, the bowed heads of those sitting in a circle opened out. Peggy asked me to introduce myself.

'I'm John Haden,' I said. 'I've come to teach science at the Secondary School.'

'Welcome,' said the man with the Belfast accent. 'I'm Stuart. This is Margaret. Next to her is Christine who teaches English at the school, then Donald who works with the Diocese. Seton and Peggy I think you know.'

The only other event that week was a Staff Meeting at the Old Site. The members of staff were to meet in what I still thought of as a small shed. The notice on the door said that the meeting would be at 4 pm so I went across from the Maclure's house just after half past three. There was no-one else there. Well after four, Lewis arrived clutching a folder of papers and let me in to the hot, airless room. Corrugated iron roofs without any insulation do not make for comfortable meetings.

A European couple arrived first. The man was bearded and broad chested in open-necked shirt and khaki shorts with an arm around the thin shoulders of a pale girl with that burnt-out look of too much sun-shine and too many late nights.

'I'm Des and this is Hilda-Mary,' he said. 'Who are you?' I explained and Lewis added that I'd come to teach Science.

'And a bit of Maths and some English and some RE – you'll soon find out,' said the girl. 'Where are you living?'

'I'm staying at the Mission with the Maclures.'

'You're not another bloody missionary are you? That's all we need.'

'No, I'm on a government contract.'

That seemed to cheer her up and she turned to greet the three Ugandan teachers coming into the Staffroom.

'Hi, Dison. Hi, Silas. Hi, Guy.' They all smiled and sat down. 'This is John – Science he says.' They shook my hand and offered their own welcome.

There were two more Ugandan teachers by the very English names of George and Dick, another English teacher called Christine, and Margaret, the Biologist.

'We're still short of three staff,' Lewis announced. 'There's another John coming to teach English, Gordon to teach Maths and TD and his wife Grace, also English. They should all be here in a day or two. That'll bring us up to fourteen including me, so that if everyone turns up we shall start the term with just a Mr X to teach the Art and a Miss Y to cover the English. Perhaps the Peace Corps will send us someone by half-term. If we get really stuck, we'll find some Makerere students to tide us over until the end of the year.'

The meeting got under way with the usual 'Minutes' and 'Matters arising', none of which seemed very interesting to me. Then we moved on to the allocation of 'duties and responsibilities'. It seemed that, in addition to teaching, there were boarding duties, and a lot of miscellaneous duties which I had not come across before: 'i/c Girls, i/c Boys, Food Liaison Teacher, Games Master and Games Mistress, i/c Uniforms[2].' Lewis read down his list as the staff did their best to avoid catching his eye.

Some of the roles were clearly more suited to the Ugandan staff, so Guy ended up as i/c Food Liaison, and George took on Games Master. It seemed that these roles carried no sort of supplementary allowance, just a bit of relief from teaching time. Margaret accepted her usual role of i/c Girls as she lived next to Jericho and Silas, who apparently lived near to the Boys' Dormitories, grudgingly accepted a supervision role for boy boarders. No-one seemed to be interested in i/c Uniforms. Lewis looked at me. 'How about it John?' he said with a note of desperation in his voice. 'It would be great if you could help in this way.'

So before term had even begun, I had achieved my first promotion at Mvara to a role about which I knew nothing, except that it had something to do with 'uniforms'. There were two more items on the agenda. 'School Dance' and 'Head Boy and Head Girl', it said. 'School Dance' sounded like an end-of-term celebration, something of the kind that most UK schools enjoy, a disco or, for the more adventurous, a 'formal'. But this was not what we discussed.

Lewis explained for my benefit. 'Last term there was a request for a mixed school dance, which we as a staff refused to allow as it would break another rule which the School Governors have agreed, forbidding mixed dances. We did say that we would discuss this again at the next staff meeting, so will someone put forward the reasons why they think that we should have a mixed dance at the end of this term? How about you, Guy? I seem to remember that you supported a dance last term?'

Guy looked up sharply. 'That is true, Headmaster, of course I want the school to dance. Dancing is important to Africans; it is part of our culture. We all dance in our villages, no matter what part of Uganda we may come from. In my Alur area we have many special dances to celebrate great events. The end of term is a great event for the students. When the students get home, they dance in the village in the holidays, so why do we have this ban on dancing? In this school, the rule says; no dancing. Why? Because the missionaries said that dancing is bad, so our Governors, the Church governors, say that there must be no dancing. But why is dancing bad? Are we afraid that our students will become bad because they dance? Some of them are bad already – can we change them by preventing them from dancing? It is the rule that must be changed. This is not a Mission school any more. It is a Government school and it must become up to date.'

He stopped as Dick, Silas, Hilda-Mary and Des nodded their agreement. Lewis looked pained, as if he had explained all this many times before.

'Our Governors have a policy. At this school they have decided that they will not allow mixed dancing.'

'But it is the Church that does not like dancing,' insisted Guy. 'And this is now a Government School. The Church should not dictate.' Silas and George muttered their agreement. Christine chipped in that the students who danced in the town in the holidays did so in the bars, got involved in drinking and got into trouble. Surely, they did not want that to happen at the school.

'That is not an argument.' Guy was becoming heated. 'We are not suggesting that students should have alcohol at their dances. But they must be able to dance.'

This had clearly been discussed so many times before. When the Staff were all European and mostly working with the Mission, it must have been easy to support the Governors' apparent enthusiasm for a dancing ban. Now that there were Ugandans and European teachers with no church links working at the school, it was much more difficult. But the Governors were, apparently, firm on this one. Lewis offered to put the point of view of some staff to them.

'How would it be if I, with Dison as my Deputy, raised the matter at the next Governors' Meeting? We'll put the points of view that the staff have expressed and ask them for a clear ruling. Meanwhile, the ban remains and can we please move on to the last item on our Agenda?'

Guy grudgingly agreed and we focused on 'Head Boy and Head Girl'. I thought that this would be a discussion about who would be suitable candidates for these roles and prepared to sit back as I had no knowledge of any of the students. But that was not what it was all about. It seemed that, at the end of the previous term, one of the S3 boys and one of the S3 girls had already been chosen. They would take over from the S4 holders of these posts for the final term of the year, to allow the S4 students to concentrate on preparing for their exams in December. But it seemed that the chosen two had celebrated their promotion by falling in love and had gone off to consummate their relationship in the privacy of the long grass around the school site.

Lewis was clearly embarrassed. 'We've not had this happen before', he said.

Hilda-Mary interrupted him. 'How do you know? For all we know, previous holders of the posts have been having it off with each other for years. And anyway isn't it the custom round here to 'try before you buy'? I'm sure I've read a poem somewhere which says as much.'

'Well it may have happened before, but I did not know. Now I do know because the girl's father has been to see me. Her mother has noticed she's pregnant. The father would be happy to simply get the boy to pay the usual number of cows and they can get married. But that's more difficult for the school. We have a rule about sex between students and now our leading lights have all too obviously broken it – what do you think we should do, Dison?'

'The girl has to go,' his Deputy said. 'That's the rule.'

'But what about the boy?' Christine chipped in. 'Surely he has to go too.'

The European Staff were divided. Hilda-Mary thought that neither should leave but be helped to finish their courses. Margaret and Christine thought that both students should be sent away as the school rule was quite clear. They were sure that the Board of Governors, all African Church leaders, would demand that both be expelled. To my surprise the Ugandan staff, all men, were equally sure that both should go.

Silas spoke for them. 'This school has a rule and that rule means that girls who misbehave must leave. This girl has been impregnated by this boy. They have both misbehaved. We may not agree with the rule, but we must apply it without fear. They must both leave.'

Christine looked across the table at Hilda-Mary and Des and whispered in my ear. 'There, but for the benefits of contraception, go our two love-birds.'

With this decided Lewis closed the meeting and released us from the hot and airless shed. I gathered my papers and walked back to the Maclures, feeling an increasing itch on the backs of my legs. I learnt another lesson that afternoon. Don't sit on the wooden slatted staffroom chairs in shorts. Across the back of each leg, I had a row of angry red bites, the work of bedbugs hiding in the cracks in the chair and excited into a feeding frenzy of my blood by the presence of two nice warm thighs. Sadly, we did lose our new Head Boy and Head Girl. She had her baby and they got married. He found a place at another school in S1. Their deputies were promoted.

Term began, according to the Ministry Circular pinned to the Staff-room board on Tuesday, September 6th 1968. So in the half light of 7 am on that day I walked across the valley to the 'New Site' classrooms to meet my first class, S1A. I was also to be their Form Teacher. The day before Lewis had handed me a list of names and a handful of forms.

'These are for Bursary applications,' he explained. 'We can only give them to the most desperate cases so can you find out who needs them and get them to fill them in.'

I had no idea how I was to make judgments on need but for once I understood what he wanted. S1A classroom was new, spacious and utterly bare of any display, just a large room with thirty five desks and chairs and a table for the teacher with a more comfortable chair with arms. At least it was clean and airy, businesslike with windows down both sides. Not a student had appeared so I looked at the list, 35 single names, twelve A's Aate, Abelia, Adraga etc, then more variety with Bongo, Burua, three Candias, each with an initial, Endreonzi, Fetaa, no Gs, Hs or Is, Jawoko, Okunziga, Onzi, etc and then mysteriously back to A again with Acanda, Anite, Apio, Candiru and Onziru. Just single names, no John, no Mary, no first names at all, Christian, Islamic or other.

I later learnt what these names actually meant and how the individuals had acquired them. Boys born as twins were named Opio and Odongo by the Alur, and their twin sisters, Apio and Adongo. Family tragedies were remembered in Lugbara children's names like Draonzi, 'death is bad', or even just Onzi, 'bad', linked to some other bad event. Each was more than the family tag which each English child acquires at birth, linking with parentage and sometimes to UK regions. For the people of West Nile, each name had a significance in terms of an event, Fetaa, 'gift', Candia, 'sorrow' for a boy and Candiru for a girl, Bile 'grave', family fortune recorded in the names of their children. To these single names, the individual could add as many others as they wished and change them when they felt like a change. So we had 'Harold Wilson Toma', 'Milly Small Mary Candiru' but in class they were always just Toma or Candiru.

At ten past seven on that first morning, one of the cooks thwacked the lorry wheel that hung from the fig-tree by the Dining Hall, and served as the school bell. The clang announced the start of the school day and the new term. No student had appeared in my classroom. Down by the boys' dormitories, a handful of figures wrapped in lengths of cloth or almost naked in shorts long since reduced to underpants drifted about. By the running tap on the outside wall, three boys were cleaning their teeth by scrubbing them with the well-chewed end of a thick stick, and spitting vigorously into the pool of muddy water at their feet.

No other teacher was around so I sat down and tried to learn the names of S1A, puzzling over the five at the end. At about half-past seven, one of the Ugandan staff wandered in. It was George Okai, looking sleepy.

'What's the matter, John, confused already?'

'I was trying to work out this list. Why are there these five names at the end?'

'Those are the girls,' he explained. 'Thirty boys and five girls in S1A. The girls will be here when they walked over from Jericho. They have their fees because their fathers know the value of a good wife with O level when it comes to the bride-price. If the girls come at all, they usually get here at the start.'

'Thanks, that explains one thing,' I told him gratefully. 'But none of the boys are here yet. Is the start of term always like this?'

He grinned. 'School fees,' he said. 'Each student has to bring the fees at the start of the term. No fees, no school.' He watched the boys beginning to drift up to the classrooms. 'This is the worst term. The tobacco and the cotton were sold months ago. The coffee is not yet picked and so, no money left for school fees. That means each student has to go round the family to get their fees from relatives and that takes time.'

'So most of the students always miss the start of the term?' I asked incredulously.

'Some get here on time, like these boys coming up now. Some miss the first week and a few even miss the first term, all because they cannot find the money. Many of those who do sneak back have to be sent home again because they haven't paid enough. Sometimes, we even have to lend them the bus fare home so that they can get the balance of their fees. Lewis tries to help the most deserving cases but it's hard to know which these are.'

With that, George left the classroom to see which of his own class had arrived. Another loud clanking announced the start of the second period. My time-table said S1A again after the change-over so I stayed in the classroom and waited. Students began to come in and sit down. There were twelve in that first batch, twelve out of thirty five, five girls as George had anticipated and seven boys.

'Good morning,' I said breezily.

'Good morning, Sir,' they replied quietly without much enthusiasm. We watched each other for a moment or two, as I waited for any more to arrive. None did. The five girls sat in a row at the front, with folded arms across their expansive chests, staring at me with deep brown eyes. At first glance they all looked alike, strong, well-built girls with their white blouses straining at the front. But then I realised that their hair differed. One had close cropped curls, another, a knotted pattern of tightly bound skeins in straight ridges all over her head.

The boys sat at the back. One looked as if he was about thirteen, small and timid while his neighbour, lounging over the desk with an expression of apathy on his face pitted with small pox, could have been a few years older than my twenty six years. With only a third present, doing anything important seemed a waste of time so I decided to try to get to know them as their Form Teacher. Discussion seemed unlikely to produce much response so I explained who I was and where I came from.

'My name is Mr Haden and my home is in England. I have been teaching Chemistry in an English boys' school to O level and A level and I have travelled from London to teach here at Mvara Senior Secondary School. I am looking forward to getting to know you.'

All this was received without a murmur of interest, so I gave out sheets of paper and asked them to write something about themselves which they would like me as their form teacher to know. I might as well have been a member of the secret police from the looks of deep distrust that this produced, but eventually, the girl with the short hair decided to write something and the others slowly followed her lead. The tall boy at the back was the last, slowly searching his thick mat of hair to find a small stub of pencil, licking it suspiciously and starting to write.

The first girl to finish got up from her desk and brought it forward, looking at the floor. She went down on her knees and handed me the paper with both hands. She had written: 'My name is Milly Small-Mary Candiru. I have not had any failures with school life and hope to work hard for progress this term, if God allows. I have a lot of troubles in waking very early in the morning and find I have a lot of problems in Chemistry. I have failed to understand the subject completely.'

The tall boy at the back was equally candid: 'Name: Lord Sam Aspro Adraga. Achievements: grabbed more facts especially in Biology and cleared most problems which kept my brain under a blanket. I have helped to defeat all West Nile Schools in Champion Basketball Team. Hope to get good Cambridge, pass well at Higher, go to the Hill, pass BSc Agric – MSc – PhD !! If these fail and I crack my brain, then I simply go to the land. Dig hard, like the Devil, get enough money to booze sensibly. Aim for holidays: help parents with work, then the maize, groundnuts and mangoes have to be eaten!'

In sad contrast, the small boy sitting next to him, his dull greyish skin loose around his thin arms, had written: 'Name: Harold Wilson Toma. I am a Kuku. Successes: nothing.

Hope for the future: I hope that our new Form Teacher will be sympathetic to my problems because I am a refugee from the Sudan, and I think that he will help me with my school fees next term when the money from the Church is finished.'

Others who wrote had additional names which were obviously Christian, like the Marys and the Mattayos. Some were more complicated but no less biblical like Onessimo and Penina, Remelia and Manasseh. Then there were the Sheiks and Jumas from the Muslim community and one calling himself 'Coca-cola Seraphim Okumu'. However extraordinary, each had been the careful choice of an individual. Any laughter would have been inexcusable. Fortunately, they all responded to their listed names whenever the form list had to be called.

Those personal response sheets from the members of my 'Form' were the only reaction I got from the students in the first few weeks of that September term. When I eventually decided, after facing groups of less than a dozen in most classes that to wait any longer while doing 'revision' was unfair on those who had managed to pay their fees and get to school in the right month, I started to teach new material to each group in turn. The course was very familiar, the O level Physics with Chemistry of my own school days dressed up as an overseas Cambridge Physical Science course. Having spent two years developing a chatty style of teaching at Worcester using the Nuffield O level Chemistry course, I had hoped to be able to use the same approach at Mvara. It was heavily dependent on the two techniques of class discussion and finding-out style experiments, so without very much careful thought, I tried the same approach. After all, I reasoned, my contract specified my duty to innovate and to introduce the highest possible standards of teaching and learning.

To say that there was no response to my initial efforts to provoke discussion would be untrue. If I addressed a specific question to a particular student, he or she would wait for a second or two, slowly rise to his or her feet and offer an almost inaudible answer. But the overall effect was as wooden and flattening as the response to the initial cheery greeting at the start of each lesson. They simply sat, stared and remained largely silent so that by the end of each school day in the high heat of mid-afternoon, I was exhausted, frustrated and puzzled.

'When you first started here,' I asked Christine Walker one morning break, 'did you find the students passive?' She taught English and Music and I knew from walking past her classroom that her classes were as lively as mine were silent.

'I'm glad you didn't ask what one of our new staff asked,' she replied with a smile. 'Did I find the students stupid? He didn't last long! After a week, he threw himself through that door and shouted for all to hear, 'God, these lads are thick!' They put him on the next plane home.'

She stirred her coffee. 'I know that there is an assumption in England that African children are all desperately keen to learn, but just because they don't immediately laugh at all our O-so-English jokes and answer all our questions, don't assume that they're bored stiff.'

'But they don't respond, not to me anyway, so how am I to know what's going on in their heads?'

'First of all,' Christine explained patiently, 'it's your voice. You may think that you speak clear, loud, straightforward English. But it is not their English. They've had Irish, Scots, Indian, Dorset, and Oxford accents since they came to this school and it takes time for them to get tuned in to something new. They need a chance to listen to you and to learn to understand what you say. Then it's a matter of expression. I heard you say this morning, 'Right lads! Let's think about an oxidising agent. What does it do?' Silence. You told them to think, so they were thinking! In any case, all the girls would have taken umbrage at the term 'lads' – you were clearly not including them! You thought – no response, but there was a response, just not the one you expected! Another thing is that you teach by asking questions – no-one else has ever tried that here in Science. They've always learnt by writing down what's written on the board and what the textbook says. Then in the middle of their course up pops John Haden, full of questions and expecting them to make an immediate response. Sorry John, I didn't mean to mock, but don't expect too much too soon. You'll get round their mental blocks in the end.'

I felt frustrated but was grateful for her forthright comments and she was trying to be helpful. My progress against those blocks seemed very slow and was not helped by the trickle of new blank faces into each class for much of the first half of the term. I began to wonder if I would ever get these students to think more and do more for themselves. Every day I seemed to be writing more on the board, dictating more into their notebooks and demonstrating more and more practical work to a less and less active audience.

By about the fourth week, when most of the classes had reached an uneasy equilibrium of about thirty, I had lapsed so far from the discovery approach that I spent eighty minutes one morning covering the board with notes on the reactions of sulphur, without a murmur from the class. They all sat and copied as if this is what they really enjoyed doing. Some of the girls even smiled at me! At last I had learnt how to teach them in a way they appreciated. It was simply a process of dispensing information in as digestible a form as possible. The more information that was written on the board, the better was the teacher. The fact that this made them all deeply dependent on notes, highly demanding of teachers and unwilling to think for themselves mattered not a jot.

They regarded European teachers as highly expensive imports, a necessary but temporary embarrassment for a young black nation. Like the exotic Friesian and Shorthorn bulls flown in to improve the nation's cattle stock, they provided a service, nothing more. But although the students recognised the need to use expatriates to staff an expanding secondary school system, they had a deep sense that their schools should also have more Ugandan teachers, that the system should be 'Africanised', especially the leadership.

This caused another problem as they were also far more critical of the Ugandan teachers who were recruited, particularly if they came from another part of the country. Woe betide the young Makerere graduate, impeccably dressed in his white shirt and tie, pressed trousers and polished shoes, if he could not turn out as good notes as the older, scruffier, more experienced white men teaching next door. He would not be left in any doubt about his shortcomings as a teacher when his whole class boycotted his lessons and sat in a silent circle under a mango tree, waiting for the Head to find a better teacher for them. So for years, the notes of one generation of Uganda's students were solemnly regurgitated for the next, and for the most part, the results in the Cambridge School Certificate Exams were good enough to keep the process going.

My teaching steadily deteriorated, or so I thought, into a more and more arid provision of 'notes' but, in the eyes of the students, it got better and better. The teaching day, from seven in the morning until two, with just two short breaks for breakfast and what the students called a 'short call', seemed more and more exhausting. The last two periods in the roasting heat were the worst.

\*

Having arrived at Mvara in early September and been offered accommodation by Peggy and Seton in their small garden guest house, I was still there at the end of the month and wondering how much longer I was going to have to trouble them. They could not have been more hospitable, generously sharing their meals with me and even taking me on their trips to local church communities at the weekends. This was a wonderful introduction to the Church of Uganda in West Nile, travelling with them in their VW Combi, loaded with church people from Mvara, down narrow *murram* roads to distant villages. I joined them for the dedication of a new church building, a simple mud-walled, concrete floored structure with corrugated iron roof, and for the induction of a newly ordained pastor into his village living. Each occasion was exuberantly joyful and the occasion for a gathering from miles around. The Bishop, Rev Silvanus Wani officiated, Seton Maclure kept an eye on the proceedings and there were long speeches and a great feast.

We weakling *muzungus* were placed under the shade of a grass roof on school chairs borrowed for the occasion. The children of the village school would sing to us, anything from '*Is she fit to be your wife, Billy Boy?*' to '*Jesus loves me this I know*'.

Then the women of the church would come to greet us, going down on their knees to offer bowls of water and cotton cloths so that we could wash and dry our hands. Plastic bowls would be distributed and more women bring us mounds of steaming *enya*, the hot, stiff mixture of boiled millet and cassava, their 'bread of life', on great woven platters with brightly coloured conical covers. Peggy taught me how to eat it.

'You take a lump of the *enya*', she explained, 'using your right hand, left is for other purposes! Roll it into a ball and press your thumb into the middle to make a sort of scoop. You then use this to scoop up some of the stew and relish. It's really quite easy and the stew is usually very tasty. Don't worry about making slurping noises – they'll be delighted that you're enjoying their food, so have a go.'

The first of these feasts was a challenge but I soon got used to eating with my fingers and making suitably appreciative slurping sounds. Beef was fine if gristle-rich, goat more challenging, especially the fatty bits and the lumps that seemed to have come from inside the animal. Best of all was a sauce of ground nuts like very runny peanut butter. After two or three such church visits, I was happy to eat what the people of the District ate and could join the Mvara students in their Dining Room without worrying about it.

*Is she fit to be your wife, Billy Boy?*

But I was still stuck in the Maclures' guest house and I was not the only one boarded out around the Mvara community. Gordon and Grace were living in a house temporarily vacated by a missionary. John Martin who had arrived to teach English was living with Angela and Lewis, who were also sharing their house with two volunteers who had come through AIM, Andrew Dow and Richard Inwood.

On the school's New Site, the staff houses which we knew had been allocated to us were nearing completion. All that remained was the final wiring and the provision of Ministry of Works 'hard furniture'. At the start of the fourth week, Lewis told us that all was ready. John Martin and I were to share the lower semi-detached bungalow with Gordon and Grace as our neighbours.

Moving in was simple as we were all still living out of suitcases. A visit to the *dukas* in the town and a bit of help from Peggy produced some cushions for the new mahogany easy chairs. We bought sheets and towels from Arua market and John and I moved in. As if by telepathy, the trunk and teachest that I had sent off from Worcester, to travel by sea to Mombasa, train to Nairobi and Kampala, and Ministry lorry to Arua, arrived on the site and were delivered to our house. To my delight all the china had survived un-broken, the record player still worked and my books, clothes and other belongings seemed unscathed from months at sea. John Martin's trunk arrived shortly after and we could set up our bachelor household and invite visitors.

Neither of us was much of a cook and we were advised to find a 'house boy'. This sounded much too colonial to us enlightened servants of Uganda, but we soon tired of the joys of cleaning, shopping and cooking, while trying to teach in our spare time.

'How do you recruit a 'house boy'?' we asked, but it was not long before the word got out that we needed help and a queue of potential employees formed at the back door. All seemed to have letters of recommendation from previous employers, spoke basic English and all had willing smiles. We should have asked for Peggy's advice but flushed with the novelty of becoming employers, we singled out a young man who was strongly recommended in his letters and who clearly needed a job.

'I need to send money to the village,' he explained. 'I have many brothers who want to go to school.'

So Alex Candia joined our household as a fairly willing cook, a less willing ironer of shirts and occasional cleaner. I think we paid him Ug.Sh.200/- a month which seemed to be the going rate at the time. Every morning, he would arrive about seven, serve our breakfast of coffee, toast and paw-paw when we came back from the first lessons of the day, clear up and cycle off to the market to get what we needed for that night's supper. 'Meat without bones' was sold in small shops behind the market, and once we had told him to get *filleti*, he could turn it into a reasonably tender stew. Bread was baked every day in the town and would arrive back at the house wrapped in a sheet of newspaper. Carrots, cabbages, aubergines, tomatoes, potatoes and sweet potatoes were all readily available in Arua Market for most of the year and at some seasons, rhubarb and green but tasty oranges would be carried in on women's heads from the high country across the Congo border.

Alex, John Martin and I formed a team, perhaps not the most adventurous catering team, but a team which kept us fed and occasionally offered a meal to others. We soon realised that he was not talented as a chef and could not be persuaded to do more than he felt like, but at least we had a fairly clean house, three meals a day and time to get on with our teaching. Best of all, we were sometimes invited next door to share

Grace's far higher standard of home baking and hear Gordon's view of the world in general and West Nile in particular.

He was an old hand compared to the rest of us, having worked at Mvara in the Church Book Shop for a year or two before returning to County Down to marry Grace. On the surface, he had all the prejudices of the fully paid-up Orangeman, underneath, a heart of gold. Gordon referred to the Catholic nuns at the local RC Mission as 'Free State Arabs'. He told boys in school who got their Maths problems wrong that they were '*Fenian eejits*'. Fortunately, his Ulster accent was so strong that few understood these insults. If they had, he might have been deported. To everyone, staff and students, they were both as kind and helpful as they could be.

One day, I called round to see them. 'We're worried about Alex,' I said. 'He's even less energetic than he was to start with. His cooking is now getting to the level of inedible, and he has managed to burn two shirts. We've tried to ask him what the problem is but all he will say is that he's 'a bit alright'.'

Gordon's advice was to keep a close eye on Alex and to see how he got on. His work was not yet totally useless and he should be given a chance to do better. Then Alex started to turn up late for making the breakfast and on some days, not turn up at all. I found, under my bed, the torn up remains of a sheet out of my cheque book bearing an all too obvious attempt at a forgery of John's signature. We sat Alex down in the kitchen for a serious chat.

'Did you tear this paper out of my cheque book?' I asked him.

'No, Sir,' he insisted.

'Alex?' John asked him. 'Are you in trouble?'

'No,' he insisted. 'I am a bit alright.'

But he clearly wasn't. He seemed to be getting sadder and greyer and thinner week by week. We asked him if we could do anything to help. 'No', he insisted. 'I am a bit alright.'

We consulted Peggy. 'He looks to me as if he thinks he has been bewitched,' she said. 'Once a Lugbara boy thinks that he is being bewitched or cursed, there's little anyone can do to help him. Unless of course he becomes a convinced Christian and know that such powers cannot help him.'

We knew that Alex was not a church-goer but we had no idea what he believed. So one day, I asked him about why he seemed to be so sick. 'I am a bit alright,' he said yet again, but then added, 'I think that someone has cursed me.'

'I'm sorry to hear that,' I said. 'But we need you to be able to do your job. If you cannot do your job, then we cannot continue to have you as our house-boy. And anyway, I don't believe in cursing – there must be something wrong with you. Have you been to the hospital?'

'But I think I have been cursed and it is true. I am failing to do my job,' he said sadly

That left us with a dilemma. If he was sick, we as concerned employers would of course have given him time off to seek medical help and probably helped him with any charges the hospital made. But neither of us felt happy about offering him help with a 'curse' whatever that was, and wondered whether the effects of such a 'curse' was grounds for dismissal in Ugandan Employment Law. In the end, we did not have to send him away, he just disappeared. After he had not turned up for a week, we started to look for someone to help in his place. We did make enquiries about where he might be but no-one seemed to know or to be very interested. So we talked to Peggy again and she said, 'Leave it with me.'

That's how we were adopted by Onessimo. A day or two after our conversation with Peggy, an older but very spritely man appeared on our veranda.

'I am Onessimo,' he said. 'I have come to work with you.'

Not 'for' but 'with', and he was true to his word. He had worked in the past for a British District Commissioner and his wife. The Church at Mvara had persuaded him to come out of retirement to look after a couple of incompetent bachelors on the New Site, just across the valley from his house. We were happy to have his help and he soon remembered his stock of catering recipes, as taught by Mrs DC.

'This is Queen of Pudding,' he would announce with a flourish, serving a perfect sponge with marmalade running down the side. 'This is 'scollop of filleti', which turned out to be a delicious fried steak. We were delighted to have him working with us and our house soon became a model of cleanliness.

Onessimo took a dim view of the state of our concrete floors. The builders had left them smooth but unsealed, so the concrete dust built up and blew everywhere. Onessimo set about covering them with red Cardinal Polish and then polishing them by skating around with dusters tied around both feet. For a grandfather, he had amazing energy and balance and our floors were soon up to his high standards. 'Muddy feet,' he would mutter if either of us forgot to take off our shoes by the door. We learnt to wipe our shoes more thoroughly.

If progress on our housing was good, the same could not be said for the school buildings on the New Site. It seemed that the World Bank Project, so boldly advertised on the hoarding by the roadside, had ground to a halt. Gaunt rows of concrete beams stood like gallows in place of finished buildings.

Gaunt rows of concrete beams stood like gallows...

In some Washington architect's office, the designers of the new structures had chosen a form of reinforced concrete for the main load-bearing beams, to be made on site. This required aggregate of specific size, high quality cement and precision made timber casting moulds into which the reinforcing steel could be fixed and the concrete poured. The Italian contractor who had been awarded our job, started on site in January 1968, when the world of West Nile was as dry as a bone. Aggregate was bought, Tororo cement came up on trucks and the Italian engineer in charge set out hardwood frames for casting the beams onto the bare earth. When the concrete was dry, the first batch of beams was inspected by the project Building Inspector who came up in a smart 4x4 to check the job. The beams passed and up they went to form the first of the new structures, the school's offices, classrooms and labs.

But by April, the rains had started. The timber-moulds warped, the cement ran out of the moulds and even the aggregate was too small to be acceptable. So the whole job stopped, the contractor withdrew his engineer to another school site in the south. The boys living in the New Site Dormitories, put up in a month or two by a local Asian firm using local labour and materials, took to wandering around the site in the hour before sunset, inspecting the sad rows of beams

'Local is good,' George said to me one evening as we shared a duty. 'These Asian contractors can put up good buildings. using concrete blocks in just a short time. That's how our houses will be built. Local is good.'

Since we were enjoying our new bungalows, put up without any finance from New York or expertise from Washington, I had to agree. As John and I settled in, each of us with his own bedroom and a shared bathroom, kitchen and living space, I began to feel that God's provision for my needs was very generous. Teaching in the school was challenging but we had expected that. We had the same salaries as the Ugandan teachers on the same grade and a generous overseas allowance to bring the total up to the UK level. Since there was very little to spend money on in Arua, we were well provided for. The house was comfortable and adequately spacious and life was good. We listened to Brahms on the record player and enjoyed the two hours of evening light provided by the town generator.

But some of the power sockets in my room did not work. I had no bedside light, hardly a major deprivation compared with the rest of West Nile's population, but irritating as there was a socket. So I used a chair on a table to get up through the access hatch into the roof space and hauled myself up. The beam of my torch showed three neat wires running along the tops of the timbers, one bare copper, one black and one red. Carefully avoiding stepping on what I thought might be the live wires, I walked across the joists and stepped on a length of bare copper earth.

There was a flash, a bang and a smell of burning as I was thrown onto my back across the joists. 240 volts is more than enough to kill you so I was very, very lucky. Perhaps the damp sandal had somehow reduced the shock but had also ensured that my foot flew off the wire. Very cautiously, I got back to the hatch and lowered myself down onto the chair and table. I was not so sure that 'local is best'.

When the Asian contractor who had built the houses was told about the live earth wire later that day, he rushed round with his electrician. Both were full of apologies.

'I am so sorry, Sir,' he said. 'I will check all the wiring of the houses myself.' It occurred to me that he might have done that before we moved in, but it seems that our rush to be in had meant that he cut corners.

'Please check all the new buildings now, the dormitories and the new classrooms as well as the new houses.'

'Certainly, Sir, it will be done today.'

Better a shocked teacher than a dead student, I thought, that evening, and vowed not to go into unknown roof spaces again. I had been warned about snakes, about using a mosquito net and taking the tablets. I had been told to boil all drinking water and to wear a hat in the noon-day sun. But no-one had mentioned avoiding bare wires in the attics of modern houses. I would just have to be more careful.

## 2.2 Science and Uniforms

One of the books I had read before leaving England was E. B. Castle's account of encouraging students' to take responsibility for their own learning[3].

'That's all very well, Professor,' I thought, 'but how do you stop your students being dependent on you when they have nothing else?'

Teaching science on the New Site was difficult as there was no lab, just a couple of large, bare, classrooms. S2 Physics was the easiest to manage as they had got to the 'conduction, convection and radiation' section of the course and it was possible to improvise. Hot kettle handles and the smoke rising from fires were part of the students' daily lives and it was easy to get them to find lots of examples of heat transfer which they could write about. But I struggled with radiation from hot dark objects. Then walking home one lunch-time, I felt the heat from the walls of the classroom block warming my bare legs. The rough concrete had been painted alternately dark grey and white. After a morning under the hot sun, they were acting as perfect illustrations of the principles of radiation; white surfaces reflect heat and do not absorb it, dark surfaces absorb heat and then radiate it, teaching problem solved.

Chemistry in classrooms was even more difficult. The school had a set of small spirit burners in place of Bunsen burners, just a glass bulb of methylated spirit and a wick. We had test-tube racks and boxes of test-tubes, a supply of distilled water and a range of basic lab chemicals. But we only had one set of this equipment, kept in the prep room next to the old lab at Mvara and guarded closely by the school lab technician, Mr Opio. To offer any sort of chemistry practical work on the New Site or even in the Old Site classrooms when the lab was being used by the Biologists, all this equipment had to be moved. Mr Opio tried to be helpful but was clearly unwilling and unable to transport all the kit we needed from one site to the other. He could be persuaded to load it onto a trolley and wheel it across to another Old Site classroom but even that was clearly beyond his job description. 'It is too heavy,' he would mutter, pushing and pulling the pile of equipment between rooms, watched by a gaggle of students totally unwilling to help with such demeaning manual labour. What I needed was a car.

I had planned to save some money and then perhaps buy a second-hand car around Christmas. Now I needed one urgently and I fished out the file of contract papers which had been given to each of us during our Kampala induction. A car loan scheme was mentioned. It appeared to be limited to new cars and to be administered through the national agents of each car company in Kampala. So, I got permission from Lewis to miss two days of school, hitched a lift to Kampala on the next car going down and went to Cooper Motors (Uganda) Ltd. They were the VW agents for Uganda and their salesman knew all about the car-loan scheme. Yes, they had new VW Beetles, yes, I was eligible for a loan and yes, no deposit was required, just a standing order to transfer monthly payments from my Uganda bank account. It all seemed too good to be true, but it was true. The following morning I signed the papers, picked up a brand-new white VW and set off for Arua with a map and a full tank of petrol. Three hundred miles, and a lot of pot-holes later, I drove my now murram-brown Beetle onto the New Site and proudly parked it next to our house. I had a car!

This made teaching much less complicated. The car became my mobile prep room, loaded up by Mr Opio with all the kit needed for the day's lessons on either site. The boot at the front was good for papers and piles of books, the back seat for plastic boxes of chemicals and solutions, spirit burners and test-tubes. It even had a spare front seat for colleagues going my way. With an air-cooled engine at the back producing an impressive roar and a cloud of dust in my wake, I could rush around the roads between Old Site and New while the students made their leisurely way on foot across the valley. If the first lesson was 'Old Site', I would leave the house as dawn was breaking through the mists over the Nile valley far to the east. By the time I was nearing Emmanuel Church, the great red orb of the sun would be sitting on the end of the Mvara Road.

With teaching settling into a manageable and rewarding pattern and most of the school back from their village homes, I had more time to get to know other staff and talk about what we were trying to do. Gordon, Grace, John Martin and I were the newcomers and we shared evening duties on the New Site with Dison, Silas, George, and Guy. On our evenings together, in theory on patrol but often over a cup of coffee in one of our homes to escape from the mosquitoes, they would tell us about what it had been like to struggle through primary, secondary and higher education to reach the status of a graduate teacher, with a house and a regular salary. Dison was the most ambitious, already a Deputy Head, he had almost completed his in-service Headship training. It was only a matter of time before the Ministry took him off to join the handful of Ugandan Heads leading one of the other eighty Senior Secondary Schools.

'It won't be Budo or Mwiri,' he grinned. 'They're the flagship schools and a *muzungu* will be Head there for a long time yet. But this expansion programme has produced eight new schools all over the country and I'll probably be sent to one of those. Building delays are just part of the training!'

It was a Friday afternoon, never a good time in any school, when I finally decided that teaching the way the students wanted to be taught, giving them notes to be slavishly copied without any thinking on their behalf, would eventually drive me mad. I had to persuade them that there was a better way. I had a Physics class for Period Eight that day and I had already taught the first seven. They were desperate for notes on the mechanical equivalent of heat. I was bored, tired and sleepy. The hands of the clock seemed stuck at five to two. I had covered the board with formulae and units, definitions and explanations. The metal roof of the old lab at Mvara radiated down on our heads. The rows of expectant faces wanted more. I could not think of anything that made any sort of sense. So I stupidly decided to lighten the last five minutes.

The Flanders and Swann song on the Laws of Thermodynamics came into my head. I cleaned the formulae off the board and wrote:

'$1^{st}$ *Law of Thermodynamics: Heat is work and work's a curse*'

Seventy trusting eyes followed the chalk and thirty-five neat copies of the jingle were safely recorded in their notebooks. Not a flicker of a smile, not a single puzzled look, not a suspicion that I had written anything other than a vital piece of Physics. It was of course a gross betrayal, and as soon as I had done it, I regretted it. But I never admitted what I had done to any of them and no-one ever asked me about it. I had proved how much, or rather how little, actual thinking went on in the note-taking process but the deliberate misleading of the class was inexcuseable.

That weekend, I slaved away at text-books and the syllabus for Cambridge Overseas Physical Science. I worked out an outline for a course based on a discovery approach and hammered out the duplicating stencils for the first few sets of work-sheets and teaching notes. By Monday morning, the Mvara Secondary School Science Project was born. In a flush of brash self-confidence, I created a complete Physical Science course for the four years of Secondary School. It was to be delivered through worksheets, most of which asked questions. On Monday morning I consulted Lewis, explaining my frustration at what I had been doing. I did not tell him about Flanders and Swann and I did not consult the other science staff.

'Look John,' he said with a resigned look. 'You're in charge of Physical Science. You do what you think best but you'll have to sell the idea to anyone else who teaches Physics and Chemistry and you'll have to explain it to the students. The last thing I want is a strike over a Science course. So why not start with S1 and S2 and work through up to S3 next year. For the current S3 and S4, you'd better keep plugging away with the notes which seem so popular.'

With that limited support, I made a start and spent an evening that week talking to the other staff. Lewis himself was one of them, although he did not say much. Mr Avutia was in his second year of teaching and had heard of discovery methods during his course at Kyambogo National Teachers' College. The other teacher was a young AIM volunteer, Richard Inwood, who had the same Oxford Chemistry degree as me but had decided to do a year's teaching in Uganda before going into the Church of England ministry. He and the Mr Avutia could see the advantage of having lessons set out for them in my teaching scheme and were happy with the idea of worksheets. As the students had no text books, they pointed out that getting a detailed work sheet would be a big improvement for them, even if the content was mainly questions. By the end of that week, the MSSSP was up and running for S1 and S2.

Then I hit a snag. Silas Adrabo, the Biologist and most senior of the Ugandan staff, was not happy. He had heard of my dismissive comments on the process of giving and taking notes and he was sure that this was a challenge to his professional integrity.

'This is the way I have always taught,' he told me with slow dignity. 'What right do you have to say that this is not a good way? My students have always appreciated my teaching and they have passed their examinations well. I do not understand why it is necessary to change.'

In the end we settled for a compromise. I would stop making disparaging remarks about 'note-taking' and limit the MSSSP to the Physical Science course. Biology would stay 'traditional' under his leadership. But the damage had been done. So the scheme got under way with my Junior classes and those taught by my two young colleagues. The younger students began to enjoy doing more experimental work. Avutia was right in saying that they liked the Work Sheets. For students who had no books, the sheets which they could keep stuck into their notebooks had a sort of mystical significance. We found that the Old Site lab had a collection of old equipment in the back of the Prep Room and I wrote the work sheets around what we had rather than what would be desirable. The scheme started well.

A few days later, I passed Silas Adrabo on the path between the Old Site and the New. We were both carrying armfuls of books and I was not keen to discuss the new Physical Science scheme. I was ready for lunch and a gentle siesta. But he saw the meeting as a chance to make his grievances clear!

'Mr Haden, it is not right that you should be so proud.'

'I'm sorry,' I said, genuinely puzzled. 'I don't understand what you mean.'

'You come to Uganda; you are full of new ways; you are proud to show us new ways, but we do not need your help.' He went on, his voice rising with indignation. 'I have taught for many years, many more years than you. I understand my students and they have respect for me. I have too much work to do at my house. I have my wife and my children to be with and to feed. But you have none of these things. It is not right that you should tell me what I should do, that I should change. You are too proud, Mr Haden.' His eyes burned with resentment, but he kept his control.

As we stood there, a queue of boys was building up behind him and a similar queue of girls behind me as they tried to get from one school site to the other. It was not the moment for open conflict. I felt that I had acted in good faith although it was true that I had little respect for this senior colleague. I was too proud and there was now no turning back. But I could walk past Mr Adrabo and ignore him, so I did. With frustration and anger showing on my scarlet cheeks, I squeezed past him and the embarrassed students on their way to their lessons. We never discussed science teaching again even though we taught alongside each other for three years.

The S1 students took to the new course with enthusiasm. My two colleagues did a good job in selling it and they enjoyed the clear structure of the work-sheets. The S2s started well but began to resent the demands that the new approach made on them. They set up experiments as slowly as possible and wrote an absolute minimum in response to all my work-sheet questions. I tried to cajole them into a better attitude, full of my own importance as the initiator of the scheme and safe from further interference and criticism. It was three hundred miles to the nearest Inspector of Schools in Kampala, so I could bounce around looking out hitherto unused apparatus and writing an enormous number of work-sheets.

The S2s stepped up their passive resistance. One Monday morning, I handed out their work-sheets ignoring the atmosphere of tense expectation.

'Right,' I said, 'now get on with it.'

No-one moved.

'Come on; you know where to find everything you need.'

Still no-one moved. Then a boy slowly unwound himself from his stool.

'Excuse me, Sir.' They all looked at him in support. 'Excuse me, Sir. We think that you will teach us today.'

'What do you mean, 'teach you'?' I asked, knowing that I had either to convince them now or else abandon the whole project.

'I mean that you will teach us properly as our teachers did last year.' He swallowed and cracked the joints of his fingers in embarrassment. 'We think that you will teach us properly, as you have been teaching your students in England.'

So that's it, I thought. They have got the idea that what I was offering them was not what I would have offered English students, that I was providing a second best scheme. I was sure that I knew the source of this bizarre idea, that somehow I was selling them short. If only they knew, I thought, how far I had gone the other way. I told the boy to sit down, which he did with obvious relief, and I spent the rest of the lesson patiently explaining to them about understanding things, not just learning them. I asked them why it was that they had to spend so many hours each night reading and re-reading the notes they had made so that they could memorise them. I asked them why they used such expressions as 'cracking my head' and being 'tortured by Science'.

In the end, they agreed to co-operate with the new scheme and try to understand. I agreed to spend more time explaining things that they found hard. Somehow, I had avoided open revolt and it was not until much later in my time at Mvara, that I realised just how much I had asked them to accept. The middle class children I had taught in England were very practised at asking questions. Their child-centred, discovery orientated Primary Schools had encouraged them to challenge, to wonder about their world, to show a lively interest in their surroundings. If anything, they had too great a confidence in the face of the unknown.

For the African child, especially in an area such as West Nile still largely dependent on shifting subsistence agriculture, the largest community a child would know with any confidence was the extended family village. This cluster of mud walled grass roofed huts surrounded by patches of cultivated land was his world. His Primary School, perhaps a few miles walk across the countryside, offered little more in the way of stimulation. A a teacher and a chalk-board, hours of rote learning of English and Arithmetic, all in preparation for a Primary Leaving Exam by which perhaps 10% would be selected to go to a secondary school like Mvara.

It was not just that poverty prevented him from enjoying all the material advantages that a Western child takes for granted, good food, tasty soft drinks, access to motor transport, books and toys. It was not even that the poverty of his country prevented him from seeing anything more technological than a bus or a diesel generator. The root of the problem was a cultural one, in the attitude of his parents and all adults to children. African children should not ask questions. My Mvara science students had been through years of positive discouragement of questioning. George Okai put it simply.

'Children who ask questions are beaten by their fathers. They learn not to ask questions.'

Obedience and respect for adults was what made life easier for a child. It would not occur to the Ugandan father to encourage his son, and even more his daughter, to ask about the names of the dozens of insect that fluttered around the pressure lamp at night or how the transistor radio or the bicycle gears worked. The idea that 'finding out is always exciting' did not apply. For the boys, it was more likely to be painful and for the girls, who would always present things to an adult male while kneeling with their heads bowed in respect, saying anything at all was frowned on.

And yet.........if the experiment was sufficiently interesting, their imagination could be fired and they could express the wonder of a discovery in often surprisingly graphic language. A class was looking at the migration of ions across an electric field. One of them wrote:

'We grasped the glass in the jaws of the crocodile and applied the electricity. Very, very slowly, the colour of blood began to walk across the moistened paper. It was escaping from the minus jaw.........'

I was not alone in wanting to introduce more discovery methods into science teaching in Uganda. Others who had been involved in the UK Nuffield curriculum developments had come to Uganda and Kenya and started a School Science Project based on the Nuffield 'learning by discovery' approach. It was already being used in the leading secondary schools, Budo and Gayaza in Uganda and Alliance High School in Kenya. The British are good at telling other people how to do things and the University Eduation Departments and National Teachers' Colleges were promoting the scheme vigorously. The difference between their version and the Mvara Secondary School SSP was that ours was low-tech, work-sheet driven and very cheap!

\*

Mvara Secondary School had been founded by the Church of Uganda through the efforts of AIM Missionaries like Margaret Lloyd and the influence of the Church was still strong as I had learnt at that first staff meeting. The Board of Governors was made up largely of Church members and chaired by the Bishop of West Nile, Silvanus Wani. They had appointed Lewis Stephenson as Head when he transferred from the Mission to Government Education Officer status and they continued to look to him to maintain the Church influence in the school. As a result, our school rules went far beyond the normal attempts to restrain teenage temptations, such as drinking, smoking and dancing, and they insisted on compulsory worship on Sundays. This was for me the ultimate irony as I thought that I had escaped compulsory morning worship when I left the Cathedral School at Worcester but here, there were differences.

Firstly, only a minority of the Mvara staff turned up, and secondly, Lewis did his best to find a way of making the service interesting. He encouraged the students to take part, especially the thriving Scripture Union Group, and he invited speakers whom he thought the students would listen to. Margaret Lloyd did her best to help, as did Christine and those of us who arrived at Mvara with a church-going commitment. Of the Ugandan staff, George Okai came most weeks, Guy Kerunen some weeks and Dison Anecho would lead the service if Lewis was away. For the students, attendance was in theory compulsory. As the last crashes from the kitchen announced the end of breakfast, the first few students, smart in their weekend white, would wander into the Hall. Outside, the Duty Master, with his pink face already streaming with sweat, would start to round up the rest from their hiding places all over the school sites. Each week a good number always 'got away', finding a sudden need to go to the hospital in the town or a pressing urge to visit the latrines.

We usually started late. 'Excuse me, Sir, the breakfast was late.' 'There was not enough water for washing.' 'I could not find my white shorts.' The same excuses were offered every week. Eventually the last few would amble in and those leading the service would appear from the side store where they had been praying amongst the schools stock of toilet rolls, spare kettles and cheap cough mixture.

'Brothers and Sisters in Christ, the Bible tells us in many places ………'

We would begin our simple, direct service. A few late comers would amble in, wander down the central aisle, select a friendly looking neighbour and settle down. It always surprised me that those who were there took such a full part in the service; somehow the act of worshipping together helped them to forget that they had to come. They concentrated on what was said and read and there was none of the deep resentment that had destroyed the services in Worcester Cathedral. Every so often, one of them would walk out for a 'short call' but the majority stayed and sang with enthusiasm. The hymns that were familiar to them, those which had been translated into Lugbara or Alur for use in the village churches at home, were sung in English with real enjoyment. They just liked to sing.

When I had to stand up to preach, as I did several times in that first year, I was always anxious. Would I be able to build on the bond we had established between teacher and taught over long hours in the classroom and lab? Would my words, so carefully prepared at home before the service, bring them to the door-steps of their lives and actually meet their need? Somehow, my helplessness in that situation, feeling utterly inadequate and empty, was the key to real communication. Only when we accept our own need of God can He fill that need. Only then can His Spirit give us the words to say. Only then can those who hear have the hearts to understand. Each time it happened, it was new and wonderful, the same rich gift that had swept into my life years ago in Oxford, except that now it was made even richer through being shared with young men and woman of another Continent, another race and another world.

\*

Those who have worked in boarding schools know that the best times to really get to know the students are outside the formal teaching day. Some of us had been boarders ourselves and so knew how boarding 'worked' from the inside. But for European teachers at Mvara, school life outside the classroom also exposed all our inadequacies. It was bad enough in England, when at least we all equally visible and spoke the same language. But in Uganda, the pale young European teacher would soon find himself on evening duty, responsible for hundreds of boys and girls who could simply melt into the darkness of the African night and who used a range of at least six languages, none of which we could understand.

They were often older than we were and sometimes larger. They knew every corner of both sites of the school which some of us had hardly begun to explore. All around the unfenced, un-hedged school, African villages offered welcoming hearth-sides and copious supplies of millet beer. Yet the duty list told us that we were responsible and in charge and must walk around the school sites 'on duty'. In the pitch blackness, our torches, white shorts and white faces, acted like mobile beacons warning of our coming, small islands of order surrounded by the potential chaos of the night.

The Ugandan staff had more sense. They largely stayed in their houses and expected the Prefects to run the school. They had better things to do with their families. Why look for trouble? But we *muzungu* were made of sterner stuff. If we were asked to be 'in charge', we would do our best to be 'in charge' no matter how foolish we looked. I soon learnt that it is good to have a well-developed sense of one's own ridiculousness in such situations!

I remembered David Gill's lines about 'trying to ban the bomb through jumble-sales….. ideals are fine – in vacuo, it's the imbecilities they land you in which hurt you so[4].'

Every Saturday evening, after the evening meal of millet and stew had been cleared away in the Dining Hall, all the tables were moved to the side and as many chairs as the school owned brought into what became a temporary cinema. The projector was set up, the electricity supply connected and the 'entertainment' began. This was, in theory, compulsory and had to be supervised by two Duty Staff looking after hundreds of young men and women crammed into the small hall. It was my turn after just two weeks. Lewis explained to me what needed to be done and said that he had asked George Okai to be on duty with me so that he could explain what should happen.

'We've got a Shell documentary and a film about Hawaii tonight – something about Pacific wildlife,' he said. 'It should be fine.'

George and I turned up at the Dining Hall as the students wandered in. Fortunately, the power was on and the projector rattled into life. We showed them the documentary first, a film made by Shell on the use of fertilizers in India, or that's what we thought it was about. They had actually filmed famine conditions in Bihar State, intending to show how such tragedies can be overcome by the effective use of fertilizers. That point was lost on the school. As soon as the first starving Indian peasant staggered across the screen, pandemonium broke out. The students roared with laughter, slapping each other on the back, rolling off their seats with tears streaming down their cheeks. The girls ululated with joy as each pathetic skeletal family crawled to the emergency feeding station.

Deeply shocked at their reaction, I was even more surprised to find George Okai, sitting next to me, joining in the general hilarity.

'What's so funny?' I shouted to him over the wave of noise.

'Look,' he said, 'a poor Hindi. I've never seen a poor Indian before. How can they be starving? All Indians are rich and fat around here. They cannot be starving.'

When the documentary ended, the students were still chortling with glee. Forget the benefits of fertilizers; the entertainment of starving Indians was much better.

The roll of film which we then put on the ancient projector was labelled '*Blue Hawaii*'. Any link with Pacific wildlife was marginal. It soon became clear that this was an Elvis Presley film which had taken seven years to get from Hollywood to Mvara. The students loved it, an ideal blend of treacle romance, surf-boarding hunks, loud Afro-American music and compulsively gyrating hips. All the girls shrieked with delight and the boys started to stand and swing their hips with looks of glazed rapture on their faces. Outside the hall, villagers had gathered to share the fun, pressing closer and closer over the wire grids that served as windows, sealing off the fresh air for the students inside. It got hotter and hotter as Elvis and his girl-friend expressed their passion in more and more intimate terms.

The projector started to clatter. Those wiggling hips in glorious Panavision slowed to a frozen gyration and the film stopped. For a second there was silence in the Hall. Then a roar of pure frustration swept through the mass of shouting, stamping students. Someone turned the lights on. We were on the edge of a riot and I knew I had to do something.

'Sit down,' I bellowed over the noise in the Hall. 'Sit down at once. The projector is broken so we shall have to see the rest of the film next week.'

'Sir, we think you will mend it now,' snarled a very tall boy leaning over me.

'I'm sorry, I can't mend it. Please calm down. Everyone, leave the Hall and go back to your dormitories.'

To my amazement, they did. The noise level dropped. The villagers blocking the doors and windows melted away into the night. The disappointed students slowly filed out of the Hall and back to their dormitories. Sometimes, it seemed, a loud, confident instruction could cut through confusion and potential disaster. But it was not authority that had cut through their anger. It was gratitude. I had unwittingly provided the most entertaining films they had ever seen and had for the first time shown them a film with dancing in it. In a school where dancing on Saturday nights was banned, my reputation as a worker of miracles was made.

\*

My other job, as Master i/c Uniform, was less successful. It started a week or so after the beginning of term and went on for my first two years at Mvara. In theory, each student received a new white school shirt or blouse, a new pair of khaki shorts or a brown skirt and a pair of school socks, short for the girls and long for the boys, together with one set of games kit, each year. These should all have been provided in January but, by September, it seemed that some had still not been issued. It was the Master i/c Uniform's job to manage the supply, which involved establishing good relations with the school tailor for the shorts and skirts and with the Asian suppliers of the ready-made items.

House and transport for the Master i/c Uniforms

Kefa was a short and ancient Lugbara with bandy legs and bad breath. He was established in the School Tailor role well before I arrived and advertised the fact on a board above his corner of one of the Asian *Duka* verandas in the town. '*Oficial Tailor to Mvara best shorts and skrits*,' it announced. He not only supplied the school, but also the Staff and the Board of Governors, and all their children, with whatever clothes they needed at a very good price and very short notice. This ensured that his contract was secure but it also meant that he was way behind with the school uniforms. Some of the S2 students had been measured for shorts and skirts in January and were still wearing their old clothes in September.

Kefa saw me as an enemy from the start. He strongly resented any interference from the young *muzungu* who had suddenly arrived. If any hints of criticism reached him, he would start our meetings by straightening his legs to push his greying hair up to his full five feet six and exhale a stream of Lugbara. This sounded as offensive as the blast of halitosis which accompanied it. But this acute phase of our 'conversation' seldom lasted long. As he ran out of breath and curses, his knees would bend and separate and Kefa would revert to the pathetic old man who took on too much business without a hope of fulfilling his promises.

Every boy and girl was measured at the start of the school year in January and, over the next six months, Kefa would arrive on his bicycle at the school with a pile of finished shorts and skirts strapped to his carrier. Each pair would be tried on by their designated owner in the privacy of the New Site stationery cupboard. In the early months of the year, the students were pleased with their new uniform. Kefa's measurements were about right. His eye for minimum cloth and maximum profit produced an effect a little on the tight side, showing off the boys' thighs and the girls' bottoms pleasingly. But by May, months of regular school meals had an effect for which Kefa had made no allowance. No amount of breathing in would work and the shorts and skirts were rejected. He would try to offer the smaller boys and girls clothes made for their larger friends only to provoke incensed reactions.

'Our fees pay for new uniforms', they shouted. 'We will not accept the rejects of others'.

It was then my job to negotiate a compromise. Some I did manage to persuade into a smaller pair of shorts. I even suggested to a few girls that by having a button moved it might be possible to squeeze into a smaller skirt, which had the added bonus of having a shorter hem-line and no need to roll up the waist-band as all schoolgirl wearers of school skirts love to do. But most students settled for a few more months in last year's ragged uniform, on the promise of a new item of the right size.

Under pressure, Kefa made more mistakes. Shorts were offered with no fly buttons, or even worse, with no opening at all. Some had no pockets, some double seams, and one pair even had one leg in khaki and the other in white. Each faulty pair was solemnly returned not to Kefa, who left the site on his bicycle as soon as he could hand over the pile of uniforms to the Prefect in charge of distribution, but to me. When, not long afterwards, the supply of cotton cloth made in Jinja began to get too expensive, Kefa found a cheaper Chinese source. Unable to resist the temptation of using every inch of the material, he produced his masterpiece of tailoring, a pair of school shorts with a golden sun trade mark across each buttock. The boy who got the sun-shine shorts was delighted!

As the term got under way and the flow of new shorts and skirts dried to a trickle, it became clear that many students needed new items of clothing if they were to remain properly clad. If the item had worn out or got lost, replacing it had to be at the student's own expense, although Lewis did say that I had a bit of leeway for the more desperate cases. It appeared that it was my job to sort out the opportunists from the genuinely unfortunate. The reasons for loss became more and more creative, with the two favourites implicating the Army or a cow.

'Excuse me, Sir, my skirt was eaten by a cow.'

'Excuse me, Sir, my shorts were taken by an Army man.'

I never witnessed a case of theft by the military, but I soon believed in consumption by cow. A large black heifer strolled through the school compound. She ignored the lush grass growing all along the drainage ditches and headed for the girls' washing line where brown skirts flapped gently in the breeze. One by one, she removed them with a sharp tug and much chewing, before sinking onto the grass with a contented 'moo' and chewing the cud of brown cotton, broken buttons and all.

After that, it seemed more than likely that, if cows eat skirts, soldiers should steal shorts, although I had my doubts about the soldier who was said to have stolen a skirt. But the most graphic excuse came from the boy who explained that he had been washing his uniform in a stream near to his village home, when heavy rain in the hills above caused the water in the stream to suddenly rise.

'The water came up, Sir,' he explained with great solemnity. 'Myself and my clotheses were swept off the rock and carried down. By the will of Allah, I was saved but my shorts were taken away from me and trapped beneath the waters.'

Owning as little as they did, and being in constant fear of theft, the boys thought it quite normal to wear both their pairs of shorts simultaneously. For class use, their games shorts went under their khaki ones and, for games, the other way round. By this means, they enjoyed the luxury of 'under-wears'. The girls thought this very unfair. They only had a second small games skirt which hardly met the same purpose. So it was one day, after I had issued the New Site boys with their games shorts, I returned to the Old Site with the spare pairs of bright royal blue games shorts folded up on the back seat. Most were too large to be acceptable to any of the boys. I ran straight into trouble.

By the side of Old Site road were the magnificently tall and well-built girls of our school Senior Netball Team, burly young women, strong from years of doing all the digging and water carrying for their parents. They had taken no prisoners as they elbowed their way into the District Netball Finals. They were not just unhappy. They were very angry with the Master in Charge of Uniforms. Eight girls formed a very threatening circle around the car.

'We think you will give us our under-wears' said the Captain menacingly. 'The boys have under-wears and you have not given them to the girls. We think you will give us our under-wears, now.'

I tried to explain that their school-fees covered a school blouse and skirt and a PE top and skirt, made to measure by the school tailor but no undergarments, an area of clothing I felt ill-equipped to discuss, let alone supply. But, having watched the team, I appreciated that for many of the best built, their games skirts were strained to the limit and the absence of underwear was becoming increasingly obvious.

Eyeing the back seat of the car, the Captain insisted, 'We think you will give us our under-wears. How can we play tomorrow in the final without under-wears? Our skirts are now too short.'

Then, I understood. They had spotted the oversized royal blue boys running shorts. I obviously must have brought them to be issued to the girls as their 'under-wears'.

'I think you are right,' I said trying to sound as if the plan had been there all the time. 'We must not embarrass our team. You will have to wear 'under-wears'.'

The girls were ecstatic, ululating loudly and waving their 'under-wears' around their heads as they ran across to their dormitories to tell the sisters that all was now well in the world. They had won a victory as least as sweet as the District Netball Cup would surely be. To preserve the modesty of the Netball Team, eight pairs of oversize running shorts were issued for their District final. A raid on the school sewing kit produced enough large safety pins to hold them up, although the African fashion for large behinds helped as well. An emergency order was placed to supply all the other young women with their underwear. Lewis said that the school budget could stand the strain better than the school skirts. Decency was restored when 'under-wears' arrived for all.

Our team did win their District Cup and stepped up their training. They were determined to defeat 'those small brown, banana-eaters' as they disdainfully referred to the Southern teams in the National Finals. They were confident that when they won the national cup, they would be appearing before their President, Dr Milton Obote, resplendent in the brown PE skirts and bright blue 'under-wears' of Mvara Senior Secondary School.

When I told colleagues in the staff room of my success as a supplier of ladies underwear, one of the women teachers encouraged me to branch out further.

'I'm impressed, John, she said. 'Next year you'll be supplying bras for the girls. Did you know that in Nigeria, they call them 'knickers for up'.'

## 2.3 Christmas and Easter

Schools may be, as African politicians and United Nations 'experts' continuously asserted, the building blocks of a new nation, but they could also destroy a people's confidence in their own culture. So many fine schools in Uganda have in the past done just that. The products of European energy and missionary zeal, the elite boarding schools of Buganda, perched on their hills above the *shambas* of the common people, grafted a veneer of Western values on the deep cultural assumptions of the African village. Some, like Budo and Gayaza, had done a thorough job and their graduates learnt to sing the madrigals of Elizabethan England, dance the Gay Gordons and play Rugby and Hockey while gaining a superb Western education, even if they failed to learn to run a village dispensary or cook over a charcoal fire. The new schools were not so confident of imported culture, staffed so often by a patchwork of races, nationalities and cultures – they had no united front to offer, no clear cultural teaching, be it the ideals of western humanism or the precepts of Islam. So they found it more difficult to replace what they inevitably destroyed.

Dr Milton Obote put it bluntly in a speech in Kampala. '*Education therefore became, in a way, a process through which the African has been increasingly denying and rejecting his origins, his culture, his characteristics and his way of life*[5].'

Mvara struggled between the two extremes. As the 'flagship school' of the Church of Uganda in the West Nile District, our Board of Governors aspired to match the quality of King's College, Budo or Gayaza High School, the best of the

Church schools in the south, but we knew that this was a faint hope. Dison Aneco, our Deputy Head, was more realistic.

'We should be as good as we can be and we should encourage our students not to turn their backs on the village.'

\*

By mid-December, the heavy storms that swept up from the Nile valley to fall in torrents in the hill country around Arua had begun to ease. There were still occasional downpours which washed the earth from the hillsides and tore the bridges out of the river valleys, but they were dying away. West Nile was becoming a bone dry brown land. The bright grass began to wither and the air filled with the smoke of grass fires as the villagers burnt off the high grass around their homes to leave a black strip free of snakes and rodents.

Towards the end of term, the growing water shortage at Mvara reduced the kitchen to dependence on the bore-hole. In our Assemblies, it became obvious that washing clothes and bodies was increasingly difficult. When we reached the end of term, Lewis was called away to Kampala to be told of next year's admission numbers. Dison Aneco led our final Assembly and spoke to the whole school.

'Remember,' he told them, 'remember all of you, to show respect to your parents. Do not speak to your mother in English when you know she does not hear it. Do not refuse to work in your parents' *shamba* when you know that they need your help. It is not shameful for an educated man to work with his hands so dig and help them plant when the rains come. Do not speak to your father until he speaks to you. From him and from your mother, you have the gift of life. Remember the words of our Acholi poet, 'no one wrestles with his father, no one on looks down on his mother. You cannot abuse your mother because it was that woman who hewed you out of the rock.' Remember those wise words when you get back to your homes[6].'

We sang the National Anthem and the term was over. The students queued for the buses with their luggage. Packing had not taken long, a rolled up mattress secured with a length of string and a bag stuffed with notebooks and spare clothes. They owned so little that travelling to and from school, even on a bicycle, was very easy. A handful of boys had been allowed to stay on, to earn a few shillings by cleaning and re-painting parts of the school. For the staff, there was a chance to relax for a few days before we began to think of Christmas.

The VW Beetle meant that I could get to know the West Nile District beyond the immediate vicinity of Mvara. About ten miles to the south, AIM had established a hospital at Kuluva, set up by the Williams brothers, both of whom Jenny Peck knew through her parents. So as soon as I could I went down to Kuluva to meet these two doctors.

Peggy Maclure had told me how Ted Williams and his wife Muriel had come to work with AIM in West Nile in 1941, just before she and Seton had arrived at Mvara. They started a small hospital at Mvara but soon found that it was not the best place. The Arua Government hospital was already established, serving much the same population, and the growth of schools at Mvara meant that there were hundreds of school pupils on the site, many of whom thought they needed treatment. Ted Williams was not convinced that they did.

There was also a need to establish a leprosy treatment centre somewhere in West Nile as the disease was distressingly common and cases had to have consistent long-term treatment. So Ted Williams looked for a site the Mission could lease on which a new hospital could be built. He found it on a hillside south of Arua, not far from the main road to the south. The place was called Kuluva and the local Chief allowed them to lease two hundred acres of land and to start building a hospital. They were soon joined by Ted's brother, Dr Peter and his wife Elsie, and Mr and Mrs Williams, Senior, came out too. By 1950, the first leprosy patients were being treated in a chain of small villages near the hospital, on land which they could cultivate to support their families. Each village housed people from a different part of West Nile so that they were always amongst people who spoke their own language.

Kuluva[7] continued to grow through the 1950s to a general hospital of forty beds, with a church and accommodation for both European and African staff. By the time Uganda became independent in 1962, it had sixty-two in-patient beds, three hundred and forty seven operations had been successfully completed in the year and over one hundred thousand out-patients treated, all thanks to the team of doctors and nurses which the Williams brothers had built up. Kuluva became the hospital of choice for Church and non-Church patients alike, a major centre for eye-surgery and for research into the cancers most common in Northern Uganda.

When I first visited Kuluva in 1968 and met Ted and Peter and their colleagues at the hospital, it seemed to me to represent all that was best in Christian love and service. There were obvious tensions and imperfections, occasional cruel bluntness and blushing embarrassment, irritations and tiredness, but the whole place conveyed a concern for people and a single-minded desire to serve them. Some of the *muzungu* who worked there seemed still to be locked into the paternalistic attitudes of an earlier generation in a way that Seton and Peggy Maclure were not. Their home was open to all, and especially to the local people. Kuluva homes were more private, more limited to the close circle of European colleagues and family contacts. But in every other way, they lived and worked with and for the people of West Nile.

Dr Ted Williams, by the Kuluva pool

The hospital was not impressive, long single-storied wards with walls of mud bricks and rusty corrugated iron roofs. Smaller buildings housed an operating theatre and a dispensary. The in-patients each came with a family support team to feed and look after them, some of whom slept on the floor under their relative's bed, others shared the simple accommodation behind the ward. Apart from the two doctors and a handful of English nursing sisters, all the other staff were Ugandan, dressers, nurses, office staff and chaplains, all trained by Ted or Peter or their wives and colleagues.

Many had little more than basic Primary education but they shared a loyalty and commitment to Kuluva which kept them there on minimal wages and long hours of duty. This was no gleaming modern health centre, no multi-storey hospital with architect designed medical school and nurses' home, rows of new ambulances and white coated specialists. Kuluva just had two old Land Rovers, a few stretchers equipped with bicycle wheels and a collection of simple buildings set in a purple riot of bougainvillea. A lone, pale figure in ridiculous flapping khaki shorts strode around his wards of suffering humanity. They came to Kuluva because they trusted him.

It also had a small swimming pool built by the Williams families for their daughters and their friends who came for school holidays and which they generously shared with any of the Mission community who needed to cool off. The Mvara Mission and school staff were invited to use it and we would gather there on a Saturday afternoon to meet the hospital, church and Mission workers based there or passing through. It seemed that Africans were not invited. When, on one relaxing afternoon by the pool, Peter Williams was asked about this, he explained.

'We had to decide. If we included everybody, we would simply be overwhelmed. So we agreed that this was a family pool and friends of the family would be invited. It may look odd, but ever since we started to enjoy it, we've found that this was the best way.'

In every other way, Kuluva, Mvara and all the other Church of Uganda activity in West Nile was open to all. If the pool stood out to us as an example of segregation, the Williams brother did not see it that way. It just made sense to them so we accepted their invitation to enjoy it and they were gracious enough to ignore our implied criticism.

The expatriate communities of Mvara and Kuluva joined forces for Christmas celebrations. For that year, it was Kuluva's turn. We preserved our British traditions with dogged determination in the face of an African climate. We sang carols around the hospital wards, avoiding the more obvious nonsense of 'See amid the winter's snow', but unable to resist 'Silent night, Holy night' against a chorus of frogs, drums, howling dogs and buzzing mosquitoes. Turkeys arrived from Kenya miraculously preserved in a semi-frozen state on the roof of Chawda's Bus. They were roasted by Calor gas and served to a sweating gathering under the throbbing iron roof of Ted and Muriel's living room. Christmas pudding, solid with local suet and maize flour, sealed off what little appetite was left and soaked up the coffee which ended our meal. No wine, no brandy butter, no televised message from Buckingham Palace, just a quick pull at a soggy, sweaty cracker and a brave attempt to decipher the Queen's thin high voice from the whistling static of the Kuluva short-wave radio.

However hard we tried to think of home, we knew that we should join all the other people of Kuluva for their African Christmas. And so after the Queen, we went down to the church to share their service. Packed like ebony sardines onto the concrete pews of the grass-roofed Hospital Church, they sang and prayed their thanks to God for all that was good in their lives, and especially for being their Emmanuel. In spite of the heat and the dust-laden air, they flaunted every stitch of their new clothes. Children wriggled in itchy woollen vests as multi-coloured as Joseph's coat, knitted by gnarled arthritic fingers in some Home-Counties Prayer group. Two old men in overcoats sent out by an Italian relief agency, quarrelled over a woollen hat that each wanted to pull over their greying hair. Youths in Obote shirts and skin-tight trousers sat down stiffly, trying not to split their seams, while women in a solid block down the left hand side of the church chattered and laughed and shouted whenever the round and damp Reverend paused for breath. These African Christians turned their Christmas thanksgiving into a celebration of joy and generosity that was humbling in its intensity and sincerity. But as we shook hands with so many of them and wished them a very Happy Christmas, I could not help feeling a stab of nostalgia for the carols from King's College and the bite of frosty air on red and cheery scarf-wrapped faces.

*

Harold Wilson Toma, who had told me on the first day that he was a Kuku from Sudan and a refugee, was one of the boys allowed to stay in the school for the Christmas holidays. He kept his mattress and a few books in a corner of the boys' dormitory, the only place he had as home. By doing odd jobs around the school, he managed to earn enough to buy his food in the town. After Christmas, when I had time to explore the country north of Arua I took him with me up to the Sudan border. He was keen to come, if only to look into his homeland from the safety of a teacher's car on the Uganda side of the border.

We drove past the market and out of the town on the main road to Moyo, far to the north. The women living just on the edge of Arua were wrapped in much more brightly coloured robes than the Lugbara women around the town, and they kept their heads covered.

'They are Nubi,' Toma told me. 'They are Muslims who came from the Sudan many generations ago and they like to live here by the Mosque. They have their own language.'

All the faiths clustered around Arua, the Protestants to the south-east at Mvara, the Catholics to the west across the Anyau River and the Muslims to the north. I knew a lot about the Protestant community but realised that I had very little contact with the Catholics who had been in West Nile for just as long. I had even less with the Islamic community who had been there since the 19$^{th}$ Century. Some time, I would find out more about them, I thought, as I drove on towards Koboko. I knew that Joy Grindey, one of the AIM missionaries, spent much of her time there, living in a grass-roofed hut among the Kakwa and working on the translation of the Kakwa Bible.

The first twenty miles out of Arua is all Lugbara country, a land of scrub and rock with small fields of tobacco and brick curing barns. Most of the grass had already gone, no-one worked in the fields and no-one walked along the road in the orange dust. We found one of the students in Boma's class at Maracha, embarrassed that we had come to his village without warning. He dived into his hut to find his clean clothes so that he could greet us five minutes later immaculately dressed in white shirt and shorts. He looked so wonderfully incongruous, in neatly ironed splendour in the centre of his father's village, surrounded by his younger brothers and sisters in their tattered shorts and ancient T-shirts. We did not stay long, not wanting to put his parents to the trouble of offering us food, and drove on to Koboko. It was little more than a double line of small bars and *dukas* with a scruffy Post Office and a single pump garage, but it is the centre of the Kakwa world. Once we had found out from a helpful Asian shop-keeper that Joy had gone back to Arua, there was little to keep us there.

Toma sat silent beside me immersed in thought as we got nearer to the border. His hungry eyes gazed ahead up the straight road, searching for the first glimpse of the brown hills that still meant home. The wide orange ribbon of the road ran due north straight into the heart of Equatoria, beyond the frontier. We came to the last settlement in Uganda, the small cluster of huts and new dispensary at Kaya overlook the valley. We drove past the long patient queue of human suffering and stopped at the Police Post. A tall constable deterred us from going any further.

'The army boys are very rude, Sir. You have no permit to go down there and it is better that you should not annoy them.'

'Who are all these people?' I asked pointing to the Dispensary queue.

'They came across last night, Sir. Some of them are very sick.'

We followed the policeman's advice and drove no further. Toma and I got out of the car and stood in the road. It ended just beyond the Army post, halfway down the hill. But it is not the end of the road that I remember so vividly, it is the high brown burnt ridge beyond the river. Like a blockage of the mind that ridge formed the line that said so clearly, here freedom ends. Toma looked at me sadly.

'That is my country, but I shall never go back. My people have run away from our home.'

He told me of the group of over four thousand who had come when he escaped, walking over that ridge in the night. Their villages had been bombed, their huts burnt to ashes, their cattle stolen and their leaders taken away to be shot. They had walked in families, desperate to save their lives, walked through the bush in the heat of the day and through the peace of the night. Some had walked for weeks on end, for hundreds of miles, always south, always avoiding the roads, the villages and the towns where the Sudanese Army kept its iron grip on the feeble pulse of South Sudan. Like a man slowly bleeding to death, the province of Equatoria was dying, bled of her people, driven out by hate and fear and sucked across the Uganda border by the hope of peace.

Whole villages had walked, men carrying sheets of cardboard to shield their children from the sun. They rested when they could walk no more to wait for the cool of the evening. Pastors carried their vestments, their Bibles and perhaps a precious chalice wrapped in an old cloth. Churches were a popular target for the MiGs of the Sudanese Air-force. Women carried babies on their backs and bundles on their heads, perhaps a hoe blade and a few handfuls of groundnuts, millets or beans, the seeds to start a new life.

Over the ridge they had come until they could see the tiny lights of Kaya, and down that final hillside, the scruffy tents of the Sudanese Army post one last hazard to be avoided at all cost. They had reached the river well upstream of the gaping ruins of the road bridge blown open to the sky, and waded across to reach freedom from the Arabs and their guns.

Freedom to me was a symbolic torch-bearing figure, an idea to play with in after-dinner conversation, but to those weary Sudanese who reached Uganda in their tens of thousands it meant a road to walk along, a millet garden to dig and harvest, a roof of grass to build over exhausted heads and swollen bellied children. And for all of them, including the schoolboy who stood and watched beside me, it meant an endless ache in the heart for that empty land beyond the barrier of the burning hills.

No-one knows how many Sudanese refugees reached Uganda at that time. It was easy for a Sudanese Kakwa to merge into the Ugandan Kakwa villages around Koboko, but by the end of the 1960s there must have been tens of thousands in refugee camps right across the north or scattered in the countryside. Some will go back when peace comes as it surely must some day, but many will stay in their adopted homes, especially those like Toma who found places in Ugandan schools supported by the Church of Uganda. For Uganda has succoured refugees from the three troubled neighbouring lands of Sudan, the Congo and Ruanda. For many, the West Nile District has been a place of peace and hope.

\*

When school started again towards the end of January 1969, a very frustrated Lewis Stephenson was grappling with the next problem thrown at him by the Ministry of Education in Kampala. Mvara Secondary School was one of the 'expanding' schools, provided with a major building project to accommodate an extra stream of pupils in each year group. In fact the construction of these new 'buildings' had got no further than rows of concrete beams sticking up out of the red earth of the New Site. In allocating an extra stream of S1 pupils to the school, the Ministry had assumed that the buildings were ready to be used.

However hard Lewis tried, the Ministry would not change the allocation. The pupils had been told that they were going to Mvara Secondary School and go they must. So it became imperative to work out a way of finding space for the extra class for January 1969 and for another in January 1970. There was no space on the Old Site and none yet finished on the New Site. The District Education Officer in Arua, always keen to show that West Nile was an imaginative District able to cope with sudden demands, came up with a novel idea – why not turn a two site school into a three site school. There was, it seemed, a small redundant Primary School just under Arua Hill, about a mile from each of the existing sites.

'There is a good road,' the DEO said to Lewis when he went to the Office to discuss this novel idea.

'A good road is still a mile of road for students and staff to walk,' retorted Lewis, but he knew that the decision had already been made.

So from January 1969, what had been the three empty classrooms of the Madhvani Primary School became the Madhvani Site of Mvara Secondary School. The only way it could be run was to have the three S1 classes taught there for all subjects and for a temporary kitchen and dining room to be added to the classrooms. There was also clearly a need for two temporary sets of long-drop latrines for the mixed classes. It seemed madness to ask over a hundred new S1 students to walk across the town to three hot bare classrooms each morning and then to try to teach them the full secondary curriculum in former primary classrooms with no facilities. We would have to cook them a lunch, teach them again through the hot afternoon and then get them to walk back to their dormitories on the Old and New Sites. But we did.

Term for the new intake started two weeks late but eventually the new arrangements started up and the teaching staff spent much of the day cycling around Arua. As I had a car and there was no lab at either the New Site or at Madhvani, we tried to timetable science lessons in pairs so that I could at least take another teacher with me and all the kit we would need, but it was exhausting. For the students, the excitement of having got to Secondary School kept them going for the first term. The inadequacy of the accommodation was not so obvious to those who had endured years in Primary schools with even worse conditions.

*

While we were struggling to make the three site school work, at Mvara, the Arua Demonstration Primary School, next to Arua TTC, was welcoming a new teacher, John Ondoma, born in Maracha County in 1948, the grandson of the KAR soldier. John had completed his Primary schooling and gained a place at Arua TTC to be trained as a Primary teacher. The College under its experienced and very capable Principal, Stuart Cole, was regarded by everyone as a 'tight run ship'. John has written an account of what happened to him at Arua TTC:

'The Kenyan evangelist Joseph Kayo ran a fiery evangelistic campaign at Arua TTC in 1966/7.One of the songs the students sang was:

'I have decided to follow Jesus, I have decided to follow Jesus, No turning back, no turning back……..'

Many college students committed their lives to Jesus Christ and genuinely confessed Him as Saviour and Lord. They joined in singing joyfully as they walked up to the front of the College Chapel to confess their allegiance to the Lord, while the rest of us who were rather sceptical sat glued to our chairs, counting and noting who had decided to join the Lord's fold. Many of them, such as Bishop Henry L Orombi (later Archbishop of Uganda), Isaac Anguyo, John Milton Anguyo, Moses Adraiga, Asnatha Ocokoru, Rhoda Mindreru and others have remained committed to the Lord to this day and are effective witnesses to the faith they confessed all those years ago.

I was not unmoved by the messages, but I remained uncommitted because deep down in my heart was another voice saying, 'not now'...... I felt that I was still too young. If I committed my life to Christ then, I was bound to fail because of the numerous problems, temptations and challenges that afflict youth in their Christian lives. I should therefore wait until I had married a 'beautiful' wife because I thought Christian girls were 'ugly'. Besides, lingering in my thoughts was the idea that I would outgrow the youthful pleasures of an 18-year old. When they were no longer a problem, then I would have total commitment for the rest of my life. Satan creates any reason he thinks is convincing to bar people from committing their lives to Christ so as to be saved from sin and all its effects on everlasting life. So, I remained at the back of the Chapel gazing at what was happening but afraid of commitment. I should have listened to the preacher's advice to young men: 'Remember your Creator in the days of your youth, before the days of trouble come and the years approach when you will say, "I find not pleasure in them"...' (Ecclesiastes 12:1-2)

But because of God's abundant and immeasurable grace and love which is ever seeking sinners such as I was, He confronted me while I was alone, on the morning of August 4th 1967. I was a final year food monitor and it was my job to make announcements during meals. This was the last day of term and we had been busy packing to go home. At breakfast, a student brought a book entitled 'Be filled with the Spirit' which he said had been found but whose owner was unknown. As soon as I made the announcement, my table mates interpreted this (and rightly too) to mean that God had brought this book so that I should be filled with the Spirit.

After breakfast, I remained glued to my chair in the Dining Hall reading the divinely-sent book. Hardly had I read two pages when the Holy Spirit convicted me of my need of a Saviour there and then. I could not but yield and pray that the Lord would forgive me for my stiff-necked behaviour and my other sins, and that He would come to take control of my life henceforth. I had to make a choice that would ultimately determine my future relationship with God and others. This was imperative because what we do with Christ in this life here and now determines what He will do with us when He returns in his glory. Having done that, I left the hall to go to my dormitory while staggering as if I was drunk. In fact, I was filled with the Holy Spirit of God who had taken residence in me. News had already spread throughout the College that I had become an 'Oluganda' as one student came running to check if it was true. 'Oluganda' was a derogatory term to make students who got saved feel 'out-dated. It literally means 'brethren'. My immediate neighbour in the dormitory, Moses Adaiga, who had got saved in a dramatic way earlier, quickly came to pray with me. I then felt relieved and forgiven and could confidently sing: 'No condemnation now I dread, I am the Lord's and He is mine; Alive in Him my living head, and clothed in righteousness divine....' And join in with the singing: 'I have decided to follow Jesus......'   We left for the second-term holiday and I was singing, full of joy, all the way home.

The day after I arrived home, on August 6$^{th}$, there was a Christian convention nearby in a church called Olorokua. I eagerly went to attend in an expectation of being warmly welcomed as I now identified with the saved group and I was given an opportunity to testify what the Lord had done for me. But instead of welcoming me with joy and enthusiasm, some leaders took no time at all to start judging my physical appearance. I had trimmed my hair and parted it according to the youth fashion of the time. That looked unacceptable to the older Balokole to say the least, if not abominable. I felt dejected. To compound my problems, the young people who had gathered round to hear me testify, said that it was only a matter of time and that I would drift away from following Jesus.

However, my experiences since then have proved that when Jesus saved, He saves us completely. The same Spirit that had filled me from the very beginning of my salvation history, enabled me to see those discouraging remarks and the way I was received as challenges to my Christian walk. They led me to pray that Jesus would help me to stand and live for Him, so that my life might be a stepping stone for others to know and love Him, rather than a stumbling block. I prayed that I would never yield to temptation but fight manfully onwards, looking to Jesus, the pioneer and perfector of our faith.   The Lord has honoured that prayer and never let me down for a single moment. My home church at Uliapi in Maracha archdeaconry has been such an encouragement that it kept us living the faith by enabling us to participate fully in all church activities. When the third term of 1967 began we had to go for our final school practice. The three of us, John Milton Anguyo, Asher Andama and I, went to teach at Alua Primary School. We were all zealous for the Lord. We prayed together, worked together and cheered each other in the Lord until we successfully completed our school practice by the Lord's grace.

Asher Andama and I started our teaching careers in January 1968 at Opia in Vurra County. We were posted to teach new Primary Six and Seven classes respectively, and when we arrived, the 'new staff house' had just been mudded. There was hardly any dry place even to put a papyrus mat. The situation was pathetic but there was nowhere else for me and my brothers and sisters who had come to live with me in pursuit of their studies. We had to endure the cold and dreadful night in the house. Thank God that none of us fell ill. The Opia community then came in full force the following day to complete the muddying of the house and it dried as we lived in it, from the heat of our bodies.

Part of Andama's problem and mine was that our youthfulness did not amuse the Opia community at all for fear of what we would do to their mature girls. We were being judged by what other youths in our age bracket had done and possibly were doing. To make matters worse, the classes we taught were those where the girls were mature enough to be romantically attracted to us. But the Lord Jesus held us firmly to live and have our being in Him. Our lifestyle was 'odd' because we engaged in church activities. We never went to the markets with a view to seduce girls as other young men were doing, nor did we join other teachers, who were older than us, on the drinking sprees that were their daily routine.

The only discouraging factor for me was that I never felt as welcome at their fellowship meetings as other, older, people seemed to. I was looking for human approval rather than God's and I decided I would not join in the fellowship but read the Bible and pray at home. But by God's providence, I had been a regular reader of a magazine called 'Africa Challenge' and that month its theme was fellowship with other Christians. 'Let us consider how we may spur one another on towards love and good deeds, not giving up meeting together, as some are in the habit of doing, but encouraging one another...' (Hebrews 10:24, 25) I read. From then onwards, I resolved that I would attend fellowship meetings with a view to listening to what God would tell me through hymns, testimonies and sharing from the Bible. Since then I have reassessed such meetings as a great source of encouragement.

I only completed one year at Opia Primary School as I was transferred to Arua Demonstration School from January 1969. The Arua TTC Principal, Mr Stuart Cole, thought that I should join a secondary school to pursue academic studies because he thought from my earlier performance at the TTC, I could cope very well. But I underrated my own ability and preferred to study for O level as a private student by correspondence. Through Mr Cole, I registered with Rapid Results College in London and he was kind and generous enough to pay all the tuition fees on my behalf at once. While doing this, I was an active classroom teacher at Arua Demonstration School, and by the end of 1970, I was able to sit for the East Africa Certificate of Education Ordinary Level examinations. God enabled me to pass the examination well enough to be able to register for the Advanced Level studies.

While I was studying for A levels, I decided to attend an upgrading course at Canon Lawrence College at Boroboro in what is now Lira District. Before I sat for my final Grade III (secondary teaching) exams, I took the mature entrance examinations for Makerere University. It was amazing how the Lord had prepared me to pass all those exams with ease and I only taught as a Grade III teacher for a month before joining Makerere as an undergraduate for a Bachelor of Arts degree.'

*

Meanwhile, as John Ondoma was starting his Primary teaching career, for those of us struggling at Mvara Secondary School, there were signs of hope. The building work for the New Site which had stopped before we arrived in 1968 showed signs of coming to life again as the dry season came to an end at Easter 1969. A new contractor, based in Kampala with a largely Sikh team of building supervisors and foremen had got the job and they sent men up to make a new start. Had they begun three months earlier, they would have made better progress as the rains started and the foundations of the new buildings filled with mud. But they were made of sterner stuff than the Italians and soon worked out a way of ensuring that the aggregate was of the right size. A row of grass-roofed shelters was set up along the road-side and a team of rock-breakers recruited who sat in the shade and used club-hammers to break large lumps of rock into the right size to pass through a grid-iron, in a good imitation of Dartmoor convicts at work. Persuading the timber frames for the concrete beams not to warp in the wet proved more difficult but the Sikh engineer cracked that problem too. By setting out huge boulders of rock along the timber moulds rather than the conventional short pegs in the ground, he devised a way of preventing any movement at all. The problem was solved.

Slowly, beams were cast and the concrete set around the steel reinforcing. Very slowly, the New Site buildings were going up. I asked the Foreman how long it would take to finish the job. 'About another year or more,' he said grinning. 'Now we've got the job, there's no great hurry, Sahib.'

*

Guy, Dick and George were all just starting their teaching and they too had been allocated houses on the New Site, so they were our neighbours. They were all from West Nile, Guy an Alur from Goli in the south-west of the District, George and Dick, Lugbaras from around Arua. They had been through Margaret Lloyd's Junior Secondary School and then to Sir Samuel Baker Senior Secondary in Gulu. All three had Makerere degrees, had trained as Secondary Teachers and were still single.

'Saving for the bride-price,' said George. 'I need many cows for the best woman in West Nile.'

I liked George. He was keen, frank and very helpful. He was also a member of All Saint's Church, the English speaking congregation that met in a simple building in the middle of the Golf Course, halfway to the town. We both had an interest in the student Scripture Union group who met, much as the boys of the group at the King's School had met, for an evening Bible Study during the week. It was at one of these meetings that we had to deal with the first really drunk student.

We were in one of the classrooms after evening Prep had finished, for an hour of quiet Bible Study and discussion. It was immediately obvious from the beery fumes filling the room that someone had prepared for the meeting with a stiff drink.

'One of you has been drinking.' George told them. 'That person must leave now.' Since drinking was against School Rules, I wondered if we should not enforce the rule, rather than get rid of the problem.

'Keep quiet,' George hissed at me. 'I shall deal with this.' One of the boys got to his feet.

'It is not right, Sir, to say that I have been drinking. I have been to my relative and we have had porridge together. I have not been drinking.'

He was swaying from side to side, still muttering 'It is not right', when George took him by the arm and walked him to the door.

'Please get on with the study,' he said to a S4 boy and, beckoning for me to follow them, led the boy out into the night.

His name was Ndubayo, an Okebu from the Congo/Uganda border and George knew him well.

'Where have you been?' he asked.

'I have been taking food in my Uncle's village,' Ndubayo said, leaning against the classroom wall for support.

'You have been drinking,' George said. 'You stink of beer and you cannot stand straight.'

'I have been taking food,' the boy insisted. 'My uncle gave me some porridge. It is our custom to be given food when we visit relatives and it was the porridge that makes me feel ill. My stomach is now paining me; I think that I will vomit.'

George and I stood aside just in time to avoid his stomach contents spewing onto the grass.

'You have been drinking, Ndubayo,' George said sternly, 'and you know what the rule says about drinking.'

'Yes, Sir, but it does not say about taking porridge. I think that I will now go to rest in my dormitory. I am very sorry, Sir.'

With that, the boy shuffled off down to his dormitory and George let him go. He explained on our way down to my house for a much needed cup of coffee, that Ndubayo had a point.

'If you go to Arua Market, you'll see that at least half the space is taken up with mixtures for making beer, millet, sorghum, maize, even some barley from the high ground over the border. Every village brews beer. If he calls it porridge, then that's not a bad word for it, a thick grainy brew in a large pot to be shared around the fire in the evening. The local name is *kwete* and it is also true that it is the custom to offer beer to visitors. It is nutritious so it could be called 'food', but it is also quite strong and boys can get drunk very easily.'

'So what should we do about Ndubayo?' I asked.

'Leave him to sleep it off now. I'll talk to him tomorrow and tell him that for a Pastor's son to be seen by the *muzungu* in such a state is a great shame to his father. He was drunk at school but he did not drink at school. He will not get caught again.'

But others did get caught. When one of my Form, a boy called Onzi, got drunk one evening, Lewis decided that the time had come to send him home. Not for ever, but until the end of the term.

'We have to show that getting drunk is just not acceptable, John. Can you take him to his father's village, it's in Wandi near Mt Wati?'

Wandi was about ten miles north of the town along a narrow *murram* road which was not much more than a bridle path. With the erring boy giving me direction from the back seat, I drove very cautiously down the track. Beside me in the front seat sat one of the cooks, asked by Lewis to come with me as interpreter and, it seemed, body guard. As we drove further and further into the countryside, the boy on the back seat slumped lower to avoid being seen by any who might know him. It was a huge disgrace to be taken home to the village.

We reached a cluster of huts with a grass-roofed church and a house with an iron roof.

'This is the place,' said a quiet voice from the back. 'What is your father's name?' asked the cook. 'It is Dradria.'

We stopped by the church and the cook got out and went into a house, the home it seemed of the village pastor. We waited outside.

'Will your father be here?' I asked the boy, not wishing to spend the rest of the day here.

'They will fetch him from the fields.'

A small boy ran out of the house and disappeared. The cook came out of the front door with a tall, elderly man.

'This is the Reverend,' he said. 'He would like you to come in to take tea in his house.'

'My home is yours and you are welcome,' the tall, broad shouldered Pastor said as he shook hand and gestured to the chairs in the living room of his house. 'It is a sad day when a son of the village comes back to us in disgrace and we all share that shame.' The boy crept in behind us and sat on the floor. 'His father is away in the town, but his mother will come from the fields. Will you take tea with us, Mr Haden?'

'I would like that,' I said. 'I am sorry to have to bring this problem back with me but the school has a rule and Onzi has broken it many times.'

'That is true,' the Pastor said solemnly. 'He has brought shame to us all.'

The earth floor was cool in the semi-darkness of his home, but the air under the thin iron roof was heavy and hot. There was little to ease the starkness of the bare mud walls, just a plain wooden table and a collection of old wooden chairs at one end. Above the curtained off doorway which led to the cooking room at the back, a faded diploma announced that Enoka Yada had been ordained Deacon in Arua in 1956. Beside the diploma a cracked sheet of glass protected an old photograph of a tall thin man of about thirty rigidly upright in his clerical clothes. Beside him an older-looking woman, her head wrapped in a coloured cloth and her hip supporting a large baby whose mouth was still screaming more than twenty years later.

'That is our son,' the Pastor said proudly.' He is now with the United Nations in New York. He has done well.'

'You must be very proud of him,' I said as an elderly woman carrying a tray of cups swept her voluminous skirts through the curtained door.

'This is my wife, Candiru, Mr Haden. She does not speak English well but she wishes to greet you.' She took my hand between her gnarled and blistered palms and without looking up at all, poured out a stream of earnest Lugbara. The Pastor explained.

'She says that she is too sorry that a son of this village has caused so much difficulty at school that he must be sent away. But she thanks you for bringing him home safely. She prays that you will forgive him for the trouble he has caused.'

With that she let go of my hand. 'Thank you for your welcome,' I said. 'When the time comes, he will be allowed to return to school, but he must not drink.'

She picked up a kettle of water, a cheap plastic bowl and a cake of soap. Kneeling before each of us in turn, she handed us the soap, poured water over our hands and held the bowl under our dripping fingers. The 'tea' that followed turned out to be far more than just a cup. It was a full meal of *enya* and meat stew, probably the food that she had prepared for the whole family and was now offering to an unexpected and uninvited guest. The Pastor gave thanks and he, the school cook and I sat round the table.

I tried to eat some of the *enya* and a little meat but I was all too conscious of the hungry children peering into the room through the window spaces. We ate in silence. Eating in an African home is a serious business best kept uncluttered with unnecessary talk. The two men ate well, and licked their fingers in appreciation once the food on their plates was gone.

I did my best to show a similar enthusiasm for *enya* and stew but I don't think they were convinced. When we had had our fill, the rest of the food was taken back into the kitchen to be shared by Candiru and the family, and we waited for the mother of the boy to arrive. She had been hoeing in a distant field and needed to go home first to wash and change before meeting the *muzungu* from the school and her disgraced son.

When she arrived, she refused to come into the house. The Pastor met her on the steps outside and exchanged greetings. They spoke in Lugbara with many sighs and silences. He came back in.

'Onzi, your mother has come. You must greet her and tell her how sorry you are that you have brought disgrace to your family.'

The shame-faced boy got up and slunk out of the house. I heard them exchange greetings and her long stream of parental disapproval. We stayed inside to make it easier for the boy to listen to his mother's pain. Then he came to the door.

'My mother wishes to speak to you, Sir,' he said. So with the school cook translating, I listened to her saying how sorry she was that this boy, her son, had broken the school rules so often. I should forgive him and allow him back to school as soon as the Headmaster could agree.

'Go with your mother and stop the drinking,' I said as sternly as I could to Onzi and they went off home, the teenage boy, nearly a man, walking behind his mother in the reversal of the usual procession.

'He will not misbehave again,' was the only comment from the Pastor, and then he said, 'And you Mr Haden, you will come back to our village one Sunday and share the word of God with us, you will speak at our service?'

Like most of the Church in West Nile, Enoka assumed that as a teacher at Mvara, I would also be a member of the AIM and would be happy to preach at his church. I had taken short services in Oxford hospital wards with Oxford Christian Union[8] teams, and I had spoken to young people's group at Church Pastoral Aid Society[9] and Crusader camps, but I was not planning to join the clergy and I had no training or authority to preach in an Anglican church.

'Are you sure that it would be alright for me to help with your service?' I asked him. 'I'm not a member of the Mission and actually work for the Government.'

'Even Government men can preach the word of God,' he said with a broad grin. 'When you come to take Onzi back to the school, come and stay with me and help with our service.'

'I would like to do that very much,' I said, although it seemed more likely that the boy would make his own way back to school at the start of the next term.

*

I did go back to that village to help with a service, but because I had commitments in school on most term-time Sundays, I could not join them until the Easter holiday and was invited to spend Easter with them. I drove back to the village on the Saturday evening so that we could be up early for the Easter Day dawn. After the inevitable enormous supper of *enya* and goat had been enjoyed and cleared away, Enoka and I held court on his veranda well into the night as each member of the village came to greet the *muzungu* visitor. Once we had exchanged greetings to the limit of my Lugbara, I sat in silence as they each expressed their thanks to me and to the school for what the school was doing for their children, translated into English for me by the Enoka. Then we just sat in silence, sharing each others' company as the villagers around us prepared for the big day until each of them went home.

He had arranged a bed for me at the end of his veranda, under an ancient mosquito net, a cool but public place, partially screened by a papyrus mat. A man with a bow and arrow, settled down at the foot of the steps up to the veranda. His job was to guard me and the house but first he greeted me and, I assume, wished me a good night's sleep. In spite of the drones of mosquitoes, humming around my net, I slept like a log until the first village cock greeted the dawn of Easter Day. After a brief wash in a bowl of cold water under the silent gaze of a ring of children, breakfast arrived on a tray. Somehow, Enoka had the idea that his visitor would need tea and biscuits to face the day and had sent a boy to walk five miles to the nearest *duka* to buy some plain biscuits to satisfy my hunger and delicate digestion.

Eventually, we started the service in the grass-roofed village Church. It was a joyous Easter celebration as warm and as enthusiastic as any I had ever experienced. Having been welcomed by the packed congregation and smiled in what I hoped was a sufficiently friendly fashion at the rows of faces smiling back at me, I took part as best I could, standing up and kneeling down at roughly the same time as everyone else.

When the time came for the sermon, I was escorted to the front of the church and introduced by the Rev. Yada. My attempt at a Lugbara greeting produced an overwhelming response, woos-woos from the women, thanks from the men and excited muttering from the mass of small children sitting on the floor.

'They are so happy that you know our language,' Enoka said with a grin, but from then onwards, I was in English. He stood beside me and translated my short and simple sermon. Each English phrase was followed by a stream of vehement Lugbara with much waving of his arms. If I referred to a particular verse, he found two or three more on the same theme. When I pointed to the visual aid I had pinned to the mud wall of the Church, he stabbed at it with all the vigour of a hungry woodpecker until the large sheet of paper was full of holes.

Enoka included everything in that sermon, the countryside outside, the congregation, and even me until the 'ehs' and 'ahs' convinced him that they had got his message, even if mine was still a bit obscure. My ten minutes of carefully split up short phrases became a half hour torrent of words in his translation. When I reached the last sentence in my notes, now smudged and soggy in my sweating palm, he turned and took my hand, leading a chorus of Lugbara cries of 'Praise the Lord!'

'Truly you have brought us the word of God,' he beamed. 'This is a very Happy Easter for us.'

After that, the simple Easter communion was quiet and dignified. They took the bread and the wine from Enoka and his Deacon with quiet reverence and returned to their seats for the last part of the service. It had long been the custom in the village churches of West Nile to give the collections on Christmas and Easter Days to the Pastor of the church. Often these formed the major part of his income for the year. So after the communion was finished, a man and a woman stood up at the front of the church and each harangued their respective sides to be sure to be generous in their giving. The congregation then formed two long queues to bring their gifts forward and to leave them in piles on the Communion Table or on the floor in front.

Some brought cash: collections of coins ties in a cloth that had to be rattled impressively and tipped into a large basket. Some brought bundles of grubby bank notes. Others brought gifts in kind: sheaves of millet heads, leaking bags of cassava flour, cobs of maize and handfuls of eggs. Chickens with their legs tied were carried up making loud squawking protests and then settled down to peck at the grain. One proud and generous lady led up a bleating and excreting goat which she proudly tied to a leg of the Communion Table with a length of sisal string.

Lugbara women cooking enya for an ordination feast

At intervals, the two leaders would call a halt and assess the relative value of the contributions of each side, the men and the women, and the trailing gender would get a stream of encouragement to catch up. That year, several thousand shillings were given to the Pastor, together with a mound of food and a menagerie of livestock which he was free to eat, breed from or sell. These African Christians turned their Easter celebration into a Harvest Festival of joy and generosity that was humbling in its intensity and sincerity. As we shook hands with so many of them and wished them a very Happy Easter, I could not help feeling a stab of nostalgia for the feel of Spring in the air and the sight of daffodils and lambs on fresh green pasture that came each Eastertide at home.

When I got into the car to drive back to school, I found that the over-whelming hospitality that had been shown to me as a visitor went on, to a departing guest. The back seat of my car was filled with two bunches of sweet bananas, a bag of groundnuts and two live chickens, just in case I had an accident on the road and felt hungry!

\*

When there was no school morning service, I would attend the English service at the little Township Church. After a month or two, a message arrived from the Bishop's house.

'The Bishop is not able to preach at St Philip's this Sunday. Would Mr Martin or Mr Haden please preach for the English service?'

John Martin announced that he had already agreed to take the school Scripture Union group meeting at that time. I would have to go. So with considerable trepidation, I prepared to stand in for the Bishop, my next experience of preaching in Uganda. It was a real challenge as I had little in common with the people who worshipped there. They were mainly Ugandan Government Officers posted to departments in the town, the Police, the Hospital, the Ministry of Works and the rest, and their common language was English. The service itself made straightforward use of the Anglican Prayer Book but the finer points of idiom and pronunciation would often defeat the young enthusiastic clergyman who led our worship.

'Spear thou them, O Lord, who confess their faults......,' he would pray earnestly, as the handful of British members of his congregation looked up anxiously. The prayer for the Queen's majesty, still in the prayer book the Church of Uganda used, caused problems even when the President of Uganda was officially Protestant.

'Most heartidly we beseech thee with thy fever to beholdy our most gracious er Excellency, the President, Dr Milton Obote, and so replenish him with the grace of the Holy Spiriti that he may always incliny to thy way and that he may attend everlasting joy and facility, through Jesus Christ our Lord.'

'Amena,' came the deep resonant response from the loyal congregation.

But it was easy for us to be amused by errors in our language by those whose languages we made so little attempt to learn. Few of us learnt any KiSwahili, the language of the Army, or Luganda, the language of the Baganda. Neither was spoken widely in West Nile. With all school teaching in English, there was little incentive for us to learn any one of the five main languages used in West Nile, Lugbara, Kakwa, Madi,

Okebu or Aluru. We could always claim that we had to avoid speaking one local language to avoid giving offence to those who spoke the other four. The Ugandans with whom we worked and whom we taught had no such inhibitions about exposing their English to criticism and all wanted to improve their mastery of this key to future employment in Government. When all of us at Mvara received a duplicated letter headed 'A Christmas Massage from your Pastor', he was as amused by his mistake as we were.

Sometimes, it was just too difficult to explain what was funny. On the Sunday morning when I was to preach in the Township Church service, the hymn was announced: 'Glorious things of thee are spoken, Zion city of our God', which was fine, until the Pastor sung the third verse at the top of his voice:

'Round their habitations hoovering
See the cloud and fire appear…..'

Trying to keep a straight face for the rest of the hymn proved quite impossible.

'Are you adaptable?' the elderly interviewer had asked in the ODM selection process. He cannot have foreseen that the greatest test of my ability to adapt came as I turned up to preach one Sunday at the Township Church. It had been a long and busy school week and I had little time to prepare for the service, so I brought with me a sermon I had used in the school service on the text 'God is like a refiner's fire', a theme which appealed to me with my background in Ferrous Metal Oxides! Judgement, condemnation, the fires of hell, offer of forgiveness and the refining fire of the Holy Spirit, they were all in that sermon, of which I was not a little proud.

The Pastor announced the first hymn in his usual jovial way and we sang 'Blessed Assurance, Jesus is mine' while the late-comers arrived, including a middle aged family with five children who settled down at the front of the Church.

'Friends,' beamed the Pastor. 'This is a most happy day. We welcome to our church our brother and sister who have come to the Lord and now want to be really and truly married during our service this morning.'

A chorus of 'Praise the Lord' greeted the good news.

'And even better than that very good thing, they want an even better thing, to have their children properly baptised as well.'

`A murmur of approval rolled around the packed church.

The happy couple, a sheepish stooping man with mottled grey hair, uncomfortable in his new orange shirt with dark patches of sweat spreading across his back and under his arms, pushed his shy and ample bride towards the Pastor still smiling down at them. Marriage ceremonies don't take long and as it was dawning on me that I might have to preach a sermon to offer my congratulations to the happy couple, I began to panic. 'Refiner's fire' just would not do and I needed fresh inspiration, quickly. The Pastor completed the wedding and exhorted the Almighty to add yet further to the row of silent solemn children standing behind the newly-weds.

Then the Pastor changed gear into baptism mode and cantered through a multiple baptism as if he was washing down a wall, scooping handfuls of water from the simple wooden font over the foreheads, faces and feet of each child in turn.

'Erinesti, I baptise thee, (splash), Onessimo, I baptise thee, (splash), Silas, I baptise thee, (splash), Penina, I baptise thee, (splash), Benjamini, I baptise thee', (splash), until the family was once again united in a common faith and a pool of consecrated water, steadily spreading down the cement floor of the Church. The English speaking Anglicans of Arua rose to their feet and sang 'Now thank we all our God, with hearts and hands and voices, who wondrous things hath done, in whom his world rejoices.'

All rejoicing that is, apart from me, knowing that my turn would come very soon. 'Guide us when perplexed' was never a truer prayer as I finished off my mental conversion of the Refiner's fire to a Wedding word to the happy couple. But I need not have worried. The euphoria of the occasion and the distraction of the ever-spreading pool made even my brief and muddled contribution acceptable to the Pastor and his people and, as I realised when offering my personal congratulations to the newly-weds after the service, they hardly spoke English anyway. The Pastor thanked me for my very appropriate sermon and demanded to know why it was that I had not yet found a wife.

\*

If the residents of Kuluva seemed to us to be sometimes living in a world of colonial assumptions, another group in West Nile seemed completely impervious to the feelings of the local people. They were the Asians, the business community whose help I needed if I was to get supplies of uniform for the school. Lewis let me know, just before the end of term in December that supplies of socks, shirts and games kit had been ordered in good time for the new intake. This was a relief as I had not realised that this was one of my responsibilities as Master i/c Uniforms. Lewis also suggested that I should call in to meet the suppliers next time I was in Kampala to check on how things were going and whether a better deal could be agreed.

I spent hours in the Asian stronghold of Kampala's industrial area trying to track down the cheapest suppliers of school uniforms. White shirts and blouses were relatively straightforward. Lewis gave me the contact details of our supplier and I found his shop easily – it had a sign over the entrance – School Shirts Here. The smiling Asian owner could not have been more helpful.

'We can supply any size of shirt in any number and we can supply blouses for the girls too.'

I checked the order he held for Mvara and adjusted it to allow for the anticipated S1 entry.

'Just assume that the sizes are in the same proportion',I told him, 'there won't be much difference between one form and another.'

He also supplied the badges which students sewed onto their shirts or were supposed to. Boy's games shorts were similarly ordered from the same supplier, but school socks were a more specialised job.

Our school socks were long grey knitted nylon with coloured bands at the top. Most students wore them with flip-flops although they were supposed to wear shoes. By the end of the year, there was not much left of the feet but the leg lengths lasted longer, provided that the owner made a neat job of stopping the unravelling of the nylon yarn. The supplier was an enterprising Sikh with a factory in Kampala and we needed a lot of pairs of socks. I did try to get competitive tenders from different suppliers, but there was only one reliable machine knitter of socks in Kampala so I ended up going to the same place every year.

Placing the orders was the easy bit. The Asian shop-owner or manufacturer would seal the deal over a cup of strong brown cinnamon tea, an acquired taste, and offer me a suitable gift. Most of these I politely declined but the more persistent dealers would arrange to have their shocking pink plastic salad-servers and cheap Hong-Kong thermos flasks delivered to the staffroom at school by one of their network of business contacts in Arua. But as soon as I was out of the shop or the factory and three hundred miles up-country, the supplier would appear to have forgotten the vital order. Frantic 'phone calls from a school desperate to pacify dozens of angry students still wearing last year's tatty shirts and socks, would produce further promises of delivery, all too often with a price rise.

The Asian community's reputation for efficient business was often marred by every sort of sharp practice. One year, having secured our order of a thousand pairs of socks of a new design for the school, the Asian supplier waited for the first year's stock to be issued. The smart socks found their way to every village in West Nile to be admired by relatives of our bona-fide students and coveted by every youth who had failed to get into the school. The market was now primed and the supplier of our socks changed the coloured bands by adding one extra insignificantly small strip of blue before producing thousands of pairs of 'almost Mvara socks' for sale in every *duka* in the District, at twice the price he charged me. Now everyone could wear the symbol of success and nearly everyone did. Even the oldest of the school cooks, a wrinkled old lady whose job it was to keep the cooking fires going with eucalyptus logs, sported a dashing pair of 'school socks'. There was nothing we could do about it except change the design of the sock top yet again so we left it as it was. Next time we ordered socks from the same Sikh, the only source of knitted socks in Kampala, he promised faithfully not to make the same 'mistake' again.

In Arua, the Asian business community provided much of what we as teachers needed. Stankya's Supermarket, about the size of an English convenience store, held the prime site on the corner of the main street running into town. Mr Stankya's shelves offered the usual range of tinned and dried foods, much of which was produced in Kenya, and some 'fresh' supplies. There was usually one variety of cheese, slightly melted after a long journey up on a bus or lorry. Sometimes he had fresh butter and his freezer offered frozen meat. This was always a bit of a risk as there was no guarantee that the item had not thawed out and been refrozen several times since it had set out from a distant source but Mr Stankya always claimed that it was 'fully frozen, Sir'. Much of the time we made do with Blue Band margarine, Kimbo cooking fat and red jam, possibly from plums.

Further down the street, the smaller *dukas* supplied the things that the Ugandan population needed: dried goods like rice and flour, (frequently with a protein bonus in the form of weevils), paraffin oil and basic hardware. Shopping in these *dukas* was sometimes embarrassing as their owners had a habit of spotting a *muzungu* customer in the queue of patient Africans and beckoning you forward to the front. As their customers sometimes included students from the school or Ugandans we knew from church, I always found this blatantly racial preferential treatment embarrassing.

On a side street was Chawda's hardware, suppliers of every sort of building material, tools and almost anything you could possibly need to run a school or build a hospital. Ted and Peter Williams got on well with the Chawda brothers. They had come to the District at about the same time after World War II and had helped each other in all sorts of practical ways. Although as Hindus, they did not have any interest in the Christian Church, they were generous in their support of the practical work of Mvara Mission and Kuluva Hospital and they were expert businessmen.

On a back street, Kawa Motors provided essential support to the fleet of Land Rovers used by the Police and Government department, and most of the cars of the Mvara and Kuluva communities. Mr Kawa was a friendly stocky Indian whose pockmarked face showed he had survived smallpox as a child. He was an expert at keeping ancient Land Rovers on the road with a scrap-yard of old models for recycling spare parts. We came to rely on Mr Kawa and to avoid asking too many questions about where the necessary spare had come from. When the time came for the Ugandan equivalent of the MOT test, a worn part could be replaced temporarily from his scrap-yard or from one of the Police Land Rovers in for a service.

Arua also offered bread shops and meat shops, both supplying daily essentials in sheets of newspaper, the bread just one variety either in small loaves or rolls, a little sweet but we were pleased to have it. The meat was beef or goat, slaughtered that day and butchered into rough hunks, no topside joints neatly rolled and tied, no neat T-bone steaks, just cow or goat, 'meat with bones' or 'meat without bones'. If you arrived early enough to get a piece of *filleti*, you got a relatively tender piece of beef which made a good casserole. If not, you cooked it for a very long time and vowed to get up earlier in future!

At the end of the main street, by the bus-park, Arua Market opened early every day and sold eggs and chickens, bananas, green and yellow, cabbages and all sorts of beans. There were piles of tomatoes, groundnuts in their shells and, on good days, avocados, guavas, pineapples and oranges from the Congo, mangos from the south and all sort of strange delicacies such as grasshoppers, best avoided. If you had the time to haggle with the market women, it was a bustling friendly place, but Onessimo usually went down for us by bicycle to collect what he thought we needed.

Arua had a branch of Grindlays Bank Uganda Ltd next to the Agip filling station on the way into town. We used it to get cash and kept an eye on our accounts. Usually the bank was very efficient, providing monthly statements of the small amount of activity we managed to generate, but on one occasion, their system went haywire. I received a bank statement which showed that my account was in the red by a string of 9s which ran right across the page. The amount owing was larger than the Ugandan gross domestic product, larger than the UK National Debt, so huge that the daily interest alone would be more than my annual salary. I rushed round to Grindlays to have the record put right before my financial future was ruined. The Asian manager was most apologetic.

'We are very sorry, Sir. Our printer has developed a fault – I hope that this has not caused you an inconvenience.'

'It might have caused a heart attack,' I said. 'Fortunately, it didn't - just put it right, now.'

The Asians, or rather Indians for there were very few from Pakistan or China in West Nile, owned almost all the businesses in Arua. They ran the bus system, the lorry transport to Kampala and much of the black market trading that went on across the border with the Congo. They had businesses in the towns on the other side and could move freely to and fro, so that when things got difficult in Congo as they did during the *Simba* rebellion, the Asians could move their assets, especially in the form of gold hanging around the arms and necks of their women-folk, to the more secure side.

Every evening, before sunset at 6 pm, the Indian families would walk on the edge of the Golf Course in an Arua parade of elegance as ostentatious as any *passeggiata* along an Italian sea-front. They flaunted their wealth and separateness in a way that was bound to annoy the Ugandan population. Men in smart shirts and pressed flannels, women in gorgeous saris, they would stroll along or sit in circles on the mown grass by the road-side. Children played games and teenagers giggled as the heat of the day died away with the setting sun. Further down the road, under the street lamps beginning to glow with light, ragged African children would be beating on up-turned aluminium *sufurias*, drumming with sticks to persuade the flying ants to come out of the earth, fat termite drones to catch in handfuls and fry over a small fire. Two worlds close by each other and yet totally apart.

**The district of West Nile in the 1960s**

## Part 3: Living and Working in Arua
### 3.1 Impenetrable Hides

Ted Williams was an expert on most things connected with West Nile, including the birds and animals of the area. I discovered that the Uganda Wildlife Authority had made him an honorary Game Warden. One lazy afternoon, when he took an hour off from the wards to sit by the pool with us, he told us what this meant.

'Just down the road from here, on the west bank of the Nile, there is an area called Ajai, near the village of Inde.

The land is not very fertile and the people living there weren't able to grow much apart from a little low-yield cotton of poor quality. The Madi Chief Ajai agreed to set it aside as a Game Reserve because there was a population of rhino there, not many but important.

'a splendid full grown rhinoceros, with the long thin horn of his rare tribe upon him – the famous white rhinoceros – Burchell himself – strolling placidly home after his evening drink' (Winston Churchill)

They're white rhino, not the usual black rhino you get in Kenya and Tanzania, and in some of our big game parks, but the large, grazing rhino variety which you also get in the north of the Congo. They also occur in South Africa south of the Zambezi River and that's why they're called white – it's a corruption of the Africaans word 'weit' meaning 'wide' because they're grazers not browsers like the black variety. They're also called Burchell's white rhino.'

'We came past Inde on the way up to Arua,' said Andrew, one of the AIM volunteers. 'It looked flat and hot, with scrubby trees and ant hills.'

'That's the place,' Ted said. 'We have a small Ranger post down there to keep an eye on the rhino. They're very vulnerable to poaching. People have been trying to shoot them for generations although they're not very edible. Three and a half tons of Africa's second largest mammal inside an impenetrable hide – except to a high velocity bullet. Our West Nile rhino became famous when Winston Churchill[1] wrote about them in his account of travelling down the Nile. I think he shot four at a place he called 'Hippo Camp' which might well have been our Ajai's Reserve. They've being dying ever since.'

'So how did you become involved?' I asked.

'The Wildlife people wanted to save a few by taking them over the Nile into Murchison Park,' he explained. They asked me to help as I knew about the ones at Inde. They were the most accessible rhino although there are a few left in the north up by the Sudan border. We managed to trap them in a stockade, tranquilized them and loaded them into crates so that they could be taken across the Nile at the Pakwach ferry and released in the delta area of the Park. That's why they made me an Honorary Game Warden.'

'Wasn't that very dangerous', Andrew asked. 'Trying to capture such huge animals?'

'They're actually quite placid,' Ted explained, 'much less dangerous than the black rhino, which will charge at anything. Provided you know what you're doing and keep an eye out for a good tree to climb into, it's possible to walk around the reserve and get quite close to them. Would you like to have a try? I can contact the Game Warden at Inde and arrange for you to be taken to see them.'

A few weeks later, when Ted had set up the visit, John Martin, Andrew, Richard and I went down to Inde in my nearly new VW Beetle. We stopped at the Ranger post on the edge of the village, parked the car and locked it, put on our hats and found a Ranger waiting for us. He seemed pleased to see us and explained what we had to do.

'You walk behind me, stay close and follow my signals. If we get to the rhino, we'll try to approach down-wind. They will not know we are coming. If I stop, you stop; if I wave my hand like this, we go back. OK?'

'What if they charge at us?' asked Andrew obviously expecting the worst.

'They cannot see well, but they can hear. We should try to be very quiet and get behind a big ant-hill or into a small tree.'

So we set off across the dusty plain of cotton-grass. There were plenty of huge ant-hills, which seemed reassuring, but every small tree we passed seemed well equipped with large thorns. We walked silently in single file for nearly an hour in the blazing sun, grateful for hats. The Ranger put up his hand for us to stop. About a hundred yards away, grazing an open patch of dusty grass was a rhino. It was at least six feet tall at the shoulder and as long as a family car from square snout to the base of its thin swishing tail. Its low slung head carried a yard of straight sharp horn with another horn above. By its side, a small grey calf snuffled around in the dust.

'It is a mother with a child,' whispered the Ranger, somewhat unnecessarily. 'We must be careful not to disturb them. But the wind is blowing towards us so we can creep a bit closer.'

So we tiptoed closer, to within about forty yards and then froze. The female rhino swung her great head in our direction and produced an explosive fart.

'She is peaceful,' grinned the Ranger. 'She does not know that we are here.'

We were happy to stand stock still and just enjoy being so close to one of Africa's great animals. For half an hour we watched them graze together and then backed off slowly trying as best we could not to make a sound. It was only when we got back to the Ranger post that we felt the tension lift. We thanked him for giving us such an unforgettable experience and pushed a roll of shilling notes into his hand as Ted had suggested we should. Walking slowly back to the car, we were hot and happy with our two hours in the sun.

I then discovered that we had a real problem. Not the charge of a rhino but the breaking into an equally impenetrable VW Beetle. In my hurry to make the car secure, I had stupidly locked the keys inside the car. All our water was inside. The tsetse flies were beginning to bite. It was a long walk back to Arua. Four young men, one future Anglican Bishop, two future Anglican Vicars and one very careless teacher, were stuck by the roadside in just about the middle of Africa, on the edge of Ajai's Rhino Reserve. We tried to force the doors. Nothing budged. We tried to swivel open the quarter lights of the windows. They were as secure as a bank.

'I think we should pray about it,' said Andrew.

So, three of us did pray, the future Bishop and Vicars, fervently asking for God's help. One of us went to look for a rock big enough to break a very Germanic window. I found something suitable and, feeling very stupid, brought it back to be used if no other answer to prayer arose. We sat by the road-side and wondered when, if ever, any other transport came along the road from Pakwach to Arua via Inde. No car appeared. It got hotter. A troop of baboons ran across the road and laughed at us.

'At least it will get cooler when the sun goes down,' said John helpfully. 'But that's about six hours away and there's bound to be a car or a bus passing through by then.'

A man on a bicycle rode slowly past. We wished him good afternoon and by his cheerful Lugbara response deduced that we had no language in common. I decided that the time for action had come. It was after all my car. I bashed the car window, just the quarter light. It smashed at the third blow of the rock. My beautiful new car was damaged in the cause of getting home. We got in and drive off without another word. The others never told the Mvara staff of my stupidity, but when Ted asked how we had got on, Andrew told him it was wonderful, but a bit hot!

\*

There were three other White Rhino Sanctuary Reserves in West Nile, one along the Nile north of Ajai, and the others in the mountains up by the Sudan border. I visited one of these, on Mt Otzi on another of our hill climbing expeditions, 'mad' in the eyes of the Ugandan teachers, but saw nothing larger than a buffalo. There was very little game in most of West Nile. For generations, most of the area had been used for subsistence agriculture supporting very small family units, clusters of huts and grain stores. There was spare land and in these pockets the refugees from the fighting in the Sudan and from the Congo eked out a precarious living. It was as if the borders of the modern states of Uganda, Sudan and Congo were no more than lines on maps in offices and so very porous on the ground. People could simply leave one country with what they could carry, move across the border, find a space, build a hut and cultivate a patch of land.

Some frontiers, like the Uganda/Congo boundary south of Arua, ran down the mid-line of a watershed road. The story was told of the young Survey Officer in Colonial times who was sent to check the accuracy of the map of the border including the road. When he asked how he would know where the border was supposed to run, he was told to urinate in the middle of the road. If it ran down the middle, he would know that the road followed the border exactly. If his urine ran to the West, he was too far west, in the Congo River catchment, if to the East, he was in the upper reaches of the Nile. From the air, this road still marks the boundary, a rust red line across the land. To the British, it said here Empire ends, beyond lies Congo, the Conradian Heart of Darkness of Central Africa.

*

Around the school, on the edge of Arua Township, there were few mammals, apart from dogs, cows and the occasional fox, but the birds were wonderful. In the long grass around our new houses and by the path across the valley, colonies of yellow-collared and golden-backed weavers built their hanging nests, chattering like a gaggle of school-girls in the cool of the evening. In the early morning, red bishops produced a flash of scarlet as they flew across our windows. Fan-tailed widow-birds, jet black with orange shoulders, fluttered like feathered butterflies displaying to each other.

The established gardens at Mvara Mission had an even wider range of birds. Malachite sunbirds, wings beating faster than you could see, keeping their iridescent emerald green bodies quite still, sipped nectar from the hibiscus flowers outside Margaret's window. Peggy's gardens had a resident pair of woodland kingfishers, turquoise above and grey below with a vicious black and red bill, good for grabbing insects, grubs and small frogs. Everyone had their own dusky flycatcher or its blue cousin, and those who were lucky would spot a visiting golden or black headed oriole skulking through the guava trees.

But for real game watching, we had to go down the Pakwach road and across the Nile ferry into Murchison Falls Park. I never lost the buzz of excitement at the thought that to get to Kampala by car or bus you had to drive through some of the best wild-life viewing in Uganda. Right by the ferry-dock on the east bank of the great river, herds of elephant would be grazing in the reeds, dozens of them, great bulls with huge tusks and muddy flanks and smaller cows sometimes with tiny calves at their feet.

If you then took the rough Tangi Track into the Park itself, past the Swahili sign that warned you *'Pole, Pole, tia gear moja'*, 'Take Care, Engage First Gear', to crawl across the switch-backs of erosion through the high grass, you were never sure of what you would meet around the next corner. Perhaps another elephant or an angry buffalo still covered in mud, or a herd of waterbuck, blocking the track and then charging off into the swamp.

Once, we met the white rhino that Ted had helped to save. Two of them came bursting out of the grass to canter across the road, their great horns carried low like the battering rams of ancient iron clad ships, off to make war on some lesser enemy. On other journeys we would branch off the track onto the circuits that took you right down to the flats by Lake Albert, where white rhino grazed amongst the herds of Uganda cob like huge armour plated cattle. It was always exciting to go through the park, even though we seldom had time to stop for the boat trip which took visitors right up to the foot of the great Murchison Falls. That experience had to wait until we were there to take friends or relatives 'on safari'.

*

If we found it hard to understand our Ugandan colleagues' views on enforcing school rules, they found our behaviour equally strange, for example, our interest in climbing hills. Gordon and I shared a love of walking to high places, he from his home by the Mountains of Mourne and me from holidays in Wales, Scotland and the Lake District. So it was inevitable that we should feel the urge to get higher than the plateau on which Arua stood. We knew it would be hot work but argued that the heat was not as oppressive as we had expected and the nights could even be cool at 4,000 feet above sea-level. So we planned weekend walking expeditions, to climb the hills of West Nile, *Wati* and *Liru*.

*Wati* was the nearest, a rocky outcrop 4661 feet above sea level according to the old survey map we found in the school store. It lay a few miles north of the *murram* road from Arua north-west into Terego County. So we asked who else wanted to come and soon had a 'Climbing Mount *Wati*' party of teachers and mission folk. None of the Ugandan staff wanted to come. They thought that we were mad to even think of climbing mountains. 'Why get hot going up a hill?' they argued. 'We can see *Wati* from here and there's nothing there except a few baboons. Those are the places of our ancestors and we should leave them in peace.'

It was a mixed group of Mission and School *muzungus* who drove from Arua north to Paranga, the village nearest to Mt Wati. We set off through the scrub and crossed the River Anyau towards the peak. On the way I asked Seton Maclure about the theories of origin which the anthropologist, John Middleton, had included in his book on the Lugbara[2].

'Well, you have to take them with a pinch of salt,' he said puffing slightly at the steepness of the climb. 'Sometimes, the people know that European visitors want a good story. So they tell them about the ancestors coming from a Great Spirit, a creation myth if you like. They may tell stories about how the first man and woman came to be, and how the first woman gave birth not just to boys and girls but also to antelopes and goats, all the animals of the Lugbara world. *Jaki* and *Driburu* are certainly important to the Lugbara but who they were and what they were like is very complicated. '*Driburu*' means 'the hairy one' and he is also sometimes called '*banyale*', Eater of Men. They also say that he married a woman with leprosy and cured her with local medicines.

Mvara party on the top of Mount Wati –with local guides

The trouble is that the Churches have been telling the people about the Bible stories for more than two generations since the 1920s. If you ask the Lugbara now what they believe about their ancestors, the answers may be a mixture of Biblical stories and their own myths. The anthropologists like to say that this shows that Biblical myths are universal human stories but I'm not so sure. Perhaps, they got their 'human stories' from a half-remembered Bible story. What interests me is how the language links can tell us about where the people came from. Lugbara, Okebu and Madi are all related languages from a common source in the Sudan region. That's why we call them 'Sudanic', and the language of the people to the south, the Alur, we call 'Nilotic' from a different language stem.'

A cluster of family huts under Mt Wati – the way of life of many Lugbara in the 1960s

We made it to the top of the hill, hot and tired, and stopped to look out over the land of the Lugbara. There were no large settlements, just small clusters of round grass-roofed huts with areas of cultivation around them. Back towards Arua, you could just make out larger fields which had been used for tobacco growing and the iron-roofed tobacco curing barns which the British American Tobacco Company (BAT) had financed for the village farmers. But most of the activity in the fields was subsistence farming, millet, cassava and beans, with clusters of bananas and paw-paw near to the huts.

'It looks as if it hasn't changed for generations,' Margaret said. "Development' down there means a corrugated iron roof or a bicycle, or perhaps a radio to listen to while you can afford the batteries. That's the world from which most of our students come.'

When we got back to school, I asked the Lugbara boys in my form to tell me what they knew about Mt Wati. They said it was the place where their father '*Anguandria*' lay buried but they had little interest in their people's past. They knew that the Lugbara had no written history and they had heard the story of the man who lived across the Nile 'long ago'. He was said to have a craving for liver. For a while he satisfied this by stealing cows and goats from the herds of the Acholi people over the Nile but they valued their cattle and chased him down to the river. He swam across and being lonely began to look for a wife. Because he was a stranger and had no cattle to pay a bride-price, he could find no-one so he climbed Mt Wati to end his days alone.

Half way up he met a leper woman, an outcast like himself, who demanded neither cows nor a respectable past so together they climbed the mountain and set up home just below the summit. From there they could see right across to the Nile to the land which the man had come from and the herds of cattle belonging to his people. Together they whistled as loud as they could until the cattle over the river heard them and came across the river and up the hill. Now with a wife and many cows, he could people the land around the hill with his own children, the Lugbara.

*

Ted Williams was as good a source on the history of West Nile as he was on the wildlife. I asked him why there was a very neat road-sign by the entrance to the New Site: 'Weatherhead Lane'. It would have done justice to any English suburban street but who was Weatherhead? Ted explained.

'When the British transferred this area from the Sudan to Uganda in 1914, they appointed the first District Commissioner, A.E. Weatherhead[3]. His name is remembered in Arua because he laid out the town. 'Weatherhead Lane' is the road which runs around the government housing area, or 'Senior Quarters'. He had been brought up in the tradition of 'indirect rule', the system of using local systems of control and taxation which the British had adopted with such conspicuous success in India and other parts of their Empire. Weatherhead knew that indirect rule had also worked well in the Kingdoms of Buganda and Bunyoro to the south where the British could govern through the African kingdoms with their systems of control and taxation. But within much of his West Nile District, there were no kingdoms and amongst the Lugbara living around Weatherhead's headquarters at Arua, there weren't even any chiefs. The Lugbara's traditional community life is still based on the clan, with an elder in charge of one cluster of family huts.

Although this part of the West Nile District was fertile and well-populated, the Lugbara seemed to be able to avoid conflicts over land and water without having anyone in overall charge. They were never very interested in cattle and so had little need for the cattle-raiding which the Karamajong love. When there were disputes between clans, the elders could usually settle them relatively easily. The Lugbara lived alongside the Alur, the Okebu, the Kakwa and the Madi for generations without much inter-tribal violence.'

'When the British came, Weatherhead needed labour to build roads, tax money to pay for schools and hospitals, structures through which he could run the District. He was a vigorous man and set about his task with admirable energy considering he had very little outside help. In this area, the Lugbara and Kakwa stubbornly resisted the pressure to conform to British ideas of how best to do things. DC Weatherhead needed to 'persuade' them and he did not shrink from using force. When he decided a road was needed, and the necessary local labour was not forthcoming, he simply used his armed Police to impound cattle owned by the people along the line of the road and only returned the cows when the job was done!

'Arua' means 'little prison' in Lugbara. This was the place where Weatherhead locked you up if you did not pay your taxes, provide your labour or quarrelled with your neighbours. When we first came here in the 1940s, the town was a typical up-country District Headquarters with Government housing clustered around the higher land by Arua Hill. There was a string of Government offices, a Post Office and a hospital, set out along the road which ran from the Hill down to the double row of Indian owned shops. These small shops soon developed into a thriving business community. Weatherhead built the golf course, a squash court[4] and the inevitable 'West Nile Club', to provide gentle exercise and a restorative gin and tonic for the District's officers.'

'But where did he get his police from, if everything in West Nile was new at that time?' I asked Seton.

'Some of them came from the Nubi down at Wadelai. There was an old fort there which Emin Pasha had garrisoned with Sudanese soildiers. They were Muslims and had fought against the Mahdi rebellion in the Sudan before they were brought down here. Weatherhead found that they could be trained to make good policemen and soldiers, just what he needed to sort out the Lugbara. Although they had married local Madi women, they kept their own identity as the 'Nubi', speaking a form of Arabic, KiNubi. You can still find a community of them living on the edge of Arua on the road to Moyo. Their women wear colourful cloth wraps over their heads.

Another thing Weatherhead did was to persuade the Lugbara to pay their taxes. He encouraged many of the young men to go down to the south to work in the Lugazi sugar plantations. This meant they could send money home and the Lugbara had cash for the first time – they could pay their poll-tax. That's when the tradition started for many young men from West Nile leaving to work in the south of Uganda.'

## 3.2 Mountains and moving to the Left

Once Gordon and I had explored the West Nile hills, our ambition grew. We dreamed of real mountains, the great extinct volcano of Elgon to the east, Moroto in the north-east, the Mountains of the Moon along the western border with the Congo, and the Virunga chain of volcanoes that ran into Ruanda and Congo in the extreme south-west. None of these Ugandan mountains were as high at the great East African peaks of Mt Kenya and Kilimanjaro. But they were less well known, more remote and more mysterious. I wanted to climb them all, but wondered how. Would our network of AIM missionaries and school teachers include others with an interest in mountains?

Gordon and Grace were busy for that first Christmas holiday so I explored the possibility of going over to Kenya to try to climb Mt Elgon from the Kenya side, which was said to be easier – not much more than a moorland walk. The nearest AIM community to the eastern side of Elgon was the AIM Teacher Training College at Eldoret where Gordon knew two missionaries, Julian Jackson and Ronnie Ferguson. It soon became clear that they would be very interested in a walk up Elgon, their local mountain, and I set off for Kenya in the early days of the New Year 1969 with Andrew Dow who was keen to come with us.

Elgon is a huge extinct volcano straddling the Kenya/Uganda border. Imagine Mt Kilimanjaro with the top blown off in an enormous explosion leaving the massive base of the cone and a huge caldera where the peak once was. We climbed to the edge of this gaping hole from Endebesse, first driving up the forestry road through plantations of pine trees. At around 6,000 ft, the bamboo zone began to cover the flank of the mountain, a forest of thick canes through which the track had been cut to form a tunnel into the green. Higher up where the bamboo thinned out to scrubby bush, we drove onto the shoulder of the volcano. It seemed remarkably like English moorland, short grass gently sloping up into the mist. We could have been on the upper slopes of the Cheviots. We pitched camp at about 10,000 ft beside a stream of clear water, cooked supper and prepared for a cold and damp night with no sign of humanity for miles around us.

Stiff and cold, we crept out into a misty bright dawn, packed up our camp, stowed everything in the car and set off to trek up through the grassy tussocks of the moorland to the next band of vegetation. Above 11,000 ft, a wonderland of alpine giants, tall heathers of over thirty feet, proteas and everlasting flowers, giant lobelias and giant groundsel covers the mountains of East Africa. Green towers of lobelias and cabbage topped candle-sticks of groundsel push up into the mists to form a weird primeval landscape.

We reached the edge of the great caldera bowl just to the west of Koitoboss peak at about 13,500 ft by the middle of the day. The thin, cold air caught in our throats and Andrew was struggling, complaining of a bad head-ache and feeling sick, the classic symptoms of high altitude sickness. We paused to let him have a rest on the edge, looking down and across the massive open space to the rim on the Uganda side, nearly five miles away. By the time we got to the dome buttress just before the Lower Elgon Peak at over 14,000 ft, time was running out. The cloud was thickening and the temperature dropping fast. It was time to turn back although we had completed less than a quarter of the circuit of the crater rim. The light was starting to go as drove down the darkening forestry track to the post at the Chorlim Gate.

\*

Once we could claim to have got up Elgon, or almost up it, what was the next mountain to attempt? Gordon and I thought that Moroto looked interesting, a jagged ridge to the east of Moroto town. At 10,010 ft, it was not very high, but what it lacked in altitude it more than made up in remoteness in the north-east of Uganda. It lay in the exotic surroundings of the Karamoja District, home of the naked Karamojong, famous for their herds of cattle and their endless raiding over the border into Kenya. Best of all, nobody knew anyone who had ever been to the top of Mt Moroto, although the Forestry Department was said to have built a road from the edge of Moroto town up into the mountain area.

There were no AIM missionaries on that side of Uganda but we knew from Gordon's contacts that the Bible Churchmen's Missionary Society (BCMS) had a base at Lotume not far from Moroto. This Mission had broken away from the CMS, in 1922, but they worked alongside CMS in Uganda and had been working in Karamoja since 1929. Their position was very similar to that of AIM in West Nile, committed to evangelism and to planting an African Church which would remain within the Anglican Communion. Gordon had met a BCMS missionary from Lotume, Stan Ablewhite, at a Church conference and got in touch with him. Did he know anything about Mt Moroto and if he did would he like to join us in an attempt to get up it on a break from Mission/School duties.

Stan was interested and generously invited us to stay overnight at Lotume on our way to the mountain. Gordon and I, John Martin and Richard Inwood set out at the end of the dry season in our Easter holiday, driving by VW Beetle from Arua south to Karuma and east to Lira and Soroti. We crossed the hot dry Lango plains until we could strike off north east up to Karamoja. This seemed to us to be almost Wild West country, dry valleys and bare hills with nothing more to see than the occasional herd of scrawny cattle guarded by a handful of tall, thin men. They carried nothing but their ten foot spears and a head-rest or a stool. They looked threatening and suspicious, their eyes half-closed against the glare of the sun. Behind them, the jagged ridge of Mt Moroto, miles away to the east, looked equally threatening. Was trying to climb it in this land of spear-throwing cattle thieves really such a good idea?

Lotume proved to be a major centre for Mission and Church work in a surprisingly green valley about fifteen miles south-west of Moroto. The Ablewhites found beds for four visitors and in the morning we set out for the mountain. Stan insisted on bringing his Renault 4, the tough little car of French villagers. With four young men from West Nile, the expedition soon developed into some sort of ridiculous contest, AIM versus BCMS, West Nile versus Karamoja, VW Beetle versus Renault Roho. We drove into Moroto town, the same collection of Post Office, Hospital, Police post, Rest House and two streets of Asian dukas that graced every District centre in post-colonial Uganda. There was also a military barracks and many soldiers in the town and many women in the bars. Not a place for five respectable *muzungus* with Church connections to spend any time at all. So we made one stop at the largest of the *dukas* to pick up supplies and then drove out past the football field and rubbish dump into the river valley running up into the hills. The heavy-shouldered marabou storks picking over the rubbish took one look at our dusty cavalcade and launched themselves lazily into the air to glide across to a new perch on the football goal-posts, safe from alien invaders.

Karamoja is an area of semi-desert, a harsh, unforgiving land used only by wandering cattle grazers who leave their wives and children in thorn protected villages to follow their cows in the search for pasture. They had a well-deserved reputation as fierce cattle thieves, running long distances in raiding parties into their neighbours grazing areas to steal their cows and bring them home. For as long as anyone could remember, the Karamajong had raided the Turkana over the border into Kenya, in spite of the efforts of the Colonial Police Services on both sides of the border. Even within Karamoja, each sub-tribe had traditional enemies, the Jie raided the Pian, the Pian raided the Suk and everyone who could, raided the Pokot. Cattle-raiding was as much a part of their way of life as football is to men in Manchester. 'Away matches' meant tall, naked warriors running through thorn infested scrub for miles in the night, then attacking the 'opposition's' *manyatta*, spearing the young boys who guarded the cattle kraal and stealing women and cows. When the stolen cattle were found by the Police, their new 'owners' would be fined and the herd driven back again by a few Constables to their original home. It seemed to be almost a game, discounting the deaths of boys and any others in the *manyatta* unable to run away in time. Within Karamoja, according to Stan Ablewhite, the chiefs would meet in an annual *baraza* with the District Commissioner, to tot up the numbers killed and the cattle stolen to agree a balance of 'blood money' to be paid in cattle to the losing side.

'So, what about Mount Moroto', we asked Stan. 'Is it safe to wander up the mountain without an armed Police escort?' Stan, who lived and worked amongst the Karamajong, dismissed our worries.

'They've never attacked a *muzungu*. We'll be fine.' The fact that his wife was happy for him to come with us up the mountain was reassuring, and he knew the way, at least for the first part.

From the dirty, dusty edge of the town, the mountain ahead looked very inviting, a long ridge leading up to a rocky pinnacle, Sogoloman, with the highest point, Sokdek, a rocky mound beyond. At over 10,000 ft, Mt Moroto catches enough rain to turn the brown rocks green with forests and pastureland.

Lunch break while driving up Mount Moroto

The Forestry Department had built a road out of the river valley up towards the ridge and a 'forest station' was marked on Stan's old map borrowed from a friend in Moroto. At first, a sandy track wound through the candelabra euphorbias into the band of acacia trees still able to suck a little water out of the desert soil. Then after a zone of protea trees, the track got steeper and rockier.

We were by now crawling in first gear across rocks and gulleys and decided that two should walk and two ride, while Stan in his Renault bounced along behind. Much of the surface of the track had been washed away, but by moving rocks into the larger holes, those who were walking could keep the cars moving until we came to a very steep section where the track was filled with boulders. Gordon in the VW crept up a ladder of rock, cautiously inching each wheel forward until the track levelled out a bit. Stan in the Roho tried, but it was just too steep. We lifted the light body round and he tried to back the car up the hill. Whether it was the 9,000 ft altitude, or the Renault's lack of power, even in reverse it would go no higher. Stan sadly decided that his attempt to uphold the honour of BCMS and French engineering would have to accept defeat and set off down the mountain track back to the home comforts of Lotume.

Three of us then walked to leave the lightest of us driving the VW and up we climbed, determined to get this solid little masterpiece of German motorcar as far up the mountain as we could. When it got stuck with the flat chassis poised on a rock and the back wheels spinning in holes, the three of us just lifted up the back and threw in rocks until we were off again.

Eventually, late in the afternoon as the sun was setting behind the Labwor hills a hundred miles to the west, we reached the top of the track and the Forestry Station hut. This turned out to be a falling-down shed fouled by sheltering cattle and best avoided. Just beyond, a green meadow with a gentle slope down to a small stream offered an ideal camp site so we pitched our tents, cooked our supper and gazed at the stars. It was a cold, clear and perfect night without a sound and with no sign of human habitation for miles. We had driven up Mt Moroto.

In the early dawn, we crawled out of our sleeping bags, brewed tea and chewed toast and packed up all our portable belongings in the car. We left the two tents up to make it easier to spot the camp site in case it was misty when we came back down, and set off up the last slopes of Sogoloman. It was a glorious climb, cool air, wonderful views across the Karamoja plains and grass underfoot. The last part was a bit of a rocky scramble but by mid-day we were on the top of the mountain, Gordon found a rocky niche and fell asleep in the sunshine, John walked out to the edge to look back south to Kadam and Elgon in the clouds beyond and Richard and I rested in the clear air, the perfect contrast to the hot dusty drive from Arua to Moroto.

When we got back to the tents we found that we had company. Three young men wrapped in their cloths against the rising wind but otherwise naked, were sitting on tiny stools a few yards from our tents. They were armed with long spears and bows and arrows. A few cows were grazing the rich grass just above the tree-line. We were not at all sure what sort of welcome we would get from them, but they did not seem to have touched the tents or the car. They were just sitting waiting.

When we were close to them, Gordon offered a greeting in Kiswahili, not having any idea what the Karamojong version of 'Good Evening, Gentlemen' might be. *'Jambo.'*

*'Jambo, habari gani?'* one of them replied. *'Natoka wapi?'* Gordon recognised this as 'where have you come from?' but didn't know how to say 'from the top of the mountain', so he just pointed, 'from up there!' *'Natoka Lotume, ninasema KiSwahili kidogo.'* 'We come from Lotume. I speak a little KiSwahili.'

This produced a chorus of *'Eh's'* and much spitting between the front teeth, but they smiled and came over to us to shake hands solemnly. It seemed that they were friendly. We settled down again, three Karamojong on their stools, four *Muzungu* on the grass. There was a long silence.

'We need to get on with cooking,' John said, 'before it gets dark.' So he lit the small paraffin stove and put on a kettle to boil.

*'Chai,'* said Gordon by way of explanation, but they knew.

*'Eh, chai.'* When the kettle boiled and John found our four mugs and three other containers we could use, we passed three of the mugs over to our three visitors, with a spoon and sugar bowl. There was much spooning and stirring and sucking of tea, but it was clearly appreciated. *'Asante sana,'*

While John cooked our supper, we sat together and tried to communicate. They made smoking mimes. We were all non-smokers. They pointed to my woollen sweater, already keeping off the evening cool. I pointed to the spears each of them had, trying to indicate that an exchange might be possible. That started a long discussion between them, until they clearly agreed that an exchange was fine.

Holding out a spear, the youngest one pointed to my sweater. I took it off. He gave me the spear and we shook hands. What more could we exchange? Did we want a bow and arrow? How about a small stool? One fleece and another pullover changed hands and we had a complete set of belongings for a self-respecting young Karamojong. *'Asante sana's,'* all round. Everyone seemed happy, even if three of us were feeling distinctly cold.

'British,' said Gordon, pointing to each of us in turn. 'Karamojong?' pointing to them. That produced a string of incensed comment.

'Pokot, pokot, pokot', the Kiswahili speaker insisted, pointing to himself and each of the others in turn. With that he stood up and held out his hand. '*Kwaheri*,' he said, and they walked down to their cattle and with a wave, disappeared into the trees.

When we got back to Lotume and described our meeting on the mountain with Stan, he was amazed.

'If they were Pokot, they were a long way from home,' he explained. 'Most of the Pokot live in Kenya, right over the watershed to the east of Karamoja. Your three must have brought their cattle across to the mountain because they knew that the high grazing was good. But they were running a big risk. It would have been easy for them to be caught by our local Tepeth who would have taken the cattle and killed the three men.'

It seems that two groups of visitors had met on Mt Moroto that day, three from Kenya and four from England. Both were anxious about meeting dangerous locals but the actual meeting and exchange of belongings was very friendly. As Stan said, we were all very lucky!

\*

Up in West Nile, the only active political party seemed to be the UPC for much of 1969. The Catholic Church had a very strong presence in the District, in fact had more members than the Church of Uganda, but the Democratic Party ceased to be in any way active – it seemed to quietly disappear. Whereas in 1968, there were DP flags and rallies on important days such as the October Independence Day parades and celebrations, by the summer of 1969, even before Obote moved to a one-party state, the DP was quiet in our area. Down in Kampala, the Pope's visit in July 1969 produced a massive celebration by all the Catholic communities. At the end of July, His Holiness Paul VI made his first visit to an African nation. He flew in to Entebbe in an East African Airways VC 10 to be met by Milton Obote and introduced to the Heads of State of Tanzania, Zambia, Rwanda, Burundi, and representatives of Congo, Nigeria and Biafra. Obote thanked the Pope for his great love of Africa and the Pope responded warmly and stressed his desire for peace in Africa. He went on to say that the Catholic Church would not remain a passive spectator but seek to contribute to development, to wage war on misery and struggle against injustice. These were brave comments in the presence of the military Head of State of Nigeria, the dissenting leaders of Biafra and his Ugandan Presidential host who had already moved to eliminate much of the opposition in Uganda.

Pope Paul had come to consecrate the memorial to the twenty two Uganda Catholic Martyrs who were killed at the time of Kabaka Mwanga. They were page boys at Mwanga's Court who had become Christians. They had refused to obey the orders of the Kabaka when these conflicted with their new found faith. Chosing to obey Christ rather than their Kabaka, they had been killed, some burnt alive. They had been canonised by the Pope in Rome in 1964 and their shrine at Namagongo near Kampala became a place of pilgrimage for Catholics. The Pope also acknowledged that there had been Protestant martyrs too by involving the leaders of the Church of Uganda in these celebrations. After three days in Uganda, the Pope left for Rome.

I missed all the celebrations of the Papal visit, as I joined Stuart Cole, his son John, and other friends on a week of trekking in the Ruwenzori Mountains of western Uganda. We recruited a team of cheerful Bakonjo porters, strode up through the bands of heavy vegetation in the Mubuku valley and crossed the tree-trunk bridge into the higher Bujuku valley.

'This is a wonderful example of glaciation,' I was assured by one of our Dutch companions. 'A deep U shaped valley choked by regular bands of moraine rocks.'

This may well have been true, but I was much more impressed by the deep and muddy bogs which had built up over the millennia behind each obstruction and the floating tussocks of rough grass which seemed to be the solution to crossing the mud. Standing on one tussock, you leaped across to the next, only to have your heavy rucksack hit you in the small of the back on landing, with the effect of knocking you off that tussock into the deep mud. It was exhausting, very muddy and very slow work.

We eventually made it all the way along the valley, stopping each night to sleep, or at least try to sleep in the sequence of small metal huts which a thoughtful East African Alpine Society had put up for anyone unwise enough to attempt the trek. It was cold, very cold. Each hut had a logbook carrying encouraging messages about the 'mud being better as you got higher' but also worrying comments about members of earlier parties with very bad head-aches. We all said we felt fine and went on leaping from tussock to tussock. Our porters meanwhile found rock shelters under which they could light a fire to cook the small duikers they shot with bow and arrow and roll up in their blankets to get more sleep than we had.

After the third night, we reached the lake at the head of the valley and the pass at 14,344 feet under the flank of Mount Baker, towering at 15,892 ft above us. Glimpses of the snow, rose-red in the setting sun, encouraged us to push on in the early morning to the highest hut at the Irene Lakes at 14,750 ft. This was far higher than any of us had ever been before. The headaches were beginning to get bad when we read in the log of those who 'had passed away in the night'. We began to get seriously worried. We had no equipment for proper climbing on the snow and ice of Margherita peak, the highest point of the Ruwenzori range and the third highest mountain in Africa. The headaches and nausea were getting worse. We had reached the limit of our ambition. The views were fantastic in the brief early-morning glimpse of the glaciers but it was time to get down. That's the only cure for altitude sickness and it works like a dream. By the time we were hopping across the Bigo bogs, we all felt fine and began to wonder if we had given up too soon.

'No,' said Stuart firmly. 'I was beginning to worry what I would say to his mother if we had lost John in the night like that unfortunate priest who died at Irene Lakes.'

\*

The Rev Aiya of St Philip's Arua had to wait some time for an answer to his question about my lack of a wife. Jenny and I had exchanging occasional letters through the first year of my time at Mvara. As the need for more teachers became acute and our one-year volunteers, British and Ugandan planned to leave in July, she wrote to ask Lewis if he really needed another Chemistry teacher. He was encouraging as the expansion of the school to include A level classes meant a lot more science teaching, so Jenny applied by the same route as I had done. She made it as clear as she could that she really wanted to come to Mvara. To our delight, the ODA and the Uganda Ministry of Education managed to agree to send her to Mvara to start teaching in September 1969. By the end of July, her A level classes at Nottingham High School for Girls had taken their Nuffield A level examinations and she was free to leave. Lewis was delighted too as Jenny and I could cover all the Physics and Chemistry classes between us.

He also heard that an English teacher by the name of Janet Watford would be in Kampala in September and might be willing to come up to Arua to teach with us. I was sent down to Entebbe to meet Jenny and to make sure that Janet did not get a job anywhere else. I met the early morning plane from London and whisked Jenny into Kampala to pick up Janet. Not long after breakfast, we were on the road to Arua, slithering through the mud via Hoima, Murchison Park and Pakwach. By the time I got back to Mvara, Lewis had badgered the Arua Housing officer to allocate a large house on the Boma to our two new teachers and the Mvara community recruited a 'houseboy' for them. Erinesti was pleased to work for the ladies and he moved into the quarters behind the house that night and in the morning helped the girls to move in.

But no-one had allowed for the cockroaches. There were thousands of them in every room. They were in every crevice in every chair and table, even in the old refrigerator in the kitchen, a biblical plague of them. The two girls took one look and moved out. Fortunately, Ted and Muriel Williams could advise on how to wage war on cockroaches and Grace called for volunteers from the Jericho girls. They attacked those cockroaches with everything Arua Market could supply in the way of insecticides, cleaning materials and sheer elbow grease. Soon the drawers were full of corpses and the floors crunchy with dead insects.

Jenny and Janet began to hope that the battle would eventually be won but drew the line at collecting dead insects. The Jericho girls were not so squeamish, shovelling up cockroaches with their bare hands and turning the whole episode into a great party. Eventually, the piles of insect corpses were tipped into the bin, every wall, floor and ceiling in the house was washed by Erinesti and the plague of cockroaches became a minor, night-time irritation as new cockroaches hatched from the eggs stuck in cracks. Just after the washing had been completed, the local Ministry of Works team turned up and painted some of the rooms. As soon as the paint was dry, Jenny and Janet moved in and were soon rushing around the three sites of the school like the rest of us.

Jenny's timetable allowed for the fact that she had no car so most of her lessons were on the Old Site in the lab or an adjacent classroom. Janet as the latest recruit and an English teacher decided to buy a bicycle and was soon pedalling vigorously around Arua with a large sun-hat and a handle-bar basket full of exercise books. She seemed to have boundless energy and great skills as an English teacher and was also our only expert on teaching English as a Foreign Language having completed her MA. She soon established herself as a vital member of the English department, got on very well with Grace and the other teachers and also fitted in to the Mvara Church community. Although the expansion to a third site was a potential disaster, the staff and students' response was little short of heroic. For the rest of that year, all the S1 pupils walked to and from the Madhvani site every day without any supervision and no-one seemed to think that this was in any way odd.

\*

As the new term got under way, in Kampala, Milton Obote was pushing through major changes. He banned the DP in September 1969 and Uganda became, *de facto*, a one party state. In Arua, we began to prepare for the October 9$^{th}$ Independence Day celebrations, including a day's holiday for the school. This was always a challenge for those responsible for hundreds of young people on the school site. Once they had marched around the Police football field to show their loyalty to Uganda, they were free to do what they liked.

On the 8$^{th}$, we heard on the radio that the President had published his 'Common Man's Charter' and the 'Move to the Left'. These policy statements were designed to foster a new more socialist political culture. Obote was following Nyerere of Tanzania's 'Arusha Declaration' of 1967. '*The heart of the move to the left can be simply stated*,' announced Obote. '*It is.... that political and economic power must be vested in the majority.*' He was starting a process which would lead to a very different result. Ownership of land, company shares, firms and even personal belongings such as cars would mysteriously transfer from their legitimate owners to government ministers. The Move to the Left introduced the principle 'what you have, we share, what I have, I keep'.

We heaved a sigh of relief that Independence Day passed without trouble at school or in the town and settled down to prepare Senior 4 for their 'Cambridge'. It was actually called the East African Certificate of Education – but the students all called it 'Cambridge' and for them it was the climax of four years of toil. In spite of all the difficulties, the delayed building programme, the challenge to find teachers, the political changes in the country, we had high hopes for our S4, two classes of very hard working young people. In the event, the examinations passed without incident and the end of term play, *Tobias and the Angel*, was a triumph.

John, Christine and Grace had rehearsed the cast to a word-perfect state. On the night of the great performance, the star of the show, the boy playing Tobit, prepared with a few swigs of *nguli,* locally distilled spirit. He was not very drunk, but bold enough to decide to improve his lines as the play developed. This made him the star of the show, but, as the rest of the cast missed their cues, the play descended into hilarious chaos. The watching students loved it. With a sigh of relief, we said farewell to Tobit and his fellow-leavers and looked forward to some good results.

Then the next Ministry decision was announced. Our application to start a $6^{th}$ form at Mvara with an Arts and a Science A level intake into Senior 5, which we had assumed would not be granted as the buildings to house them were so delayed, was suddenly approved. Senior 5 would start in February 1970 and those who wished to join us should apply immediately. We were filled with an exhausted blend of elation and terror – how was it going to be possible to start the courses on time?

Two events happened well away from West Nile just as the school year was ending. The exiled Kabaka of Buganda, living in poverty and said to be an alcoholic, died on his own in London. The Baganda were distraught and asked for his body to be flown back to Entebbe for burial. There was strong suspicion that this was no natural death but a poisoning by the forces of the Ugandan state. Milton Obote refused to allow the body to come home, breaking hundreds of years of emotional tradition for the Baganda – Kabaka Mutesa II was not allowed to join his ancestors in Kisubi Tombs but preserved by an embalmer in a London morgue.

Then, on December $19^{th}$ 1969, as Obote was leaving a cheering Lugogo Stadium where he had addressed thousands of UPC delegates who had just adopted the 'Common Man's Charter', a taxi-driver shot the President, and the President survived. If the gun had not jammed and the assailant fired again, or if the Chinese-made grenade, thrown just after the gun-shot, had gone off, Obote would have died immediately. But he was rushed to hospital and found to have minor face wounds. The bullet had gone through his cheek, damaged some teeth and his tongue, but he soon recovered. Everyone breathed a huge sigh of relief and Jenny and I joined Gordon and Grace on a holiday trip to the north of Kenya.

That trip was a wonderful adventure to the shores of Lake Turkana, again made possible because we could travel to visit AIM missionaries. Gordon and I bought a 1950s short-wheel-base Land Rover from a missionary who said that there was 'life in her yet', and off we went! The engine was fine and the body indestructible, the one problem was a leaking radiator. By adding everything we could think of, from raw egg to camel dung, we managed to slow the leak and coax the old girl all the way up the Saguta valley and into the desert to Lokori just south of the Lake. We followed an incredibly understanding Dr Dick Anderson to whom I am sure we were a thorough nuisance, but we got there and could order a new radiator to be flown up to Lokori when the next Missionary Aviation Fellowship plane came up. Christmas at Lokori was wonderful, with roast goat instead of turkey, and adventures up to Kalokol by Ferguson's Gulf instead of a Boxing Day walk. The AIM staff at Lokori treated us as 'cotton-picking tourists' but made sure that we had a thorough insight into the challenges of living and working in a desert and we just loved it all. Gordon and Grace noticed that for two of us something else was stirring, as Gordon put it at our Ruby Wedding just over forty years later:

*'When we arrived at our designated school in Uganda, John Haden soon became Head of Science. We all found that teaching in Uganda had many new challenges compared to teaching in UK. For John, this was an ideal situation – always ready for a challenge. Soon he was talking about a certain Jenny Peck and how good it would be if she would come and help in the Science Dept. Jenny and he had studied chemistry together in Oxford but he never mentioned if there was any other type of chemistry going on between them.*

*Eventually, the said Jenny Peck did arrive to join John in the Science Department. They were obviously 'very good friends' but we wondered if there was anything more. Neither of them gave us any clue. Jenny also became a close friend to us and entered fully into life at Mvara Secondary School. Still there was no clue as to what the relationship was between John and Jenny.*

*Then came the trip to Turkana in Northern Kenya to visit Joan and Dick Anderson (Grace's relations). We bought an ancient Land Rover which we called Matilda[5] in Eldoret for £300. During that trip the four of us went up to Ferguson's Gulf on the shores of Lake Rudulf for a few days.*

*One balmy tropical evening we were walking along the shore of Ferguson's Gulf. Grace and I were walking a bit ahead* of John and Jenny. At one point we glanced behind and saw that they were actually walking hand in hand. So there really was something happening - and the rest is history.'

*

We travelled back from Lokori and Lake Turkana via Lodwar and Lokichar and then south along the Kerio Valley. Matilda crawled up the rough road from the roasting hot floor of the Great Rift Valley to the cool pine trees of Kapsowar at the top of the scarp. It was here that I learnt of the Marakwet people, living in the Cherangani Hills, and famous for their iron-working. It seems that they smelted the iron and forged the sharp spears which every self-respecting Turkana, Masai and Kalengin warrior carried. We did not have time to explore this area, or the iron-smelting methods they used, but I filed it away in the corner of my memory reserved for all things to do with iron.

## 3.3 Starting a 6th Form

In the New Year, Lewis went down to Kampala to attend the annual 'auction', the selection meeting of all the Headteachers at which the allocation of places in S1 was made. There were over one hundred and eighty primary schools in West Nile District alone, and each had up to sixty children taking the Primary leaving examination each year. The four secondary schools in the District had a total of just two hundred and fifty S1 place between them, so the chances of a child getting a S1 place in West Nile, where most of them wanted to stay, were slim. Some of the District's Primary Schools had never sent a single child to secondary education. The Government set up a system of first and second grade passes in an attempt to make the process seem fairer and to sugar the pill of disappointment, only to add a layer of further frustration. Many of those awarded a first grade pass had then received no offer of a secondary place. There were just not enough. The only course open to those in this position was to change their name, their school and of course the place where they lived, rejoin a P7 class and try again. This was officially illegal and yet only 25% of our Mvara intake in one year could claim to have taken the P7 examination once. The rest had tried again and again, getting older and yet no more successful until that lucky year when they just scraped over the minimum mark for one of the West Nile secondary schools.

The best candidates nationally, often the youngest ones as well, could get into the prestigious schools of the south, Budo, Mwiri or Gayaza. The names of the less successful, still within the top 5% of all the primary leavers would be passed around the hall of Headteachers at the 'auction' until one of them agreed to add them to their list. Lewis came back from Kampala with the names of three classes and began to plan the year. News came from the Ministry in Kampala that because of the building delays, we would not be expected to admit the new S1s until after Easter, which was a relief. At last it seemed someone had seen sense.

At the end of January, Lewis had to set off south again to carry out the same process for the new entry into Senior 5. Although the New Site buildings were being completed by the Sikh contractor at an impressive rate, and the new equipment which was to go into them had begun to arrive, we still had mountains to climb. With the delayed entry to S1 we could at least close down the Madhvani site - things were getting better.

More classes and teachers meant more staff houses, or some doubling up. Janet Watford had gone back to Kampala after just one term with us, which was sad, but we were grateful for her energetic and expert contribution for the term and promised to keep in touch. Jenny had two spare rooms in her large house on the Boma and was ready to share with whoever arrived next. The American Peace Corps, who had a number of their volunteer teachers posted all over Uganda, sent two teachers up to Arua, one of whom shared with Hilda-Mary and the other moved in to share with Jenny. Pat Firer came from the Mid-West and we thought at first that her name was 'Piat' until we worked out her accent. If we found it hard to follow what she had to say, it was clearly going to take a little time for our West Nile students to tune in.

All the Uganda Peace Corps volunteers had been through a very thorough selection and orientation programme which contrasted strongly with the British VSO approach. The Peace Corps had language training, cultural sensitivity lessons and the support of a team of in-country administrators and support specialists. When our VSO friends heard Pat talk about the visit of her Field Director and Staff Psychologist, they just laughed.

'We'd be lucky to get a postcard. The most useful advice we had, was to get ourselves a bicycle!'

All the Uganda Peace Corps volunteers were given a course in Luganda to enable them to get to know the local communities to which they were sent. For Pat, this was not much help as few West Nile people spoke Luganda, the language of the Baganda by the Lake. She learnt greetings in Alur and Lugbara as we did and found that getting really close to her students was difficult. Full of earnest idealism, she told the Lugbara young men in her classes that she had come to help them and so wanted to be their friend. Many were young adults not much younger than her mid-twenties, and for them, 'friendship' with a young woman only meant one thing. The boys took a malicious delight in teasing her and mimicking her voice. She would then react with petulant irritation. 'Go away you horrid boy and stop looking at me like that!' The truth was that students, girls or boys, had no wish to be friends with any of their teachers. That was not what teachers were for.

When Pat set her S3 class of mature young men and women a holiday assignment entitled either 'My holiday adventure' or 'The best thing in my life', she was mortified to read their responses. The boys took great pleasure in describing for her in rich anatomical detail the full catalogue of conquests they had achieved in the villages, or the moment when they had finally laid a particularly coy target. 'And then I did impregnate her in the grasses!' Poor sheltered middle-American Pat, she could only turn a deeper shade of pink at each revelation, scribble advice about spelling two lines below the end of the purple passage and give the books back to their grinning owners as soon as possible. We could never understand why she wanted to show these very embarrassing essays to the rest of us – we would have got rid of them and kept very quiet.

Jenny did her best to befriend her and to share her household on the Boma with her amicably. Knowing that I might turn up and enjoy a home-made biscuit with a mug of coffee, Jenny would bake a tin-full and leave them in the kitchen, only to find that Pat had come through in the night and eaten the lot. She was not herself into home baking, although she found packets of American instant cake mixes at Stankyas. By the time these reached West Nile, the packets were so old and full of weevils the contents were not worth mixing, and had to go in the bin.

Pat enjoyed sun-bathing, lying out on the concrete top of the septic tank in the garden in her bikini and trying to add to her already impressive tan. She complained once or twice about the strange smell near her sun-bathing place but we did not have the heart to tell her what she was lying on. It never ceased to amaze me how keen white women were to plaster themselves with sun cream to achieve a slightly browner skin while their Ugandan sisters were spending much of their limited spare cash on Bu-tone cream to try to turn their rich and attractive black skin into something slightly lighter.

At the end of January, the results for the 'O' levels taken by our S4 students in November came back from the Board. They had done very well, better than any previous year-group at Mvara. Lewis went off to Kampala to the second 'auction' for places in our first S5 and we prepared to start a Sixth Form although they would not arrive until the start of the second term. Since most of the students coming back would be familiar with Mvara's inadequate facilities, we did not anticipate too much trouble, but amongst them would be a few from the south who might expect more. In the event, Lewis came back with one class of twenty-five for Arts subjects and one of twenty five for Science subjects. Amongst the West Nile O level 'graduates', there were a handful from other Districts, two boys from the far south-west District of Kigezi and two Acholi girls from Gulu.

Over the Easter holiday, the school had organised a visit for S4 students to the Jinja area, where Uganda had a cluster of industrial developments, a cement works, a cigarette factory, a smelter and a cotton mill, all dependent on the electic power generated by the Nile as it poured through the Jinja Dam. Going on school trips is not the most popular activity amongst teachers even in English schools. When all the Ugandan women staff made it clear that they were very busy over the holiday, Lewis asked Jenny if she would help look after the group together with some of the Ugandan men.

For Jenny, it was a miserable time. Travelling in a crowded bus with all the students was hot and exhausting. The food was basic and the school dormitory accommodation full of bed-bugs. The male staff had a very relaxed attitude to discipline and she found it very difficult to be in effective control of the girls. They all wanted to 'visit relatives', go out with the boys and generally avoid her supervision as much as possible, yet she was responsible for them. The visit to the cigarette factory was a particular nightmare, with the boys taking handfuls of cigarettes for smoking in the evenings and the girls encouraging them. Only when they all came safely back from Jinja, the proud bearers of photos of themselves in their best headscarfs by the Jinja Dam, could she relax and vow never to go on a Uganda school trip again!

School trip to the Owen Falls Hydro at Jinja

Without much of a break, she was soon into the new term and the arrival of the new S5 students. With forty eight now in our new Year 5, they had to be found places to sleep. The girls went back to be with the sisters in Jericho and, pulling rank as S5s, soon settled into the best corners of the over-crowded dormitories. The boys became the first occupants of the newly completed dormitories on the New Site. They were in heaven! Their new rooms had lots of space, adjacent washrooms with showers and indoor lavatories, unheard of luxury for boys used to over-crowded sheds and a long walk to the odoriferous earth latrines on the down-wind side of the site. No matter how many moon-flowers we planted to disguise the smell, 'long-drop pong' always broke through.

The New Site had a fine water-tank on a tower, pipes taking water to each block of dormitories, wash-basins with taps, showers with drains and flush toilets, all linked up to septic tanks. In the staff houses, the water pressure improved dramatically. In the new school kitchens, stainless steel electric cookers and boilers, stainless-steel sinks and cooking pots all shone under the new electric lights. A wide steel serving hatch into the huge new dining/assembly hall stood waiting for the first meal of the new system, *enya* and 'meat stew'. The cooks started to cook the meat and turned on the boilers for the *enya*. All the little red lights, showing that each piece of equipment was 'on', went out as the power supply failed. While the cooks, the school *fundi* and Lewis searched for a solution to the problem, the Uganda Electricity Board foreman from the town generator arrived on his bicycle. He was hot and angry, having pedalled flat out for the two miles to the school.

'Turn everything off,' he panted. 'You've burnt out the main generator. I'm removing your main fuses now and taking them with me.'

He was as good as his word, whipping out the heavy duty fuses at the box where power came into the kitchen, pocketing all of them and rushing back to the generator. If we were to feed the school that night, the cooks would have to go back to the old way. The fires were lit in the 'cook-house' shack behind the new dining-hall. The old large aluminium *sufurias* were scrubbed out once again, filled with water and balanced over the fires on three large stones. Cassava and millet flour was stirred in until the boiling mixture reached the consistency of a very thick, almost solid, porridge.

School bell and serving enya for four hundred at Mvara

The school 'bell' was rung and the man with the wheelbarrow loaded up the *sufurias*, steaming with *enya*, ran across to the Hall and inside to serve up supper for the hungry students, two hours late, but at least they were fed. The new kitchen equipment stayed unused for all the time we had left at Mvara.

The S5 girls included two Acholi girls who had a lot in common with our Alur girls and fitted in almost immediately. Their language was very close to Alur and they could eat our millet and cassava based food without a problem. For the two Bakiga boys from Kigezi, everything was very different. We did not serve their beloved *matoke*. No-one spoke their language and Mvara was full of very black boys much taller than them.

They were a long way from home and probably very frightened when the Mvara boys bullied them for being 'brown banana-eaters'. After a week of this, they decided that they would have to get back home.

On the first Saturday evening at Mvara, they took their mattresses and other belongings into the town intending to catch the next bus to Kampala. There was no bus until the following morning so they decided to find something to eat and a quiet corner to spend the night. They had a little money and could buy some rice and meat in a bar, and they could afford a beer or two, or three. Later that evening, when they needed to go in a bit of a hurry around the back of the bar for a 'short-call' in the pitch black of the night, the two boys fell over two local young women busy with the same urgent need. The girls squawked and rushed back into the bar in a dishevelled state.

The men in the bar assumed the worst and rushed outside to catch whoever had been interfering with their girls. Our two S5 boys ran for their lives. Both managed to reach the Police Station before the growing posse caught up with them and the Sergeant on duty put them in the cells for their own protection. The following morning a Police Land Rover came to the school with two very frightened boys in the back.

The Sergeant found a member of staff and established that the two boys were, as they had said, our students. I was asked as the Duty Teacher to look after them.

'Much better if you keep them in the cells, Sergeant,' I said. 'They may not be safe here in the light of what you tell me has happened.'

He could see the sense of that and took both boys back to the Police Station. There they stayed until the Magistrates could hear their case, on charges of attempted rape and indecent assault. They were asked how they wanted to plead. Both said, very vehemently, 'not guilty'. It transpired that the reason for the two charges was a matter of fly-buttons. The boy whose original need had been more urgent had opened his before falling over the girls. His fellow defendant had not got that far. When witnesses were called from the men in the bar, they all agreed that one boy had open buttons, one closed. No-one had actually seen any attempt at rape or assault of any kind. After their own 'two or three beers', the men had assumed the worst. The two girls kept very quiet. Perhaps they were worried that their boy friends thought that they might have gone outside for more commercial reasons!

The magistrates conferred and came up with a proposal. If the two would plead guilty to the much lower charge of 'being drunk and disorderly within the town limits after dark', they could convict them, give them a suspended sentence and get rid of them. The two boys liked the idea. After all, they had drunk 'two or three beers'. They were soon back in school but, as they now had a criminal record, Lewis felt that he had to send them home, at least for their own safety. They caught the Kampala bus in the early morning, their fares paid by the school and they were pathetically grateful. In the style of the Luganda language, they both addressed me as 'Sir, my dear Lord' as I took them down to the bus stand. Lugbara boys would have been no less grateful but would have said 'We think you will take us to the bus.'

*

It took the Uganda Electicity Board team a week to repair their generator. For the remaining time we were at Mvara, the main kitchen fuses were not returned to the school. If the power demand of the new facilities including the kitchens was greater than the output of the town generator, everything would blow again. They were not going to risk that happening. So we had power for lights and for the houses, even for the laboratories when these opened, but not for the kitchens. George Okai looked at the cooks toiling away over their smoky fires.

'Local is best,' he said, with a wry smile.

Managing the new showers and toilets was almost as much of a challenge. The town water supply would go off regularly, simply because power cuts stopped the pumps supplying the system. With no water in the cisterns, the un-flushed lavatories would fill up rapidly. The boys seemed unconcerned until such was the mess that it actually became more pleasant to go back to strolling across to the old 'long-drops'. In the end we had to lock the toilets, get them cleared with buckets of water and only open them for night-time use. That way, there was some water at some time of the day to supply most of the staff houses but it was never reliable. We all learnt to stockpile water in buckets around the house and to make as little use of the flushing of toilets as we could. Margaret introduced a mantra from the chronic water-shortages of her own school-girl days, 'if it's yellow, let it mellow; when it's brown, flush it down'. Students could be heard muttering the formula on their way to the toilets. The girls set it to a catchy little tune.

\*

Once such practical matters as food and hygiene had been sorted out, we could do some teaching. The A level Arts subjects could be covered by the graduates we had, British and Ugandan. Guy and Dison taught the Geography course, Dick covered most of the History, Grace, Christine and Pat taught the English. Silas was in his element covering the Biology with Margaret's help, Lewis dusted down his Mathematics. Jenny and I could cover the Chemistry and the start of the Physics course. Milcah, a young Makerere graduate who was engaged to be married to the Deputy Principal of Arua TTC, joined us to teach Religious Studies and the rest of the History. Although we had had twenty-nine staff changes in the previous eighteen months, as the new A level courses started, we were as strong a teaching team as we had ever been.

The new science laboratories were a huge help. They were large and airy, with proper benches and stools. Mr Opio had two large Prep rooms and needed an assiatant to help him with the new equipment. Some of this was sadly not useable as it had been in a crate which slipped into Mombasa harbour while being unloaded from the ship from Washington, DC. But a rusty circuit board was certainly better than none at all and we were grateful for the thought that had gone into the items selected to support O level Physical Science. Someone had clearly read the syllabus!

Included in the provision of new buildings was a Domestic Science room with a small flat attached, complete with bathroom and toilet, kitchen and bedroom. Someone in the World Bank Project Team had decided that our students needed to be fully familiar with Western forms of domestic life, even though many of them would have to return to their villages after leaving Senior 4. The equipment included a complete set of jelly-moulds which was odd. Even the most determined of our ex-Patriate cooks had never managed to get a jelly to set in the heat of West Nile.

We had no teacher of Domestic Science and the subject did not actually appear on the syllabus for O level so we wondered how best to use the new space and facilities. Then someone hit on the good idea of setting up the Domestic Science flat as a small medical and first aid clinic, complete with a sick-room. Even the toilet-pan found an important use. No-one wanted to stay in overnight isolation in the sick-room, so the biologists decided to turn it into a frog store. It held their stock of dissection specimens, nice, fresh, and still alive, until they were needed.

Dison Aneco, as Deputy Head, decided that the school needed a football pitch and led an army of boys and girls armed with slashers into the sea of elephant grass that covered most of the site. Soon a line of singing students were slashing their way across, clearing a great swathe through the grass with Dison setting the pace.

'Sir, you are really sweating,' panted an S2 boy grappling with the novel idea that as important a man as the Deputy Head should soil his hands with physical labour.

Dison was determined that the job would be finished by the end of the dry season and slashed away even more vigorously. Piling the cut grass high around the edges of the pitch, they set it alight and watched with delight as the smoke and flames leapt into the air. Most of the singed grasshoppers were caught by the birds or by small boys from the surrounding villages who came to eat the ones that fell back to earth. In less than a week of after-school slashing, the school had a rough football pitch which would grass over well when the rains came and from then on provide more than enough detention slashing to keep all the miscreants busy.

Allocating staff housing was more difficult as there were bound to be winners and losers. Lewis introduced a points system to try to make it fairer. If you were single and could find someone to share with, you got a house bigger than the basic one bedroom semi. If you had a wife and a family, you got a larger house. Academic status counted for nothing, once the Head and Deputy had been housed. The focus on family size led some colleagues to adopt additional children and claim them as their own, until it was pointed out that having children a lot older than your marriage raised some questions. John Martin and I continued to share our small semi-detached bungalow, with Gordon and Grace McCullough living next door. Guy Kerunen, who had been married for a year, moved into a house with his pregnant wife, clearly anticipating a larger family. Betty, the other Peace Corps girl, decided she did not want to share with Pat and Jenny, much to Jenny's relief, and she stayed with Hilda Mary.

\*

Just to the north of Arua, under a clump of mango trees by the road-side, a group of blacksmiths operated, old men with small, hot, hearths making knives and other items out of scrap iron. I stopped one day to see what they were doing and found that they were from the Okebu people, most of whom lived along the Uganda-Congo border just to the south of Arua.

It happened that the Chemistry syllabus included the industrial extraction of iron and Jenny had drawn a very fine poster of a blast furnace to decorate the wall of our new Chemistry laboratory. In my S3 class was a boy called Peter Ogani and when we were talking about iron smelting in blast furnaces, he said that his people used to make iron. He was an Okebu, the son of a sub-chief from Logiri, about ten miles south-west of Arua on the watershed road that runs right down the Congo border.

At the weekend, I took Peter and two of his Okebu friends to talk to the smiths, who spoke no English and little Swahili.

Children of the blacksmiths, with added baby!

They were suspicious of the interest of the *muzungu* teacher in what they were doing but, encouraged by the boys to talk of the old days, they told me that the Okebu used to make iron 'long ago'. It seemed that the coming of cheap Birmingham hoes had destroyed this iron-making tradition and that none of the local Okebu had actually smelted iron from rock since the 1940s although they thought that smelting had continued in the Congo into the 1950s.

'Would you still be able to make iron?' I asked them through the boys.

'Of course,' they claimed. 'We are 'Kebu!' The blacksmiths heated the metal on their forges with bellows of two small clay pots, with goat skin covers tied to long sticks. These they pumped vigorously to get the charcoal burning brightly and the iron to glow, hot enough to work with hammers. I wanted to try to get the students at Mvara interested in their own traditions, in music through *udungu* playing, in poetry through the work of Ugandan poet Okot p'Bitek, and in the making of pots and woven baskets. They dismissed all these activities as 'village things', not worthy of the interest of the educated. But Peter Ogani and his friends were keen to see whether the old smiths could do what they claimed, actually make iron. We all had our doubts. He promised to discuss this with the Okebu elders at Logiri when he went home for the holidays.

In Kampala, President Obote was fully recovered from the shooting and was preparing for the next stage of his 'Move to the Left'. At the May 1$^{st}$ Labour Day celebrations, his 'Nakivubu Pronouncement[6]' set out the immediate acquisition of 60% of the shares in eighty four major industrial, agricultural and commercial firms. This was nationalisation with a vengeance but it made very little difference to us up in West Nile, where there were few major businesses. Of more concern was the government's radical plan to provide a form of National Service for young people who finished Primary school but could not find a Secondary place. Existing secondary schools were to be the pioneers of this initiative although it was unclear how we were going to take on a new challenge on top of all the others thrown at us by Obote's government. We could only hope that this idea would eventually be forgotten.

There was one other ominous event that passed us by. After the attempt on Obote's life, in January 1970, the Deputy Commander of the Uganda Army, Brigadier Okoya, and his wife had been murdered by an armed gang in Gulu. Okoya had denounced Amin earlier for his cowardice because he ran away and hid when he heard the news of the attempt on Obote's life, rather than taking command of the Army. There were strong grounds for believing that Amin was involved in the Okoya murders but there was no effective investigation and Obote made no move against Amin. He seemed to want to protect Amin from being linked to the murders and, by September of 1970, Obote was ready to back Amin further, promoting him to Army Commander and Chief of Staff.

\*

The April to July term was always difficult to staff for Uganda's secondary schools as the English summer beckoned contract teachers home. Unlike the contract arrangements in Nigeria, where holidays were taken out of term-time, our two year contracts often started in September and ended with three months paid leave. That meant that most of us left our Uganda teaching posts at the end of May, around the middle of the term and the schools struggled to staff the last eight weeks of teaching. In 1970, Gordon and Grace, John Martin, Lewis Stephenson and others were all due to go on leave in May and they did. Grace had to go even earlier when she heard the devastating news that her father had been killed in Northern Ireland and so Gordon was left to finish off his contract on his own. Lewis went first, so that he could get back well before the start of the new term and Dison, as his Deputy, became Mvara's Acting Head, the first Ugandan to lead the school.

We all wondered what difference this change would make but the problems remained the same. Dison was actually rather stricter than Lewis, insisting on obedience to the school rules, but he had the same difficulties in enforcing this. Boys still disappeared at weekends to drink *kwete* in the surrounding villages and would be found snoring loudly on Sunday afternoons. The same staff still failed to turn up for their duties in the evenings, pleading sudden visitors or being 'not all right'. But the atmosphere was different. Somehow there was an air of pleasure at the place that was new – the school knew where we were going, who was leading it and they approved. The Ugandan staff began to take a more active role in meetings and in out-of-school activities, including helping more with football and netball coaching and we even had a cultural club which enjoyed creating an *udungu* orchestra. This had a complete set of these Alur traditional instruments, eight-stringed harps which could be tuned to a pentatonic scale and used to accompany singing. But Dison made clear that dancing still remained strictly off-limits. He made sure that he retained the support of the Governors.

One evening, just before the rains came, I was driving back along the Mvara road as the street lights came on. Under each light, people were sitting, reading. I stopped to talk to them and heard that a new consignment of the Lugbara Bible had been delivered to the Mvara offices of the Diocese. They had walked or cycled in from miles around and were now reading their Bibles in their own language for the first time. The scene reminded me of the Oxford student followers of John

Wesley who had been called 'Bible Moths' because the clustered round a lamp to read God's Word.

Less than a hundred years before, the Lugbara had no contact with the outside world apart from the raids of Arab slavers in the Nile valley to the east. Now they had the Bible, thanks to the work of Seton Maclure, the American missionary Laura-Belle Barr and their team of Lugbara helpers. Seton had chaired a committee which met sometimes in the Congo and sometimes in West Nile. The translation work continuing right through the 1950s. Each time a book was finished, it was subjected to the closest possible scrutiny by a panel of native Lugbara speakers, until the final draft was prepared, retyped and checked again. Not until 1963 was the complete manuscript of the Lugbara Bible finished and submitted to the British and Foreign Bible Society for printing in London. Eventually, copies reached Arua, to be bought by Lugbara Christians so keen to read them that they spent their evening under the best source of light, the lamps along the Mvara road.

In 1952, Seton and Peggy Maclure had left Mvara to move to Goli in the south of West Nile on the border with the Congo. In the seven years they were there. Seton Maclure established a reputation for knowing more Alur than the Alur themselves and set up a training scheme for evangelists and pastors. In 1960, the Maclures were asked to return to Mvara and Seton developed his linguistic interests by working on the Madi and Okebu languages, both related to Lugbara, and the Kakwa language. Work on translating the Scriptures into all of these languages has now been completed, thanks to the efforts of Seton Maclure, Laura-Belle Barr, Joy Grindey and others. The most recent has been the 1994 publication of the Okebu New Testament, translated by Joy Grindey. The fruits of all this work bringing the Scriptures to the people of West Nile can be seen in the many churches across the District and in the lives of men who responded to God's call into the ministry.

*

My own leave came due in mid-June. I had planned to visit my sister in Iran. Margaret Lloyd overheard me talking about this in the Mvara Staff-room and her eyes lit up.

'I'm coming too,' she said before I could suggest that I was looking forward to a long trip on my own. 'My best friend from College is a missionary in Iran, at a place called Isfahan.'

When I confessed that my sister was actually living in Isfahan, having married an Armenian Iranian, Margaret was over the moon.

'Wonderful,' she beamed. 'We'll be able to travel together!'

Mid-June saw us fly out of Entebbe on our way to Isfahan via Nairobi, Addis Ababa, Dira Dawa, Assab, Aden, Kuwait and Abadan. We needed visas to get into Iran at Abadan but there was no Iranian embassy or consulate anywhere along the route. We got to Kuwait after a number of adventures, with Margaret getting closer to driving me mad at each complicated connection. Kuwait Air refused to fly us into Iran.

'You have no visas and they will deport you at Abadan back to Kuwait,' the official at the desk pointed out.

'But we have tickets with you,' I said hopefully.

'No matter, we cannot fly you unless you take the risk yourselves.'

So, I had to sign an indemnity form on which I agreed to pay my fare and Margaret's between Abadan and Kuwait and back again for however many times it took before one or other country took pity on us and allowed us in. We flew to Abadan in the morning and on the way worked out a strategy. Since the flight back to Kuwait left an hour after our arrival at Abadan, if we could delay getting to Iranian immigration for long enough, it would have gone without us before we could get deported. That would give us twenty-four hours to make our case for entry.

Margaret was magnificent. She played the elderly and confused traveller to Oscar levels. She lost her glasses as we landed and had the whole team of cabin crew and cleaners searching for them before finding them in the depths of her hand-bag. She then needed to go to the nearest Ladies, which was hard to find in Abadan Airport but eventually the ground staff, courteous to an elderly traveller, found what she said she needed. There she stayed with me patiently waiting outside until the Kuwait Air plane jetted out of Iranian airspace.

I was then arrested by immigration and taken under armed guard down to Abadan Port as an attempted illegal immigrant, while Margaret was offered sweet tea and dates in the Iran Air First Class lounge. At the Port, the senior Immigration Officer, dripping with gold braid all over his uniform as 'Lord High Everything Else', listened to my tale of not being able to get a visa in any of the places we had travelled through. He made me wait for most of the day and then announced that he had never met anyone before who had attempted such a stupid plan as our transit of eight airports between Uganda and Iran. We should have travelled to London, got a visa and flown to Teheran like everyone else.

The indomitable Margaret Lloyd in the Kuluva pool

    I could only apologise for my extreme stupidity and appeal to his sense of chivalry, emphasizing how keen the elderly English lady was to visit his country, where her best friend had been looked after so well by such kind people for such a long time. He slowly softened and as night was falling, took pity on Margaret and her stupid escort, stamped our passports and allowed me to return to the Airport. We were just in time to catch the evening flight to Isfahan. There I left Margaret and enjoyed my visit to my sister and my new nephew.

*

    Schools like Mvara which had links to church and mission networks could use these to recruit teachers in addition to the usual Government channels. We received volunteers from AIM, from UK church and school communities, as well as from VSO, the Peace Corps, even the Norwegian volunteer organisation. While I was at home, one thing I could do, as well as getting a good rest and seeing the family, was to meet as many actual and potential teaching recruits as possible. By the time I flew back to Entebbe I had visited a number of these, including Wendy Moore, teaching in Bristol, and Lance Corker. Both taught Physics and Mathematics and could therefore fill gaping holes in our A level staffing. Both persuaded the ODA to send them to Mvara, Wendy on her own and Lance with his wife. I also met Trevor Gazard, who planned to spend nine months at Mvara when he left King's School, Worcester after taking his Cambridge exams. John Martin was not planning to return to us as he and Richard Inwood were committed to training for the Anglican Ministry. Gordon was also staying at home, now that Grace's baby had arrived.

I flew back to Entebbe in early September to be welcomed to Uganda by friends who had been at Oxford with Jenny and me. Peter Childs was the distinguished chemist who had tried to cram some understanding of the subject into my head on those walks around the Parks years before. He and his wife Margaret had come out to Makerere University where he became a key member of the University Chemistry Department and she taught Religious Knowledge in Makerere College School.

Murchison elephants crossing the road to West Nile

While I was away, Jenny had been visited by her mother and father who had a wonderful time getting to know the people in the Mission whom they had supported from home for so long. She had bought my VW when I went on leave so they were able to travel all over Uganda, visiting all the game parks and seeing the wealth of animal and bird life that the country offered.

At that time, Murchison Falls Park alone had over fourteen thousand elephants, often seen in herds of over five hundred. The signs said 'elephants have right of way' on the

Park roads and campers at the Falls Top site were advised to ensure that tents were pitched far enough apart to allow for free access by hippos on their way to the river. Jenny took her parents down to Kagando hospital in the foothills of the Ruwenzoris and to Queen Elizabeth to see the tree-climbing lions of Ishasha and the huge variety of brilliantly coloured birds. It was a wonderful holiday and they left for home disappointed that their daughter's boy-friend, who had disappeared to England, had not made his intentions clear while they were around.

That came soon after I got back to Arua as I had bought engagement presents to bring back for Jenny made of Isfahani gold. We planned to get married in England at the end of her two year contract; we owed our parents that much at least. We had to explain to the Arua Ugandan and Asian community at a party at which our engagement was announced that, although we planned to be together for the rest of our lives, we had first to complete the tasks that we felt God had led us to. That meant waiting for longer than we wanted but meanwhile we planned to share our happiness with all the friends that West Nile had brought us, the local Church, the school and Mission staff, the members of the Arua community, Government officers and Asian businessmen. The invitations had gone out ten days before the party and the Pastor of St Philip's Church in the town had chosen to tell his congregation all about our friendship and commitment to marry, exhorting all the 'boys and girls' in his morning service to follow our example!

The following Sunday, he preached a very different sermon.

'They have brought confusion to us, these Europeans,' he announced sadly looking straight at us. 'They came to bring us the word of God, but they bring bad things as well.'

At first we puzzled to work out what he meant. Then came the more direct attack. 'They say that they are Christians, but they give men beer to drink.'

Faced with a mixed crowd of Church and West Nile Club, I had thought of offering both soft drinks and beer at our engagement party, trying to ensure that no-one who did not drink got a beer. There were only a few bottles of luke-warm light ale, one of which slipped quickly down the throat of the British High Commissioner, who happened to be in town. I had worked hard to ensure that none of them reached any of the senior Mvara students who been invited. But the damage was done when one of the local church members spotted a beer bottle. It caused deep offence in the congregation. 'Christians never drink' was the rule and, although I had tried to follow it for over two years, making sure that I never drank myself while in West Nile, my hospitality to others was clearly unacceptable to the Church.

There were other, more trivial misunderstandings. The Asian traders failed to make any distinction between commitment and consummation and Jenny became Mrs Haden in their eyes from then onwards. Those who knew us well, Mr Kawa the garage owner and the Chief Clerk at Grindlays Bank were plainly puzzled why I did not move into her house which was much larger than mine. To the students, Jenny now changed from 'the woman who goes in Mr Haden's car' to 'Mrs Haden herself', addressed still as Miss or Madam as the fancy took them.

\*

That September, with all the new staff arriving and needing accommodation, there was a lot of moving house. Staff with families moved into the three bedroomed detached houses. One of the new English teachers was allocated the semi which a Ugandan teacher and his wife had occupied. It came complete with the paw-paw trees which they had planted. The ownership of trees and crops is always complicated and, in West Nile, it seems that some felt that if you planted a tree then you were entitled to the fruit it produced.

No-one explained this to our new colleague. When the paw-paws in what was now, in her view, her garden, started to flower, she looked forward to enjoying the first fruits. Young, green paw-paws began to appear just under the crown of leaves. She knew nothing about paw-paws but, always eager to learn, she levered off the largest oval paw-paw, still hard and green, and tried to cut it open. Finding it inedible, she left the remains on the ground under the tree. The Ugandan former occupant of the house, believing that she still had a claim over the paw-paws, came and found the remains. The two women had a very public row, in a mixture of English and Alur just behind the staff houses. The English teacher completely lost her temper, always a sin in African eyes, and shrieked at the Ugandan, 'Get out of my garden!'

The Ugandan, equally furious but silent, picked up the hard half paw-paw and threw it at our colleague, catching her right on the nose. She sat down with a bump and bawled, and that's where we found her almost an hour later, still sniffing with hurt and frustration. That night, she decided to escalate the paw-paw war. Standing on a chair in the darkness, with clouds of mosquitoes whining around her, she used the tip of a *panga* to prize all the small green paw-paws off all the young trees. This time, she carefully collected the evidence and hid them under her bed. Next day she scratched her way through her lessons and after school ended, hurried back to see what the Ugandans had done. All seemed peaceful at her house. If the enemy knew of the loss of all their paw-paws, they had done nothing and said nothing.

A week of peace passed and by the end of it, her legs had swollen so much that it was hard to tell where her knees ended and her calves began. The skin was covered with angry mosquito bites which she made worse by scratching to get some relief. Then she began to shiver as the malaria developed, pumped into her blood by all those hungry mosquitoes. When she failed to come to class on the following morning, we went to see how she was and found a very sick girl. She had forgotten to take her Paludrine tablets. Ted Williams called in on his way back from Arua and filled her full of Nivaquine, before sending her back to bed. There she stayed, brimming over with self-pity and bringing up what little food we managed to get her to eat. While she lay there, moaning gently in a haze of aching, sweating semi-consciousness, she may have heard the thumping sound behind the house. Only when she was strong enough to stagger to the window to check on her paw-paw trees did she discover that they had been reduced to a neat row of short stumps. The Ugandans had harvested their paw-paws.

## 3.4 Rusting Spears

We had a volunteer biology teacher for a time in the third term of 1970, a gifted teacher and one of the rare few who took the trouble to learn about the local plants and animals to make his biology lessons more relevant to his students' lives. They loved him. He had that quality of detached sympathy that they could appreciate. He did not want to be their friend, just their teacher. Knut was Norwegian and, to the British, very unconventional. He frequently objected to the Board of Governors' rules, on drinking, on dancing and especially on sex education. He decided to leave the first two for a later day and to start with the third, having witnessed another sad episode which ended with a girl leaving the school. What was needed, he was convinced, was a proper course of sex education, particularly in contraception, for both girls and boys. He consulted Lewis and was advised to keep this strictly within the O level Biology syllabus, which did include some work on human reproduction. That was enough for Knut, and he explained how babies were conceived, which they probably knew already. He then rapidly went on to tell them how to avoid conception. Methods were carefully explained, samples displayed and visual aids showing how they worked were hung up around the new Biology Lab. They became a popular Art Gallery. Classes who had not yet had the benefit of Knut's advice sneaked in to have a look between lessons.

The students clearly found this fascinating and very helpful. They began to discuss the relative merits of each method over the mid-day meal.

'If you interrupt before you erupt, then how can that be good?' argued the advocate for condoms.

'But, man, where are you going to get the covers, eh? Do they grow on trees in your village?'

'Mr Johansen says you buy covers at the *duka* where you buy the *dawa* (medicine) and then you can enjoy your girl and have no babies.'

'Does he buy them in Arua then? What does he want them for? He has no wife.'

Roars of laughter caught the attention of the member of staff on duty, one of our Ugandan women colleagues who wanted to know what was so funny. They tried to avoid telling her but one of the girls explained that the boys found avoiding making babies funny, at which she was not at all amused. What was going on in Biology reached the ears of the Governors who sent a member to the biology department to check the wall display.

'Mr Adrabo,' they told the Head of Biology. 'This is not right. We do not want this sort of teaching in our school.'

Silas promised to speak to Knut, who was completely unrepentant. He received a letter from his superiors in Kampala telling him that at the end of term he would be transferred to a new school in the East of Uganda where they had no biology teacher. The Governors decided that there was no point in demanding his resignation as he was going anyway and the students soon found out that, in fact, supplies of condoms were unobtainable in the Arua pharmacy store. The Indian lady owner had no wish to supply such things to oversexed schoolboys. The final straw for Knut was to be told by another member of staff that the idea of contraception would never catch on in West Nile where the rich fecundity of the local people was such a source of pride. They saw no need to restrict the birth of children and welcomed each new arrival, conceived in or out of wedlock.

Then an S3 boy asked Knut if he could get some of the 'many babies *dawa*'. He had read in a copy of a UK paper of the English woman who had received a drug to help her conceive during an early experiment in IVF treatment. When, to her horror, quintuplets arrived, the Mvara boys all wanted to try out the wonder drug on their girl-friends.

Knut talked to Dison about his frustration and enjoyed reading the lines Okot p'Bitek had written about 'young hunters':

> 'Let the fool continue to deceive himself!
> Who has ever prevented the cattle from the salt lick?
> .......
> But they lock you up inside a cold hall
> As if you are sheep, and they lock up
> All the girls in one cold hall,
> And the boys in another cold hall.
> ........
> And the spears of the lone hunters,
> The trusted right-hand spears of young bulls
> Rust in the dewy cold of the night[7].

'We have to look after the Mvara girls,' Dison told him. 'It's better that the spears remain rusty! Fear of getting pregnant and family pressure is the best form of contraception around here and we don't want swelling bellies in Jericho.'

Knut left us for his new school a disappointed man, with the rule forbidding sex in school still unshaken and the prohibition on sex education still firmly upheld by the Governors.

\*

Peter Ogani, the Okebu student, reminded me that I had wanted to see whether the old Okebu smiths could make iron. He had asked the elders in Logiri to tell him all they knew about the old ways and he was keen for me to go down to Logiri with him to meet the elders. Which was why, one Saturday, Jenny and I, Peter and two other Okebu boys, drove down to his village to meet his father. Over a cup of tea, we leant that the people of the area did make iron, 'long ago', but that the raw materials came from further south, in Alur country. We set off down the road to the Alur village of Zeu to meet some of their elders. They were suspicious but said that, for a small fee, they would take us to the place where the Alur 'dug the iron stones from the hill at Amonze.' After a walk of a mile or two, we found a hillside with the rock exposed where the local people had already dug up a small amount of rock and broken it up into pieces the size of walnuts.

'This is the stone for making iron. We think you will pay us for it.'

So more shillings changed hands and Peter carried a sack of the stones back to the car.

What was interesting to me was that the making of iron seemed to be an Okebu monopoly yet they were dependent on the Alur to obtain the actual iron ore. The stones we had acquired looked nothing like the Haematite or Magnetite ores that I had seen, but Peter was sure that they were iron ore. When I was next in Entebbe, I took a sample to the Uganda Geological survey headquarters and they very kindly analysed it.

'Yes,' they said. 'This is Limonite, quite high grade, about 80% iron oxide.'

So the Alur elders, and Peter Ogani, were right. All we needed now was some charcoal, a furnace in which to smelt the ore and our team of confident experts.

A few weeks later, the Mvara Okebu Iron Smelting Club met on a Saturday morning, outside my New Site house. Three of the smiths from just north of Arua started to clear a patch of my garden and to dig out the base for a furnace. All the activity attracted a large audience of students including all the Okebu boys and girls in the school. Peter Ogani assumed the role of project manager and told them all to stand well back. Then the old men stopped working. There was a long discussion between them and the 'manager'.

'Sir, we cannot have girls here,' Peter explained. 'The men say that the iron will not come if there are menstruating women here.' He looked accusingly at the posse of girls. 'They must go and we must sacrifice a cock to clean the space.'

I was tempted to say that all this was a lot of nonsense but thought better of it. It happened that the visitors had brought just such a sacrificial cock with them which, for a few shillings, they were happy to kill and to keep the carcase for use at home afterwards. We could now start properly, without any women. Boys were posted on the path behind my house to ensure no other females came near.

Setting up the *ubi* and seeing if the iron will flow

They lit the charcoal and pumped like mad for two hours, until the whole structure was glowing red-hot, and then for another two hours, until the 'ubi' got so hot that the front started to break away. A dribble of white hot liquid trickled out of the hole at the base. I was impressed! They had smelted iron. But the old men were not at all happy. The white hot liquid was not iron.

'It is just shit', they said. 'There must have been a woman here.'

Bitterly disappointed, Peter walked back to the town with the old men and for the rest of that school year, the members of the Mvara School Iron Smelting Project kept very quiet.

\*

In the middle of the term, just as the school was settling down with a full team including many new staff, the next bomb-shell hit us. Dison Aneco, our Deputy Head, was suddenly transferred to a new school in Kigezi where the Head had died of a heart attack. He had his promotion and we were glad for him but his leaving left a large hole in our staff. The school was already restless from the sudden cancellation of the Independence Day Celebrations in October. The President was said to be concerned about unrest within the Army and fear of a possible coup. But Obote made no move against Amin. When Obote was installed as the Chancellor of Makerere University, Amin turned up uninvited and was cheered by the students.

The competition between the President and his Army Commander was becoming more open by the day but still Obote made no move.

When Dison left the Governors had to find a replacement. The Deputy Head post was advertised nationally and although we all knew that the successful candidate would be a Ugandan in line with the Ministry's policy of the Ugandanisation of school leadership. Lewis made clear at the staff meeting that anyone could apply if they thought they had the experience and qualifications. The most senior Ugandan on the staff was Silas Adrabo, the Biology teacher who had so strongly protested at my efforts to improve Science teaching. He applied for Dison's job and one other external application came in to the Governors, an Indian Mathematics teacher from Kampala. I wondered whether Lewis might welcome some additional applications as it seemed that Silas would get the post by default. He and I both cared a lot about the school which the Church and the Mission had nurtured through so many challenges and which Lewis had led through a minefield of disasters.

'Ultimately, the Board and the Ministry will make the decision,' Lewis told me. 'If you want to apply, I'm not going to advise you not to. But if you do, I would try to make it clear that you are only doing so to provide some continuity in the short term. This school needs an African Head and will have one in the fullness of time.'

On that basis, I applied for the Deputy post and tried to make it clear in my letter to the Chair of Governors, Bishop Wani that I was prepared to serve as Lewis' Deputy for as long as I was needed but that I had no ambition to become the Head of Mvara. Five members of the Board, with the District Education Officer representing the Ministry, interviewed the three applicants, Mr Mehta from Kampala, Silas and me. It seemed unlikely that five Ugandans, only one of whom was a leader of the Church, would appoint a young European in the teeth of National policy and yet they did. From the opening question, 'would you be prepared, Mr Haden, if you were the Head of this school, to hold religious assemblies in the school?' to which I replied, without really thinking, 'of course', it was clear that they were looking for Lewis' Deputy to become his successor. My claim to have no ambition to lead was simply disbelieved. It was a very courteous interview which left my ignorance of the administration of Ugandan schools largely unexplored. Discipline and academic standards were what concerned the Committee and it seemed that I had a reputation for both. I began to enjoy the experience of discussing the future of the school with five men deeply concerned about it. All the time, I was pushing my head further into the noose!

The Board in fact had no power to make an appointment. Their panel could only make a recommendation to the Minister and leave him to accept or reject it. That might not happen for some time and we all had to wait at least two months before any news came back from Kampala. If the Board had recommended Silas, he was sure that this would have been accepted within a week or so, but we heard nothing. He got restless and wrote to the Ministry and the Chairman complaining about the delay. He was also increasingly disgruntled around the school and would not speak to me at all. Faced with this, I could have withdrawn my application, but I supposed it was as he had said two years before. I was too proud. I tried to get on with my job and to enjoy being with Jenny in the place to which we both believed God had called us.

\*

November came and with it the time for O level examination again. The lights burned late into the night in the dormitories. Even when the fuses were removed by tired duty staff anxious to get to bed, the tiny flickering lights of oil lamps and the fading glow of torches lit up the dancing words of revision notes held up before exhausted eyes. Boys and girls 'cracked their heads', lost weight and visited mysterious relatives known to offer strong local medicines guaranteed to improve memories. As the exams got closer, the group hoping for a lift into Arua Hospital got larger. The stomach ulcer sufferers were the most pathetic, grey with pain and worry and unable to face the mound of *enya* each mealtime, as corrosive to their stomachs as a dose of Vim. The Medical Officer prescribed a milk diet, but milk was a shilling a pint and few could afford even a little each day. What dried milk was available in West Nile went to ailing babies, not students with stomach pain. Failure in 'Cambridge' was unthinkable. Had they not all been selected for places in S1 over four years before, the flower of the District's youth? Failure could not be their fault; it had to be the school's. And yet they all knew that a form of failure was inevitable for the majority, as there were not enough A level places to carry them on to their ultimate goal, a place on a degree course at Makerere, the passport to an affluent future in the Civil Service, teaching or in politics.

The new staff members were found housing, Wendy, sharing with Jenny, the Corkers in a semi like the one I now had sole use of as John Martin had left, and a new Art teacher and his wife, the Mackays, provided with one of the large detached houses on the New Site, now almost completed. Lewis, in his usual thoughtful way, had gone down to Kampala to meet the Corkers and the Mackays, shepherded them through the form-filling and the hand-shaking at the Ministry and brought them up to Arua in his car. He stopped where the grass was high. In a jocular fashion, he explained.

'Ladies to the left, Gents to the right.'

The two young wives declined the offer and hung on until they got to 'a proper place' at Masindi where they had stopped for lunch. When they got to Mvara, Lewis took them to their houses and we all helped them to settle in.

It is always hard for the wives or husbands of teachers in boarding schools if they do not themselves have a role in the school. Lance Corker's wife was keen to get involved and found all sorts of useful things to do, even if she was not paid to do them. Betty Mackay, with no knowledge of Christian Missions or rural Uganda, found life at Mvara much more difficult. She spent much of her time at first in the house on her own, trying to get on with a succession of house-girls each of whom soon gave up trying to do what she wanted. Terrified of flying insects, of which we had a wonderful variety, she sprayed everything, including her open veranda, with 'Flit' in a vain attempt to keep Africa at a distance. Her husband, Angus, enjoyed his Art teaching and did his best to support her but it did not help that her early months of pregnancy brought on bad morning sickness and she had few shoulders to cry on. Most of us were far too busy. The West Nile Club offered a social base outside the school where Angus enjoyed planning hunting trips with other ex-patriates over a gin and tonic in the evenings. These would provide an opportunity to use the shot-gun he had quite legitimately brought with their luggage, but Betty never really felt at home.

\*

Towards the end of that term, Lewis began planning the move into the office buildings which were now completed on the New Site. He had held the school together through a series of crises that would have destroyed men of less faith and patience but accidents happen, even to experienced Headmasters. This was perfectly illustrated by the fate of the boys' latrines. Lewis decided that he should first clear out all unwanted paperwork from the old office. There were piles of old school lists, out-of-date exam papers and inventories of everything from books that had long since been eaten by termites and gardening tools which had mysteriously found their way out of the school into the neighbouring villages. Because some papers might be confidential, Lewis decided that all should be burnt and he recruited a team of S2 boys to help him. As it was the start of the dry season and the grass in the gardens around the school could easily catch fire, he chose his incineration site carefully, well away from the main buildings in a discrete corner of the Old Site. Soon there was a huge pile of crumpled paper on the bare land to the south of his office and, with a flourish, Lewis lit it.

What he had not planned for was a sudden increase in the strength of the afternoon breeze from the Nile valley below. As the pile of paper caught fire and began to blaze under the excited eyes of the S2 boys, the strengthening wind rolled the mass of burning paper across the site, heading straight towards the only other feature of that discrete corner, the boys' 'long-drop' latrines. These were a row of ten holes in the ground screened by mud and wattle walls with wooden doors and a grass thatched roof.

Lewis heard the shouts of the boys and came out of the office just in time to see the fire ball reach the latrines. Fortunately, none of the cubicles was occupied by a squatting student but the whole block was tinder-dry. The roof caught fire first but soon the whole temporary building was ablaze. All that Lewis and the boys could do was to stand in stunned silence as the boys' latrines were transformed into a very public row of ten holes in the ground and a neat pattern of ashes and smouldering stumps where the poles for the walls had been. To this day, Lewis Stephenson is probably unique amongst Headmasters in having destroyed his school's only block of boys' toilets.

When the Jericho girls heard of this exciting event and realised that the Old Site boys would have a problem with both 'short' and 'long' calls, they came laughing up from their dormitories and made a generous offer. It was only a week or two before the end of term and they were due to move out and over to the New Site at the start of the new school year. They would be pleased to offer the Old Site boys the short-term use of half of their 'long-drops'. They knew full well that this would mean the exciting prospect of boys, for the first time in the history of Mvara, coming down the hill, past Miss Lloyd's guardpost house and into Jericho. To her credit, Margaret saw the generosity of spirit which they showed and agreed to this as a very temporary, arrangement. As far as we know, the boys who used the girls' latrines behaved like perfect gentlemen until the end of term.

*

    Our two S4 classes started their exams with the Practicals. Although we now had the use of the new labs, it was easier to set everything up in the old Mvara lab and organise morning and afternoon sessions there over two days. The papers had been set and details sent to the school to enable us to prepare and we did not anticipate any problems. Biology was usually something simple, like cutting a fruit in half and identifying the different parts. We could usually find enough tomatoes and conceal them from prying eyes until the big day. But that year the Board was far more imaginative and set an observation exercise on 'the lower jaw bone of a carnivore'. No doubt some keen young Chief Examiner thought it was about time that the Africans studied the local wild-life. Lions and leopards were clearly unavailable. Hyenas, foxes, civets and mongooses were not common around Arua.

    'We'll just have to find cats,' Silas said. 'There are lots of strays around Mvara and it would be good to get rid of some.'

    So, all around our side of town, the cat population plummeted as two local young men, sworn to secrecy as to the true purpose of their nightly netting activity, killed enough cats to provide thirty six jaw bones, one each for every student taking the am and pm sessions of the practical examination. Behind the old lab, mysterious cauldrons of boiling water bubbled away as the heads were boiled to clean the bones. On the morning of the practical, the gleaming white jaw bones were set out with full rows of very carnivorous teeth. The students examined them minutely, drew their diagrams and wrote long explanations of what each type of tooth was for. The Biology Practical was a triumph.

    Physical Science, the following day started well. The Physics test was a simple lens problem which involved identifying where the image would be and drawing appropriate ray diagrams. They had all worked through a very similar exercise in class the month before and answered with confidence. The Chemistry question was, on the face of it, equally straight forward.

'A small sample of a substance X (supplied by the Board) is placed in a test tube. To this, add 5 ml of water and then add dilute hydrochloric acid, drop by drop. Record what happens in the test-tube.'

The task was simply to observe and record, to note all the changes of colour, smell and temperature and to state what occurred as X reacted with the acid. Those of us who had met such tests before recognised it immediately as the 'thiosulphate plus acid' reaction and were sure that the students would be able to make appropriate observations.

How wrong we were! Some thought that they had to identify X, although the paper did not ask them this. Others found the changes of colour confusing and wrote 'first it went less yellow and then more yellow.' They were struggling with language. Students in an English school would have some idea what ivory and cream, lemon, egg-yolk, gold, beige and brown looked like and those more interested in Art would have an even richer range of Raw and Burnt Sienna, Marigold and Marmalade. We had shown our students sulphur and told them it was yellow but had not fully understood that in both Lugbara and Alur, there was no word for yellow. The only colours in their world were red as in blood, black as their skin, blue as in the sky above and white as in the cotton cloth their uniforms were made of, although 'white' was really the word for 'clean'. Then there were the problems of describing the changes as the sulphur first appeared as a faint cloud of white in the solution which became creamier as it flocculated and coagulated until it formed a clearly solid yellow deposit. Most of them could only write 'less yellow then more'.

Many did not even notice that the tube became perceptively warmer as the reaction took place, easy enough to miss in an old lab under a hot iron roof crammed with thirty five candidates in the heat of the day. It was probably well above 30°C for much of the practical. Then there was the smell of sulphur dioxide, a sharp, acid smell which most could not identify with any confidence. They did so little practical work that only the more obvious smells of chorine and hydrogen sulphide were in any way familiar to them.

By the end of the afternoon, when the second batch of candidates was released from the lab, there was a crowd of angry boys around the door.

'Sir, I think you will tell us what the substance X is.'

'You were not asked what it is, only to write down your observations,' I said defensively, puzzled as to why they seemed so angry. 'In fact, X was Sodium Thiosulphate, a common chemical used in photography.'

'You have not taught us about this X. It is not in the syllabus,' said another boy who must have learnt the syllabus off by heart.

'But you were not asked to say what X was, only to note down what happened.'

'We think that you want us to fail.'

The crowd around the door had grown to include almost all the S4 students, including the girls.

'You have not taught us about this reaction – how can we pass if you do not teach us properly.'

I was beginning to get annoyed with this stubborn failure to understand what they had been asked to do.

'Look.' I said. 'If you think that the Chemistry question was unfair, we can make a note of your complaints and send them in to the Board.'

'But then the Board will hate us and we will fail.'

They would not be convinced that their difficulty with the chemistry question was anything less than a conspiracy between their teacher and the distant Board with the explicit aim of ensuring that they failed. It was ludicrous but I could not persuade them.

'I have to go to the office with the papers and then you have to go for your evening meal. Why don't you do that and come back to meet me and the Headmaster this evening in one of the old classrooms on this site?'

They began to drift away, muttering darkly. That evening, Lewis and I worked hard for over two hours to persuade a packed meeting that we were on their side. I started by explaining all over again what the Chemistry question had actually asked them to do.

'Then why did you tell us that the substance was this 'thio' which we could not know?'

'Because you asked me what it was.'

'So how do you know?'

'Because the Board told us so that we could put out the right things for the examination.'

'So you tried to confuse us because you knew we did not know this 'thio'?'

The pointless argument when round and round until we were all exhausted. Lewis asked me if we could go outside for a quiet word.

'I think that you'll have to apologise to them, although I'm not sure for what. Perhaps you could say that you are very sorry that they are so upset and promise to write to the Board telling them of their anger. That way we may at least get to bed in one piece and the Board may see the wisdom of setting something else next year.'

So we went back in and I apologised, promising to show them the letter to be sent to the Board. Very reluctantly, they calmed down and began to go off to their dormitories while Lewis and I walked across to where we had left our cars. While we had been in the meeting, someone had been busy. Both our cars sat on four flat tyres and some artist had tied a neat knot in Matilda's metal radio aerial. I wrote the letter to the Board, gave a copy to the S4 students who insisted on it being displayed on the school notice-board. The rest of the S4 examinations were taken without further trouble and Jenny and I were about to go away for a well-earned holiday together when two very unpleasant things happened. At the end of her evening duty, Jenny found a human turd on the seat of her car and an envelope arrived at the school office, addressed to: 'Hadens, Mvara Secondary School, Arua'. The office staff left it in my pigeon-hole.

It was typed on a page torn out of an exercise book and read: 'Hello, Hadens. This is to warn you on your behaviour. Let it be known to you that if you come out of your house after 6 pm any day, you will find yourself ……………You stupid ox of a man – you think you are superior. Mind you this is AFRICA! Be warned that if you show your unintelligent superiority etc you will find yourself…………..before you realise. Good buy till our next meeting. Mind you – we are on your track every hour of the day. Good buy – stupid husband of a buttockless woman.'

I looked in Jenny's pigeon-hole and removed the second envelope addressed to her. It read: 'Hello, Jenny darling. Be warned that you will find yourself <u>widowed</u> in no time if you don't take care in preventing your husband going out of the house after 6 pm. You buttockless woman belive it or not but our eyes are watching him closely. Just waiting for chance. May you be safe after his ………………'

I put the two notes in an envelope in my desk at home, thought about the fascination with buttocks that S4 boys seemed to have and went up to Jenny's house to have an end-of-term coffee with her and Wendy. She told me what she had found in her car, but I did not tell her about the notes. The next day, we packed for our holiday, got into the VW and drove off to the Kenya coast.

*

Another letter was waiting for me when we got back to Arua, from the Ministry of Education. Someone had at last made a decision. 'The Chief Education confirms your appointment as Acting Deputy Headmaster of Mvara Secondary School with effect from $1^{st}$ January, 1971.' There were a few more lines pointing out that as I was an Education Officer on contract to serve the Government of Uganda this 'acting' appointment made no difference to my contract or my salary. I was simply posted to serve in a new role, as disposable as my previous position.

With the school buildings on what was still referred to by everyone as the New Site now complete, we could use the week or so before term began to move the last school functions from Mvara. At the end of the previous term, the boys had moved across from their dormitories on the New Site into the new buildings. This left the dormitories free for the excited girls to move all their beds from Jericho to take over the vacated dormitories. They would no longer be guarded by Miss Lloyd's eagle eye and their new home was very close to the road.

Margaret had not been happy. 'They will be visited by every boy, army man, ne'er-do-well in Arua,' she warned. 'How will they be supervised?'

Silas Adrabo's house was the nearest and he had, in theory, been in charge of the boys. But no-one seemed convinced that making him responsible for the girls was a good idea. Lewis had tried to re-assure Margaret.

'My new house is just across the way from their dormitories and I'll keep an eye on them over-night.' So the girls had moved across and the duty roster drawn up for the new term before the buses came to take the students home.'

## Part 4: Surviving Idi Amin

### 4.1 Things fall apart

'Things fall apart; the centre cannot hold;
Mere anarchy is loosed upon the world,
The blood-dimmed tide is loosed, and everywhere
The ceremony of innocence is drowned.'
William Butler Yeats (1919)

The school re-opened towards the end of January 1971. We were all determined to make a good start to the year. At last, everything seemed to be in place. The New Site buildings were completed. The new staff had turned up and housing found for all of them, even if in a few cases in temporary arrangements. Our first Senior 6 classes were half way to their A level examinations. Jenny and I were to be married in August.

Few of us realised the true significance of what was happening in Kampala. We knew that the President had quarrelled with the Heath UK Government over British support for the South African regime and their Simonstown Naval Base. Obote had flown off to Singapore to continue his argument at the Commonwealth Conference table. His Deputy, Akena Odoka, normally left to guard the home front while Obote was away, had also left Entebbe. He had flown to London.

On a Sunday evening, as the fruit bats were chasing the last few rays of sunshine down the Bombo Road in Kampala, Sergeant Major Musa of the Uganda Army was in the Jinja Army barracks. He intercepted a telephone call from Singapore to his Army commander. It was an order from President Obote. Major General Idi Amin was to die. Musa, like Amin, a Kakwa from West Nile, did not pass on the order. He was not going to wait for the Acholi and Langi soldiers in the barracks to start the shooting. With a handful of West Nile soldiers, he seized the Jinja armoury, handed out weapons to as many West Nile soldiers as he could find and drove off in a tank to warn Amin.

Amin, the Army commander, had been out duck-shooting[1] that day, enjoying the temporary absence of his President. They had had a flaming row just before Obote left over two small un-resolved matters, the Sh2.5 million unaccounted for in the Ministry of Defence accounts and the unsolved mystery of the deaths of Brigadier Okoya and his wife. Neither problem was ever brought up again because by the morning of January 25th 1971, General Idi Amin was

President of Uganda. It was later described as a 'bloodless coup', bloodless that is apart from the Langi and Acholi soldiers who died in the Jinja Barracks and some of the crowd at Entebbe Airport. They had been standing in front of a poster of Obote at the Terminal Building. It was there, ready to welcome the President back from Singapore, but was spotted by the tank crew who drove into Entebbe to take over the Airport. Their first shell obliterated Obote's grin and with it, two Canadians unlucky enough to be standing alongside.

When the news of the Coup broke in Kampala, the Baganda went wild. At last, the hated regime of Northerners who had oppressed their people, imprisoned their leaders, exiled their Kabaka and then even stopped them giving him a proper burial was overthrown. Dancing, wailing and cheering, they drove round the city in open trucks decorated with banana leaves and filled every bar to drink to the sudden setting of Obote's Langi sun. Kampala shook with the thunderous beating of their drums.

It was all very quiet in Arua that evening. Jenny and I walked up through the school in the starlight, arm in arm, past the classrooms still full of white-shirted students, reading, reading, and re-reading. We passed a trio of girls, hands on hips, buckets on heads, swaying gently in the darkness as they took water for washing back to their dormitories.

'Good evening, Sir, good evening, Madam,' they chorused softly, with a flash of teeth and discrete approving smiles.

It was all so peaceful and so perfectly beautiful, with the Milky Way in an arc of bright, icy, majesty over our heads. Even the air seemed cool with a light breeze coming up from the great river to the east.

Usually, the school radio, an ancient Grundig clamped to the Dining Hall wall, blared out Congolese music all Sunday evening with occasional news bulletins. But on the evening of the 25th, it was strangely silent. No-one in the school heard the first self-conscious broadcast of the new regime, 'explaining' the Coup. Only after the evening meal when the experts had had time to thump the radio in all the right places and pull out and push in all the visible wires, did the radio even crackle. Then out of the rattling speaker came, not the usual repeated rhythms of the Congo, but, incredibly, a military band playing hymn tunes straight out of Moody and Sankey. The first verse of 'Blessed Assurance, Jesus is mine' passed without much notice amongst the few students propped up in the Dining Hall reading their notes. They were full of *enya* and half asleep. But by the third verse, they had picked up that something was very odd. By the end of the hymn, most of the students were clustered around the radio. Something had happened but no-one knew what. They listened to more hymn tunes that evening than ever before and it was not until much later that the music stopped. The halting English of Idi Amin, the Kakwa soldier whose home was not more that twenty miles to the north, told them what had happened in Kampala.

*'The men of the Uganda Armed Forces have placed this country in my hands by entrusting me with its government......... I will accept this task, but on the understanding that mine will be a caretaker administration, pending an early return to civilian rule.'*

After the speech, the students wandered out of the hall, confused and uncertain. Two of them passed my house on their way to take the news to the villages beyond the edge of the school site. They stopped to tell me as I hoed a corner of my garden.

'The army has power,' one said gloomily.

'Is that not a good thing?'

'We do not know,' he said. 'But we know the army.'

The other simply asked me, of all people, 'What will happen to us now?' I told them I did not know.

The reaction to the news was the same amongst most of the staff. They knew the Army and many had been strong supporters of Obote's UPC. Dick Nyai, who was already involved in District politics, was clearly worried.

'This is the worst thing that could have happened. We will all now regret that Amin had taken power.'

How right he was, but at that time, most thought it was for the better. Men, who the day before had worn red 'Obote' shirts as they worked in the fields or walked down the road, hurriedly took them off and buried them as soon as they could. Pictures of the ex-President, the day before essential in all the Asian *dukas*, were quickly hidden before any army-men arrived. The West Nile people had witnessed the barbarity of drunken soldiers in the border villages when the Sudan troubles made each *askari* jumpy and frightened of invasion. Many Lugbara and Kakwa had joined the Army but many had not. There was no dancing in Arua that night as a curfew was imposed and the school stayed silent.

We met as we always did for a Bible Study that week, led by Donald Temple, who was part of the AIM team at Mvara. He chose to study the verses in Paul's Letter to the Romans, Chapter 13:

'Let everyone be subject to the governing authorites, for there is no authority except that which God has established.The authorities that exist have been established by God. Consequently, whoever rebels against the authority is rebelling against what God has instituted, and those who do so will bring judgement on themselves. For rulers hold no terror for those who do right, but for those who do wrong.'

The Christian church in Uganda had grown under Obote's regime. There had been tensions and there was anxiety about what the future might hold as the government 'moved to the left'. But what would life for the church now be like under the incoming military regime, under a Muslim President? Paul's teaching seemed clear enough when 'the governing authorities' were those established by democratic election, however flawed that democracy might be. Donald pointed out to us that when Paul wrote his letter, the authorities in Rome upheld the Roman peace and Roman law and that stability had enabled the Christian church to spread across the Roman Empire. God had blessed his church with growth under Roman authority. But within ten years, the church had to face a wave of persecution under the emperor Nero. What would Paul's advice have been then? In fact, the church did not die although many Christians did. The blood of the martyrs seemed to fertilize the growth of the Church.

Those who first brought the gospel to Uganda and the first Ugandan Christians had shared such suffering. Had not Bishop Hannington been murdered before he even reached the Kabaka's court and many of the young Muganda pages who had responded to the Gospel were cruelly murdered. For us, in 1971, Paul taught that we had to respect the authority of the day who was now a military man, and we should pray that the Ugandan Church would follow that teaching no matter what uncertainty we faced. In St Philip's Church, Arua, where we met for worship on the first Sunday after the Coup, the change of regime involved a revision of the prayer for the President, although finding the right words to pray for a Muslim Major General was not easy.

For most people, life at first went on unchanged but, for a few in West Nile, normal life ended abruptly. They either disappeared in the early hours of the military regime, melting into the anonymous 'bush', labelled as 'guerrillas', or they were found floating face up in the Nile with a bullet hole in their forehead. Our Acholi biology teacher, Mr Oyot, was the first to go. On the morning of the coup, he was there teaching S2. By nightfall he was gone, leaving his pregnant wife sobbing in their home. The Police tried to frighten her into telling them where he was but she knew nothing. As soon as the road to Kampala was open, Lewis sent her back to Gulu on the bus. The boys insisted that Mr Oyot must have been a General Service Unit agent planted in the school. He may well have been.

The only student from Lango in the school, one of the new S5 entries, was the next to go. The Police came and searched through his pathetic box of belongings, trying to find some sign of political involvement, but there was nothing incriminating, just an old pair of shorts, last year's socks from his old school in Lira and a carefully hoarded roll of toilet paper. They found a self-conscious and well thumbed photo of a boy in very tight trousers between the leaves of one notebook and muttered to each other enthusiastically, until one of the frightened boys in his dorm admitted that the picture was of him. The policemen had to find something to justify the time they had spent searching, so they hit on his A level Chemistry notes, full of references to 'moving to the left' and 'moving to the right' in the work on chemical equilibrium. When they showed it to me as evidence of support for Obote's politics, I hadn't the heart to tell them that every S5 chemistry student had the same notes copied carefully from my blackboard. So the Langi boy joined the list of suspected GSU men who had disappeared from the school.

Later, some of the Alur boys and most of the rest of the Acholi ran away but by then even the Lugbara students, normally the most unshakable of all the boys, were frightened of the Army. More beds in the dormitories at lights out became empty spaces with a few scattered clothes that no-one wanted. We learnt not to be surprised. In Baganda, Amin sealed his popularity with a release of all the old political prisoners and announced that the Kabaka's well preserved remains could be brought back for burial in the great royal reed house at Kasubi. The Baganda went wild again, celebrating for months in an ecstasy of drumming and dancing but West Nile stayed quiet and many were afraid.

George Okai called in to share a mug of coffee on my veranda just as the sun was setting. We watched a swarm of tiny key-hole bees building their combs high up on the rough wall of the house.

'The army are like bees,' George said. 'They can bring honey to a place. West Nile will have honey from Amin. But soon the bees will go and their homes will be taken over by wasps and hornets. That may happen to West Nile as the

Acholi and the Langi in the Army come to fight Amin here. Then there will be no honey for us.'

But Amin seemed to have an iron grip on the Army. He was prepared to use his Kakwa and Sudanese allies to break the Acholi and Langi majority. Many were killed in the Jinja barracks and the fighting spilled over into other units. The curfew, imposed just after the Coup, remained in force from seven pm to six am but this had little effect on the life of a boarding school. No-one was supposed to be out at night. Some of the staff refused to do any evening duties, considering it too dangerous to leave their houses after seven pm. Fortunately, the students worked quietly into the night unsupervised. More of a problem was the poor power supply for their dormitory lights. As the dry season took hold, the water shortage worsened.

Lewis returned from the usual Kampala 'auctions' for S1 and S5 entry and about two weeks after the coup, our new S1 intake arrived. The evening queues of girls at the bore-hole pump got longer. The new lavatories and wash-rooms had to be locked and all the old 'long-drops' brought back into use. Some girls even made the journey back to Jericho for their evening needs; at least that's where they said they were going. One week later, the curfew was suddenly lifted and we could once more travel freely at night, freely that is, apart from the road-blocks which sprang up around the town and along the main road south. Most were manned by local Police who knew us well and remained quietly courteous, but the Army could be difficult. The bridge at Pakwach, which had been completed a year before the Coup, suddenly became of enormous strategic importance, guarded day and night by the Army. Woe betide any tourist foolish enough to stop and photograph the elephants feeding on the reeds around the piers of the bridge. One American arrived at Arua still in a state of shock having been pulled out of his car by the Army guards and deprived of his camera, film and spectacles, all of which sailed into the river. Only the timely arrival of a truckload of Police saved him from joining his belongings in the water. We learnt to speak very politely when the muzzle of a gun was poked through the car window.

At the beginning of February, the new S5 students arrived and soon settled in. Most were from our own S4 leavers, the same students who had caused such a fuss over the Science Practicals. Most had done well enough in the exams to get into S5 and it was agreed that the S4 prefects who had been supervising the dormitories since the start of the year should continue. They seemed to be doing a good job, under the overall leadership of the Head Boy and Head Girl from S6. With the power failures becoming more common, the evening prep arrangements were frequently disrupted and students had to go back to their dormitories to continue with what little light they could get from torches, illicit oil lamps and candles. When the power supply settled down in the third week in February, the girls especially wanted to stay longer in their classrooms to use the light to make up for lost time. This seemed reasonable, but it also meant that the duty staff had to be around for longer and longer which clearly could not go on. Lewis consulted me and the women on duty, Jenny, Milcah and Wendy. We all agreed that the girls must return to their dormitories by ten each evening, an extension of an hour over the usual time.

At ten o'clock on Wednesday 17$^{th}$ February, the girls refused to move. Jenny called me and I warned them that they must go back or be reported to the Headmaster. All but the S4 girls, including some of the Prefects, reluctantly left.

'We'll have to leave them here and tell Lewis in the morning,' I said to Jenny. 'I'm not staying with them to argue all night.'

So we left them in the classroom. When they felt like it, they drifted back to their dormitories. In the morning, the S4 girls were duly reported for their disobedience and told to meet Lewis to learn their fate. He listened to them and then told them that they must go to their dormitories each night at ten.

On the Thursday, Milcah Avinya was on duty. Lewis warned her about what had happened the night before. At ten past ten, she went to the classrooms to make sure that the S4 girls had gone to bed. They were all still studying in the classrooms. She told them that they would all be reported to the Headmaster for their disobedience and left them there. Eventually, they went to bed. In the morning, Lewis had to see them all for the second time. He discussed the issues with me and with Margaret Lloyd, with Milcah, Jenny and Wendy. We all agreed that he had no choice. The girls must be punished and be told that they would be sent home for a week, subject to the formal approval of the Governors. Lewis saw the girls and told them what would happen on Saturday. Buses would be arranged on Saturday morning, to take them to the Arua bus-park and they must be ready to go home.

Every Saturday morning, the whole school met at nine for an Assembly. We sang the National Anthem. There was a short word from a member of staff on some improving theme.

The notices for the week were given and the school dismissed. That's what normally happened, but on that Saturday, as the school assembled, they seemed unusually quiet. Everyone stood as Lewis came in and walked to the front. He looked exhausted, determination and misery competing in the down-turned corners of his mouth. 'Sit down, please,' he said, and the staff sat. Not a student moved.

Before he could say anything more, the S4 Prefects walked towards him down the length of the Hall. Impeccable, boys in clean white shirts and shorts, girls in white blouses and pressed brown skirts, all with heads held high in the rightness of their cause, they bore down on their speechless Headmaster. As each reached the table at the front, each took off their Prefect's badge, placed it on the table and walked out of the Hall. They had all resigned, and the school, row by row, in perfect, dignified order, followed them out of the Hall. It was the smartest thing that I had ever seen the Mvara students do. Only the new S1 children remained standing in the Hall, wondering what was happening, with the Staff sitting stunned and silent behind Lewis' chair. He spoke first to the S1s.

'I am sorry,' he said. 'The school seems to be on strike. You have been in this school for a very short time and are not involved. You must keep out of trouble today and go home as soon as we can arrange transport for you. Go to your dormitories now and wait there until I send for you.'

Frightened and bewildered, they drifted out of the Hall and the Staff waited for Lewis to tell them what he would do.

'We must get the students off this site as soon as we can,' he said, looking at his watch. 'We have nine hours before it gets dark and before they get beer from the villages. We must ask the Governors to close the school and get the students away.'

While the school office 'phoned the bus companies and arranged for as much transport as possible to come to the school in the late afternoon, Lewis 'phoned the Police to let them know what had happened.

'Do you want help now, Sir?' asked the Station Sergeant.

'No. It would be better to leave the students as they are quiet for the moment – I'll call you if we need help.'

Other West Nile schools had been through student strikes and we knew what we had to do. Although the students had taken the law into their own hands, we still had to have approval from the Governors before we could arrange for them to be sent home. They would be expecting to go but we needed official approval and for that we had to find the Chairman, Bishop Silvanus Wani, or his Deputy. Lewis 'phoned the Ministry next in the slight hope that someone there might be working on a Saturday, but the Arua operator's response, 'All Kampala lines are down', meant that we could not even reach the building. The Bishop's secretary was found at home near Mvara and she told us the bad news that the Bishop was out at a confirmation about forty miles north of Arua. It would take some time to get a message to him. His Deputy, the District Transport Officer, was away in Kampala. We would just have to wait, and pray. Meanwhile, the school remained quiet and at mid-day, lunch was served to the S1 students, and a few others who managed to sneak into the Hall. Lewis and I set out in two cars to ty to find the Bishop.

  I drove north that day, winding through the villages towards Koboko. Everywhere the grass had gone and the dust-devils twisted across the hard burnt earth. Nothing was moving along the road. Even the goats that grazed the verges had abandoned their search for something edible and lay panting under the leafless trees. Mile after dusty mile, I drove, stopping at each cluster of huts, looking for the old grey Diocesan Land Rover and a large man in a bush jacket and dog collar. But it was always the same answer. *'Apana Bishop –* no Bishop; he is not here.'

  It was getting near evening as I drove back onto the school site. It looked so peaceful with the neat rows of buses drawn up by the office and a few students walking from their dormitories to disappear behind the moon-flowers. The smoke drifted up from the old kitchens, supper was being prepared. Members of the Board were sitting on Lewis' veranda, sipping cold drinks and waiting for the Bishop. I called in to Jenny's house to make sure that she and Wendy were alright and shared a mug of tea before leaving them to go to see Lewis. The frogs and village dogs were just beginning to welcome the coming of the night.

  Lewis told me to go home and wait there until he sent for me. 'I don't think we can do any more, John,' he said. 'I cannot get the Board to meet without the Bishop. We had a message to say he was coming and would be here as soon as he could. We'll just have to sit and wait.'

  So I went home, had some supper and put an LP on the record player. This was a night for Fauré's Requiem, something gentle and soothing.

  'Sanctus, Sanctus....Dominus Deus Sabaoth,' 'Holy, Holy .......Lord God of hosts.'

I heard the buses go back to the town and watched as a single Police Land Rover drove onto the site, checked with Lewis that all was well and drove away again. A few mosquitoes whined against the netting of my windows.

'Pie Jesus Domine, donna eis requiem' 'Merciful Lord Jesus, grant them rest........'

I sat and listened to the beautiful sound, pouring effortlessly from a single treble voice. Outside, all seemed quiet. Fauré's lovely melodies pushed back the darkness around the house.

'Sempiternam requiem' '....eternal rest.' 'Agnus Dei, qui tollis peccata mundi.....' 'Lamb of God who takes away the sins of the world', 'Dona eis requiem.' 'Grant them rest.'

Perhaps, I thought, the school would settle down to a peaceful night and a better spirit in the morning. Then, above the volume of the music, I heard the voices, angry voices swelling in volume as they came closer down the hill.

'Libera me, Domine, de mortis aeterna,' 'deliver me, Lord, from death eternal,' 'in die illa tremenda....' 'upon that day of terror.....'

The voices were closer now and angrier as the mob of students poured around the staff houses. I locked the doors, closed the windows and drew the curtains, thinking how little protection a few louvred panes of glass and sheets of cotton offered. The voices were all around the houses now, angry voices shouting in languages I did not know.

'Libera me, Domine...' 'Free me Lord from eternal death...'

The first stone or lump of earth hit the aluminium roof over my head like a clap of thunder, and then another, and another. They were stoning the staff houses, knowing that we were huddled inside and could do nothing to stop them.

'Dies illa, dies irae.....' 'O that day, that day of wrath, of calamity and misery...'

We were at the heart of a full scale riot. To go outside would be folly until the moment of anger passed.

But someone did go out. Up by the McKay's house, three shots rang out. The noise of shouting suddenly stopped. Then I heard the roar of a car engine over the noise of the crowd. Headlights swept the houses and wheels were spinning. Then two more shots and the car engine fading into the distance. For a few moments, the shouting stopped again. The night was almost silent. Then they started to shout again, even louder than before. The noise seemed to be from further up the hill, where Lewis and Angela lived, angry voices up the hill fading away. I waited as the noise died down and then heard another car. It was driving slowly on to the site and then it stopped. More angry voices and then a loud cry like an animal being struck. After that, more cars were driving into the school and more angry voices were shouting and windows were being smashed. Then the noise of the crowd faded to an ominous silence.

I waited five more minutes but the only way to find out what had happened was to leave the house and walk up to the school entrance, past the Mackay's house to where the Stephensons lived. Near the school office, a Police Land Rover, with its engine still running, had stopped by another car. When I got closer, I could see that it was David Read's. The driver's door was open and the tyres were slashed. Fresh blood stained the dry earth by the door. Lewis and a policeman were standing by the car when they saw me.

'Thank God you're OK, John,' Lewis said, his face ashen white in the lights of the cars. 'There's been a riot and a shooting and poor David's been taken to Kuluva. One of the boys is in Arua hospital. John, it's so bad that the Police want us all to get off the site and go to Kuluva too. Can you tell the girls on the Boma if I go round the houses?'

Without waiting for any more details, I ran up to Jenny's house and banged on her door. She and Wendy were still there, unharmed and unaware of what had happened.

'Don't worry about that now,' I told them. 'Grab what you need and get in your car. Drive to Kuluva. I'll follow you in Matilda.'

Running back to the school, I passed Lewis again, still standing by the school office.

'Is there anyone else, who needs to go?' I asked him.

'The Corkers have gone', he said. 'I'll pick up Val from the Mackays' house and Liz. You get your car and meet us at Kuluva.'

When I got to Kuluva Hospital after a short drive from the school, Ted Williams had already arranged places for everyone who needed to stay. I met Lewis and he told us what had happened.

'Once it was dark, the students met in the Dining Hall. Many of the boys had been drinking and the meeting got out of hand. Someone suggested attacking the houses of the white teachers as they had tried to get the S4 girls sent home. That's what had provoked the strike in the first place. Most of the students just went along with the crowd and started to throw stones and clods of earth onto the roofs of the houses where we were all sheltering. That's when Angus went outside and fired his shot-gun. Betty Mackay must have panicked and insisted that Angus get them out of the school, so they got into the car with Betty driving. Angus must have taken his shot-gun with him because he fired twice more through the open car window at a group of boys up on the bank near the new labs.

It looks as if one of the S3 boys was hit and badly wounded. The other boys put him on a bicycle and ran with him all the way to Arua Hospital but we don't think he made it there alive. They came back to school covered in blood and very angry. They began to wreck the office, breaking the windows and trying to kick down the door, when David Read drove onto the site. He had decided that it might help to show a film of all things, to calm things down, and had brought the projector over from Mvara, not knowing anything about what had happened. When he got out of his car, the boys attacked him and they might have killed him if some of the girls had not stopped them. It was bad enough anyway as they hit David on the head with a *panga*. Just then the Police arrived in force and took charge of the site. They took David to Kuluva and came down to our house to tell us that we all had to leave. That's when I met you, John, and we all got away.'

'So what happens next?' I asked. Lewis was struggling to tell us what he knew. 'The Police say that Betty drove Angus straight round to the Arua Police Station to report the incident with the gun and Angus was put into a cell for his own safety. If the boys had caught him, they would certainly have killed him. Betty then came here and Ted has given her a sedative.'

'What happened to the boy who was shot?' Jenny asked.

'We don't actually know the details but it looks very bad and I'm afraid he may have died,' Lewis said.

'And David Read?'

'He's here, with a bad '*panga*' cut on his head which Kuluva have stitched up so he'll be alright,' Lewis said. 'There's another thing. The Police need someone to go back to the school tomorrow morning to tell the students that the school's closed and to arrange for them all to go home. Can you go John?'

It was the sort of request which I had to accept. Just before dawn the following day, I drove onto the school site and met the Police Inspector escorted by two sleepy Policemen. They had been guarding the school all night but there had been no more trouble. It was cold as the dawn broke and the full extent of the damage to the school office buildings became clear. The school seemed very quiet. Perhaps, many of the students had already gone home. The Police Inspector told me that he had a statement from the District Commissioner which I was to read to the students who had stayed on the site. He went to round them up and the two policemen got their rifles and prepared to act as my bodyguards. They must have been as frightened as I was. By seven am, most of the remaining students, almost all boys, had gathered in front of what remained of the school office. They stood, sullen and silent. The two Policemen fingered the pins on the tear gas cartridges hanging from their belts.

'Tell them,' ordered the Police Inspector.

So I read the statement, announcing the closure 'for the time being' of Mvara Senior Secondary School and the arrangements for transport for them to get home. They were to report to the buses with all their belongings at ten that morning. They listened in complete silence and began to drift back to their dormitories.

When the buses came, the students lined up to receive money for travel home. Some claimed to be going to Kampala, although we knew that they lived within West Nile. In the circumstances, it did not seem to be a good moment to argue over bus fares. By the middle of the day, the school was closed and the students all on their way home. The wrecked school office was open to the elements so I arranged for the windows and doors to be boarded up and went back to Kuluva. I was now the Acting Deputy Head of a closed secondary school, but I knew at least that all the staff were alive and safe. One was in hospital, another was in the Police Cells, but the boy who had been rushed to hospital was dead.

\*

We had gone to Uganda as teachers hoping to serve God and a beautiful country which we knew through the words of friends and the work of a Christian Mission. After three years, I had become involved in the leadership of the school, but now it seemed that everything had gone wrong. We had to face the inevitable attempts to answer the question 'why?' Why had it happened? What had gone so badly wrong? The Ministry in Kampala sent up an enquiry team. The Board of Governors conducted their own meetings and the Parents of the Mvara students put together their own investigation. Over three weeks, we had to face each in turn, asking the same questions, offering the same answers.

'Was it true that the Europeans on the staff had been plotting in Miss Peck's house even before the girls had refused to turn their lights off?'

'No, we met for coffee and for prayer for the school every Wednesday and that was why we were in Miss Peck's house that day.'

'Was it true that the S5 students had been told that the best teachers were Mr Haden, Miss Peck and Miss Moore?'

'We have no idea what the S6 students had told S5 when they arrived, but it was not true anyway and we all respected the Ugandan staff as teachers.'

'Was it true that Mr Mackay had sworn at a boy in S3 for spilling paint and had said that there would be 'big trouble' if it happened again?'

'We have no idea and cannot ask Mr Mackay now.'

'Was it true that the Headmaster had lost control of the situation?'

'We had all lost control. Once the Prefects had resigned and the school was on strike, there was nothing we could do.'

'When would the school be open again?'

'Would the students be punished now that a boy had died?'

'What would happen to Mr Mackay?'

'Mr Read should take what happened to him in a spirit of forgiveness and the school should buy him some new tyres. Was this not fair?'

We answered the questions as best we could. For a time, we stayed every night at Kuluva until the anger in the town died down. When the body of the boy was released after the necessary autopsy and coroner's report, Canon Benoni of Vurra held the funeral in the boy's home village. Lewis Stephenson, to his great credit, had the courage to go to the funeral, one lone white face in a sea of mourning and angry Lugbara. At Kuluva, David Read had a visitor. The Church Army Captain, who worked in the community, Captain Dramani, braved all the anger and rode his bicycle the ten miles out to Kuluva to tell David and all the rest of us that he and his wife were praying for us. We should not lose heart but press on.

'As St Paul teaches us', he said. 'We must press on towards the goal for the prize, for the upward call of God. We must press.'

We were very touched by his courage in coming and thanked him for his encouragement.

'Don't worry,' I told him. 'We shall not give up at Mvara. Somehow, God will find a way for us to serve Him.'

But after over a month of enquiries and questioning, some while we were still at Kuluva and then more when we moved back to Mvara, there was still little clarity about what people really thought and none about our own future. We just had to get away. The school was closed. We were told not to leave the country, but we could leave the empty classrooms and dormitories, the sullen stares of some of the school staff and the suspicious glances of the traders in the town. We knew that we would have to come back. But we had to find some distracting activity to help us through the sitting around, to fill the emptiness we felt, the feeling that it was all over, things had fallen apart and our coming had all been a terrible mistake.

So Jenny, Wendy and I flung our sleeping bags, some clean clothes and dry food into the back of Matilda, said our temporary goodbyes to the Kuluva folk and drove away from Arua and the school. We went down to the Nile at Pakwach and were surprised to receive a smart salute from the Army guard as he waived us over the bridge. There were some advantages of our dark green Land Rover with UAA registration being mistaken as an officer's vehicle. We followed the dusty *murram* road up to Gulu and set off across the Acholi hills on the way to the scruffy little town of Kitgum. Everything, the grass, the thorn scrub and the withered millet stalks in the small patches of cultivation, was burnt brown. It was the height of the dry season, the hungry season when only those whose granaries still had some grain left had food to share in the evening. Villages of neat round thatched huts sweltered beside the road. They looked so peaceful in the heat haze, a few men sitting around under a tree, drinking beer, playing *mweso* with pebbles for counters and a grid of small depressions in the dust. Women pounded millet. Chickens scratched speculatively around their feet.

We knew we were escaping; running away from the accusation that somehow, what had happened was our entire fault. We did not believe it but we needed time just to be and to talk, to try to move on and look forward. Jenny and I had planned our wedding for August. There was much to do before then. Beyond Kitgum, the road climbed into the hills around the great grey shoulder of Mount Rom.

Fine red *murram* dust had been sucked in through the gaps in the canvas back of the car and covered everything inside, bodies, clothes, luggage, everything. Rivers of sweat ran down through the dust on our faces, so we stopped in the shade of a mango tree to cool off and to top up our steaming radiator. A gaggle of Acholi women were stripped to the waist for their daily labour of pumping up water from the bore-hole for their families. When they spotted our arrival in an Army green Land Rover, they grabbed their heavy clay pots and ran, shrieking with terror. But when we got out of the car, clearly European under our pall of dust, they came back shouting and giggling, tall, black, strong Acholi women, with gaps in their lower front teeth and long legs wet and gleaming in the sun.

We tried greeting them in the West Nile language of the Alurs, hoping that they would recognise the tongue of their distant cousins from across the great river. But our efforts reduced them to helpless laughter and much Acholi comment, so we resorted to sign language. Would they pump some water for us, to wash our faces and fill our steaming radiator? They filled our plastic jerry can, laughing and pointing to our dirty clothes, so we thanked them in English, shook thumbs and went on our way.

North Acholi hills beyond Kitgum on the Kidepo road

Beyond Rom, the country got even drier and dustier. There were no more fields, just thorn scrub as we drove east out of the land of the Acholi and into the home of the Karamojong. For miles there were no villages, just a switch back road through the hills. By the road-side where the hills opened out to a semi-desert plain an old man stood to watch us pass. He was tall, naked and very black with a long spear in one hand and a small three legged stool in the other, nothing else. He had no clothes, no hat and no luggage, nothing, apart from a small herd of thin goats chewing the few thorn bushes. We waved a greeting as we passed him, which he completely ignored. We had come into his world and had passed by. He was simply not interested.

Thirty miles further into Karamoja, we reached the most remote of all Uganda's game parks, Kidepo Valley, a wildlife paradise tucked into the extreme northeast corner up against the Kenya border. The sun was setting behind the blue ridge of mountains to the west. After the dust of the day, the air was clear and cooling fast and the evening star shone bright in the western sky.

We found the ring of thatched huts which serve as rest camp rooms at Apoka and paid our twenty shillings each to the smart Acholi Game Ranger. He welcomed us politely, told us that we were his first visitors for a week and showed us where we could cook our food. It was all well organised, neat and relatively clean. We cooked our meal and sipped mugs of tea. There seemed to be few mosquitoes to bother us in this dry place but we put up our nets and the girls climbed into their sleeping bags spread across the metal springs of the single beds in one hut and were soon asleep. I spent an hour outside the other hut gazing in amazement at the brilliance of the stars. In this high and empty place, the Milky Way shone out like some stellar motorway. With no more than a hint of a sickle moon, the starlight lit up the thorn trees and the hills to both the east and the west. Kidepo, I decided, was one of those magical places, where even the disasters of the previous month seemed less oppressive.

We were up before the dawn and off into the Park. With a Ranger armed with an ancient 303 rifle sharing the front of the Land Rover, we had the best day of game-viewing of our lives. As the land dried out, the last remaining water holes along the bed of the Narus River attracted a huge range of animals and birds from the surrounding arid plains. All the ungulates, eland, zebra, hartebeest and giraffe, were there, searching for grazing. Buffalo rolled in the drying mud and pretty little oribi and reedbuck hid in the small patches of surviving longer grass.  Troops of baboons and Vervet monkeys quarrelled with each other. Families of warthogs ran daintily past, tails in the air as if off on an important journey.

Ostrich and black rhino and even a pride of lions were further away but easy to spot in the bright sunlight and the clear air.

'It must have been like this in Baker's day,' I said, as we gazed on an unspoilt world.

'We fight the poachers and the Karamojong,' said the Ranger, 'that's what keeps the animals alive.'

We were not much concerned about the ethics of preserving a vast tract of traditional hunting ground free from tall men with spears just for the enjoyment of a handful of almost exclusively European visitors. For us, as the tension eased from our tired bodies and minds, it was enough to witness the beauty of it all. In the afternoon we went even further north into the dry Kidepo Valley and there saw huge herds of gazelle and giraffe set against the back-drop of the Turkana escarpment to the east. Driving slowly back to the camp, through the deeply peaceful light of evening, we came across a group of six black rhino including a tiny calf, and another pride of lions with three small cubs. It seemed the nearest thing to the Garden of Eden.

We had agreed, before leaving on our journey to Kidepo, to try to visit a Pastor from West Nile who was serving the Church of Uganda at Kaabong, a hot Karamojong town to the south of the park. So we spent the morning revelling in more glorious game-viewing and then drove out of the Park down the Kaabong road. We were stopped at a road block set up by two very drunk Army men. The car was searched for arms.

'Where are you going and why are you going there?' they asked. We tried to explain about the visit to the Pastor but they were too drunk to understand.

'We're coming back to Kidepo tonight,' I said, perhaps unwisely.

'Our President is coming,' they told us. 'You must come to meet him.'

Eventually, they got bored and let us go and we drove into the town. Behind the small corrugated iron church, on what looked like a rubbish heap, we found the Pastor's house. This saintly man, a Lugbara from near Arua, and his Lugbara wife were trying to live in a small corrugated iron hut, one room for them and all their five children. Their survival in Kaabong was something of a miracle. They lived in the heat and flies of Karamoja, amongst people who were at best indifferent, often resentful and at worst tried to steal what little they had. With just the tiny Pastor's allowance, no land to cultivate for beans or groundnuts, no water, drains or electricity, this couple had come to work in their mission field, facing hardships far greater than the British missionaries who had trained them in the large Church community back home across the Nile. We could do no more for them than bring greetings from home, take photos to show to their families and promise to send copies. We accepted their sweet, milky tea and prayed with them for a while, feeling deeply humbled by their total commitment.

We left Kaabong well before night-fall and drove slowly back along the road to Kidepo, mulling over what we had learnt from Pastor Ezekieli. The Church in Karamoja was slowly growing in confidence and numbers. Their role as distributors of emergency famine relief had become less important as the devastating drought of the previous five years had eased and the small town developed. Now they had a church with regular Sunday services, many children came to their Sunday School and they felt that God had blessed their brave decision to serve him so far away from home. They had much to teach us about not giving up.

About half way back to the Park, we were driving along one of the few straight sections of the road when I spotted an Army Land Rover coming towards us in a cloud of dust. Lights flashing, arms waving and car weaving from side to side, the driver and his companion clearly wanted us to stop. So I did, waiting for them to do likewise.

'They're not stopping,' Jenny shouted as they got closer and closer, now on our side of the road, heading straight for us.

Fortunately, our engine was still running so when the Army vehicle was about twenty yards away, I put our car into reverse and shot off backwards down the road. They went on flashing and waving their arms, but they were slowing down and eventually we both stopped. Two very large, very drunk and very angry Army men got out.

'You did not stop,' shouted the one who grabbed the door handle on my side. 'Get out of the car!'

It seemed foolish to argue now that we were stationary. At least we were still in one piece, however terrified.

'I'm sorry,' I said. 'We tried to stop as soon as we could.'

The apology seemed to please him. 'I shall search your car.' So we all stood by the road-side as they examined what little was left in the car – most of our belongings were still in the huts at Kidepo.

'What is this?' He held up the tube which normally held a tyre pressure gauge, peering at it with bloodshot eyes.

'It is the case for a pressure gauge,' I told him.

'It is the barrel of a pistol. We are confiscating it. And what is this?' He held up the dusty remains of a Mars bar. 'It is chocolate,' I explained, 'good to eat.'

'It is explosive,' he announced. 'We shall take it too. Now you may go.' And with that, they got back into their car, drove round us and off to Kaabong in a cloud of dust.

We were still shaking with shock as we got back into our car and drove very slowly back to Kidepo. As we passed through the Park gate, a very worried Ranger stopped us.

'I am sorry,' he said. 'The President has come. The Army has need of your rooms and we have had to move you. They told me to put all your things in the huts right at the end. It is a long way from the bar. I am sorry. But they said that you should come this evening and meet the President. General Amin is having a party with the Army Band.'

By the time the band started to play and the chorus of frogs was drowned by the insistent beat of Congolese dance music, we had decided to go to bed. So we never did get to meet the President whose loyal servants we had become. By the morning, feeling less shaken but worried that we might meet yet more drunken Army men, we slipped out of Kidepo at first light and drove as quickly as we could back the way we had come, four hundred miles to the west and back across the Nile. Our experience over those few days of almost meeting the President taught us one sad truth. Europeans by and large survived in Amin's Uganda, frightened but still alive. It was very different for the Asians and worst of all for the Ugandans themselves.

## 4.2 Picking up the pieces

This time the Army stopped us at Pakwach Bridge and searched the car with drunken insolence. They stole the starter handle and the lever for the jack.

'Weapons,' they said, waiving them over Jenny's head by the roadside.

We did not argue but it was not a good beginning to our return to West Nile. Then, as we reached the corner where the road to Arua turns right in Nebbi village, we saw two girls in brown skirts carrying water on their heads and we recognised them.

'Stop,' said Jenny. 'It's Akello in S4 and the girl who won the 200m in the Sports last year.'

They had seen the khaki Land Rover and hesitated, apprehensive of the Army. Then Akello spotted Jenny and Wendy and shyly waved.

'You have come back,' she said, with a smile. We had come back and we knew that at least some of the Mvara students would welcome us. There was some hope, both for us and for the school.

More than a month after the strike, the Police agreed that we could move back onto the New Site and start to clear up the mess of broken glass and damaged buildings. At least we had something to do while the Ministry decided what was to happen. Lewis and Angela announced that they did not wish to return to the school and Lewis sent his resignation in to the Bishop as Chairman of Governors. It was a sad end to all the years he had served as Head. The Governors and most of the Arua community wanted to thank him for his efforts to lead Mvara through these difficult years and they decided to present him with a leopard skin as a fitting present to one they thought of as a 'chief'. I had to get permission from the Game Department to buy such a skin, track down a supplier and then get an export licence. All this was done and Lewis was presented with his skin by a grateful Board, before he and all his family drove down to Kampala one last time in the big black Mercedes.

Then a telegram arrived. 'To Acting Deputy HM, Mvara SS. Report immediately to Ministry.' I filled Matilda with petrol, oil and water and set off yet again on the road to Kampala. When I reached the office of the Chief Education Officer in Crested Towers, the 'Mvara Enquiry Report' lay on his desk, a green folder containing hundreds of sheets. All that 'evidence' recorded at the dozens of meeting had reached some conclusions. The CEO's finger tapped the file.

'I want you to read the marked pages,' he said, handing me the folder. It did not take long to skim through all the hate-filled comments of students, parents and some staff.

'Mr Haden is too proud…..is too rude to some teachers….behaves like a policeman……thinks he is the best science teacher ……..abuses students ………despises Africans ……..' line after line in a litany of criticism from two and a half years of striving to do what I thought was right. I reached the end of the marked section and began to read the part headed 'Conclusions'.

'That does not concern you,' the CEO said abruptly, removing the file from my hands. 'It is confidential. But are the things they say about you, true, Mr Haden?'

With a crimson face, I spluttered a reply. 'Some people may believe that those things are true. But much of it I know to be nothing but malicious, vicious lies.'

The CEO watched my embarrassment with a half-smile.

'It is interesting, isn't it, that we Africans do not blush as you do. Having a black skin helps us to hide our emotions. But with you, we see the anger on your face and we judge it. Grown men should be in control. You, Mr Haden, cannot hide your feelings and we think that such a man is still like a child. Perhaps we misunderstand you and judge you harshly.'

Then he opened a drawer in his desk and handed me an envelope, addressed to me as Acting Deputy Headmaster, Mvara Senior Secondary School, Arua.

'Read it,' he said. 'I dictated it yesterday.'

The letter simply told me that I was appointed Acting Headmaster of the school with immediate effect until further notice. I was to reopen the school within three weeks and re-call all the students except for the following S4 Boys: Onzi, Acidri, Umari A, Kiri. These were to be told in person that they are suspended until further notice and to be warned that they would not be re-joining the school. The S4 girls were to be told to return one month after the school had re-opened. The letter finished with the CEO's congratulations and best wishes for every success in my new post.

'Do you have any questions?' he asked, smiling now at the red-faced Acting Head of the school. 'You see, we do support the Heads and Deputies of schools that get into trouble with their students. You can suspend those four boys as soon as you like.'

I had no questions, just wondered how it would be possible to re-build the trust that had been so thoroughly destroyed in those hours of madness a month before.

'You will not be Acting Head for long,' he smiled. 'Just long enough to show to everyone that students who go on strike are always punished and silly girls who won't go to bed have to learn to do what they are told. We still need teachers from Britain and we don't want to cause problems for your colleagues in other schools.'

What he did not say was that he needed me, a white face with none of the ties of family, clan and tribe that

Ugandan colleagues had, to sort out the problems at the school and then be disposed of, if necessary back to England, when the job was done. I would just have to do what I could but it was with a feeling of foreboding that I drove all the way back to Arua with the keys to the school in my pocket.

Local reaction to the news of my appointment was immediate. Someone had chalked across the new Office door 'Next Headmaster must be African'. The Quartermaster resigned, the cooks followed him and the Ugandan teaching staff, my neighbours and, I thought, my friends, at first ignored my presence. Some of the students wrote letters to their new Acting Headmaster saying how sorry they were at what had happened and asking me to re-open the school as soon as possible. Letters like this encouraged us in the days when the staff silence seemed so oppressive. There was work to do and first the named boys had to be seen. I wrote to their parents and guardians, summoning them to a meeting at the school office. Three of them, Acidri, Umari and Kiri, came with their parents on the day that I had specified. They were silent as their parents spoke to me in Lugbara through the office secretary.

'They say that they are sorry that their sons have disgraced them. They ask that the Board and the Ministry forgive them for the bad things that they have done. We are truly sorry.'

I asked the boys what had happened. Why had the girls behaved so stubbornly and why had the Prefects all resigned?

'We told the girls to resist the lights-out rule and we persuaded the other Prefects to resign,' Acidri explained. 'But we did not know that there would be shooting. When the night came, we all met in the Dining Hall and got the idea that the staff houses should be stoned, just to frighten the teachers. Some of us had been drinking but we did not plan to hurt anyone. Then the boy was shot and we had to get him to Hospital. While we were away, Mr Read's car was attacked and we are sorry that he was hurt because he was a good teacher. Sir, what will happen to us?'

I explained again that they had all been suspended and that the final decision would be sent to them once the school had been re-opened. I told them that I would tell the Board and the Ministry that they had come to see me with their parents and that they had said how sorry they were. Perhaps they would find places in a different school.

When Onzi came, on his own a few days after the day I had given him, it was very different. He was the student I had taken home for drinking when he was in S2. He had behaved himself well enough since to be appointed a Prefect in S4. He came into the Office, eyes red and without school uniform.

'You say that I must come, Mr Acting Headmaster,' his sneering voice mocking me. 'I am suspended and must come to ask for forgiveness. You have been busy, Mr Acting Headmaster, running up and down to Kampala. Why do you not go home to England with your buttock-less wife?'

'Onzi, you have been suspended and the Board will decide when, if ever, you will be allowed to come back to school. My advice is for you to apologise for what has happened and to ask them to reconsider their decision.'

'I shall never apologise. This is Africa; we do not apologise to white men.'

He reached over the desk and picked up the Kakwa knife that Lewis had used for opening letters.

'I am a man, Mr Haden, I am a man.'

His breath stank of cheap alcohol. As we stood facing each other over the desk, he started to stab the surface of the desk with the knife. I picked up the 'phone.

'Miss Apio? Please get me the Police'

'But Sir, the line is down,' she said in a frightened voice.

'Miss Apio, the Police please.' I put the 'phone down, hoping that she would not come bursting in.

'They will be here in a few minutes. Now put the knife down and sit down, Onzi. You are in enough trouble already. Go home now and wait there to hear what the Governors finally decide.'

Still muttering under his breath, Onzi flung the knife at the wall where it stuck vibrating in the notice board.

'I am a man,' he said once more, and with that, turned on his heel and strode out of the door. As he left the school car-park, Miss Apio came rushing in.

'The line is down,' she bleated. 'I could not get the Police.'

'Don't worry,' I said. 'We don't need them now.'

*

We had one week after that to get the school open again, a week of frantic re-timetabling to try to cover the classes that David Read, Angus Mackay and Lewis had been teaching. We met as a staff, a tense and painful meeting at which I did most of the talking. Very little was agreed, except that we would open on the date already decided by the Board and announced over the radio. It was the day before the Ministry deadline. The school had no quartermaster or cooks, too few teachers and two full months of teaching time had been lost. If there ever was a good time for students to complain, it was now. But when they returned, quietly taking their mattress rolls and boxes to their dormitories; no-one said a word. The quartermaster sheepishly turned up at the office and asked if he could have his resignation back. I told him that I thought the office had lost it. The cooks started work again and a meal was served that first evening, *enya* for all, and unlike any previous beginning of term, they were all there.

We did not hold an assembly for the re-opening of the school. It seemed to me to be better just to get on with it. On the Wednesday of the second week back, another telegram arrived addressed to 'Acting HM, Mvara SS'. It read: 'Aneco arriving Friday to be HM of school, CEO, Kampala.' We were to have our old Deputy back, this time as Head. The good news got round the school very fast and it was as if a cloud had been lifted from us. The Ugandan staff actually greeted me in the morning and everyone smiled. In one decision, the CEO had transformed our fortunes from limping along in the shadow of disaster to a confident future. When Dison and Esther moved back into the school, I handed the school keys to him and wished him luck. He grinned.

'Just like last year, John. We'd better make a start.'

I had been Acting Head of the school for just twenty days. It was a day short of the three weeks which was the minimum period for the payment of an Acting Head's allowance – just another reminder of my status as a thoroughly disposable contract officer.

As soon as the school had settled down, Jenny and I began to plan the next few months. She was due to go on leave at the end of May, giving her the three months holiday at the end of her contract to plan the wedding arrangements and to get ready for coming back to Uganda towards the end of August. Our contract arrangements made our marriage financially disastrous. As a married woman, Jenny had to resign her contract or at least not renew it. She nevertheless agreed with Dison that when I returned to my post as his Deputy at Mvara after the wedding, she would continue to teach at the school on 'local terms'. This meant a cut of about half her contract salary and no three months leave or gratuity at the end of two years. But since my contract would be ending in 1972, this actually made some sense as we could then go home together, but the loss of half her salary was galling.

Even in that busy term, there was time for journeys away from the school. I drove one day down to the Nile to try to find the place they called Wadelai. I had been told that it was where the Inde-Pakwach road passed close by the River Nile but would be hidden now in the long grass after the rains had come. I asked some young Madi fishermen mending their nets by their dugout canoes on the Nile bank, where the fort called Wadelai was.

'Wadelai?' They looked blank but one ran off to find a friend who knew the language of the *muzungu*. He came back with a boy in his green school shirt and khaki shorts.

'Do you know where Wadelai is?' I asked him.

'I know and I will take you.'

So my guide and the fishermen walked through the grass beside the river and came to an area of low rectangular mounds.

'This is Wadelai,' he said. 'There is nothing.'

He was right. It was the place where Emin Pasha had set up a community of Sudanese soldiers. This colourful German character, originally named Schnitzer, had been appointed Governor of Equatoria by Gordon of Khartoum and became Emin when he converted to Islam. When the British Army reached Khartoum too late to save Gordon from being hacked to pieces by the Mahdi's followers, Emin retreated up the Nile. From 1885, he was based at Wadelai, cut off from the outside world. He built boats in a dock, collected specimens of animals and plants, got his followers to grow fields of maize and lived a 'Robinson Crusoe' life[2] but with ten thousand companions. His Sudanese soldiers married the local women, gathered honey and made candles from beeswax. They wore clothes made of grass when their uniforms wore out and escorted Emin in his travels up and down the Nile hunting elephant and stockpiling ivory said to be worth a fortune.

The overgrown earth banks at Wadelai had been occupied for fifty years. According to Winston Churchill, who called in at Wadelai in 1907 after his rhino hunting triumph, *'the feeble rush-light of modernity, of cigarettes, of newspapers, of whisky and pickles, had burned on the banks of the White Nile, to encourage and beckon the pioneer and settler. None had followed. Now it was extinguished... and yet I could not bring myself for a moment to believe that civilisation has done with the Nile Province or the Lado Enclave[3].... '*

For a brief time in the late 1880s, this obscure place was the focus of much interest in London. If the British had failed to rescue Gordon, could they rescue Emin Pasha? But it was not at all clear that Emin wanted to be rescued and, even if he did, whether he was still holding out at Wadelai. Henry Morton Stanley, of 'Dr Livingstone, I presume' fame was recruited to find Emin and bring him safely to the Coast at Zanzibar. After an appalling journey to Lake Albert via the rain-forests of the Congo, Stanley did meet Emin on the shores of the Lake. By then, it was Stanley who was most in need of help. After months of wrangling, these two strong characters managed to agree on a joint exodus to the Coast. Many of Emin's Sudanese soldiers had no wish to accompany them and stayed at Wadelai. Stanley and Emin eventually reached Bagomayo in December 1889.

But when they arrived at the Indian Ocean coast, Stanley and Emin attended a celebration dinner organised by the German residents. Emin fell off a balcony and it was feared that he had broken his skull. Stanley left him there to recover and returned to Cairo alone to write the story of his epic rescue, *'In Darkest Africa'*. The German doctor, meanwhile, recovered from his fall and attempted to get back to join his old soldiers in the Lake Albert region. After a succession of disasters, old, sick and nearly blind, Emin turned for help to the Arab slave-traders. They betrayed his trust and had him murdered. His head was sent to the Chief who controlled the upper reaches of the River Congo. By the time news of his death reached the outside world, Europe's interest in what was happening in the Nile valley had moved to the next phase of the 'Scramble for Africa' and Wadelai slipped back into quiet insignificance.

In 1902, when the British wanted to recruit soldiers for their newly formed King's African Rifles, they signed on many from the Nubi communities in West Nile and found that they made very good soldiers. They also recruited heavily from the Kakwa and Lugbara people and from the Acholi and Langi people of the north and east of Uganda. This fitted in well with the British Army's view that there were 'martial tribes' in different parts of the world whose men, under the leadership of the British, would turn into good soldiers. These were 'splendid chaps' to their officers, tough, strong and resilient, and not too intelligent or well educated.

\*

Before Jenny left to go on leave and to prepare for our wedding, we drove once more down to the Okebu country to see the men who had promised to come to try to smelt iron now that the Arua smiths had failed. They also wanted us to collect a supply of what they called *iza*.

'It's literally shit of iron,' Peter Ogani explained helpfully. 'They say you need it if the smelting is to be successful.'

Since the *ubi* was still in my garden although becoming overgrown with grass and weeds, I agreed to collect this *iza* one weekend. We drove down to Logiri with Jenny Burgess, one of the nurses at Kuluva. The countryside was green again as the rain had come and the high road along the Congo border gave wonderful views to east and west. We collected two sacks of *iza* from Peter's father and were driving gently back to Arua when we hit a bad pot-hole. I soon realised that something was very wrong with Matilda. The steering wheel did not seem to be attached to the front wheels; it just spun round in my hands. The *murram* road was straight, with high earth banks on both sides and for few hundred yards the car ran down the centre. Then Matilda very gradually veered to one side of the road until one set of wheels was well up the bank. We came to a gentle halt and the car rolled onto its side, with Jenny Burgess at the bottom, my Jenny on top of her and me sliding down onto both. None of us were hurt, apart from the indignity of being in a heap, and we clambered out of the door on the upper side.

One of the features of West Nile is that however empty the countryside seems, within a very short time, children appear. They stood around the car calling 'How are you?' which seemed an odd thing to ask, given that our car had just rolled onto its side. We were not a bit all right and needed help. Jenny Burgess could speak Lugbara and discovered that there was a village not far away. She asked one of the taller boys to go for help. Soon the village school-teacher came to see what the exciting event was on the Logiri road and promised to send someone on a bicycle to Kuluva to get help. We sat by the car lying on its side and waited. As the night closed in, Ted Williams turned up in one of the hospital Land Rovers. With the help of the local villagers, we tipped Matilda back onto her tyres and he towed her backwards off the road. He asked the local people to look after her until we could get Mr Kawa to tow her back to Arura.

'Hop in,' he said. 'I'll take you home.'

Next day, Mr Kawa did come with me to collect Matilda, with a tool kit and a fairly new drop-arm.

'Off an army car which had a smash and we're now mending,' he said with a grin. 'They won't miss it for a day or two.'

With the steering back in action, I drove Matilda in to his workshop in Arua and a few days later picked her up, back in one piece. The sacks of *iza* were still in the back and I showed it to Peter Ogani.

'When can we try again?' he asked.

'When Miss Peck has gone back to England and I have more time,' I told him. Soon afterwards, I drove Jenny down to Kampala to stay with a friend at Budo for a weekend before she caught her London flight from Entebbe. It would not be long before the wedding.

Meeting up with friends in Kampala, if only for a weekend, enabled me to catch up on what had happened outside West Nile since the Coup. Teachers from Jinja College told us of the immediate aftermath of the take-over, when Amin's followers eliminated the Acholi and Langi in the Jinja Barracks. As the last few soldiers from Obote's areas broke and ran from the execution squads, they came through the college campus. The teachers were trapped for a time in their houses by the army's firing until the last soldiers were shot. Other teachers had seen the truckloads of bodies that were driven down to the great dam at Owen Falls to be tipped into the white waters of the Nile.

With many of the senior army officers eliminated and sections of both the Army and the General Service Unit still on the run, and with the police uncertain as to which of their senior officers would disappear next, law enforcement in the Kampala area broke down completely. The problem of *kondos*, armed robbers which had begun to be active under Obote, was rife. People think twice about going out to visit friends or to have a meal when doing so runs the risk of losing your car and belongings at the point of a gun along the road. With the Army now 'maintaining national security' on 'anti-guerrilla operations' and the Police trying to stay out of trouble, the *kondos* had a field day.

I also learnt of other schools where the general atmosphere of insecurity had spilled over into strikes. At a boys' boarding school in Busoga, a rioting mass of students had ransacked the Headmaster's house and set fire to his car before order was brutally restored by the Army. At another school in the Eastern region, all the students had been sent home after a total breakdown in discipline. We, at Mvara, were not alone in our troubles.

I drove back to finish off the term and was soon reminded that I had agreed to return to the iron-smelting project. Peter Ogani and his friends were hoping to try again, convinced that they would succeed this time. I had discussed our first try with Hamo Sassoon, the Uganda Conservator of Antiquities and had also told him of some local artefacts, including what the Lugbara called 'thunder stones'. These seemed to be hand tools, small axes made of haematite, but no-one seemed to know much about them. While he was with us, trying to investigate these 'thunder stones', it seemed a good time to show him what we knew of Okebu iron smelting. A few years before, while he was working in Nigeria, he had seen the iron workers of Sukur in north-eastern Nigeria smelting iron and he was very interested in our Okebu project. The expert arrived and the boys borrowed a set of bellows and rebuilt the clay *ubi* ready for their second smelting attempt. We had plenty of 'shit of iron', the magic ingredient, this time and the boys made sure that there were no girls around to spoil the day.

They pumped all morning and things were looking good. An old Okebu elder from Logiri turned up and explained to the boys that now they must 'pole' the iron forming in the furnace, because the *iza* was beginning to flow. I had no idea what this meant but when the old man grabbed a green-wood pole and began to work the hot mass at the centre of the furnace into a red-hot lump, I could understand. From the partially smelted *iza*, a mass of spongy iron had formed on the end of the *lia*, the clay pipe through which air was blown into the fire. This spongy lump could be worked until the iron stuck together to form a red-hot mass which could then be lifted out by using the centre of the green-wood pole beaten out to form a strap. Out came a hot mass of iron and slag to be hammered to remove most of the slag before it was quenched in a pool of water. They had made their iron. More heating and beating reduced the lump to a solid block of about two pounds of iron. Peter Ogani solemnly took a small magnet liberated from the Physics laboratory out of his shorts pocket and held it by the lump. It sprang across the gap with a satisfying 'clunk'.

'Sir, we have made our iron,' he said proudly, with a great grin. 'We are Okebu!'

Hamo Sassoon was impressed and told them that they must ask their teacher to write a proper scientific account of the smelting process. He would make sure that it was published in the Uganda Journal[4] and the team would be true Scientists. The boys were absolutely delighted and rushed off to tell the girls.

*

With Jenny gone and my teaching load increased to cover her A level classes, there was little time to relax that term. Her letters came more regularly than mine went back and the details of the wedding, what presents people wanted to give us, who we needed to visit and where we planned to go for a honeymoon, it all passed in a blur. Just after my twenty-ninth birthday I flew home for nineteen days 'casual leave' to get married. 'Don't marry before you're thirty,' my father had advised me. I very nearly made it as a bachelor to his deadline. After a four-day whirl of suit hiring, licence applications and pre-nuptial visits to key relatives, we were married by Seton Maclure in Rugby Methodist Church in the company of all our family and friends. After the heat and challenge of Uganda, nothing seemed more natural to us than to hide for our brief honeymoon in a corner of England. We chose Durham and Northumberland, for their glorious countryside and castles. When it rained for almost three days non-stop, we found that Durham Cathedral was a good place to go for a long dry walk, hand in hand, freed from the eyes of black children who had followed our courtship and commitment.

*

Throughout those first six months of Idi Amin's Presidency, life had continued as usual for most of the ex-patriates still in Uganda. From January to March a postal strike in the UK meant that we had very little news from home and those there who were anxious about us had to make do with newspaper reports of what was happening. The UK press largely supported Amin's ousting of Obote and his brand of African Socialism and when the Baganda were burying their beloved Kabaka, the celebrations were part of a generally favourable view of what was happening. Only Colin Legum, writing in the Observer, offered a contrary view, reporting on the deaths in the Uganda Army of Acholi and Langi soldiers and of 'bodies, floating in the Nile below Karuma Bridge'.

In Kampala, preparations for the June Conference of the Organisation of African Unity pressed ahead with the building of a massive new hotel and conference centre at enormous expense. Under pressure from Tanzania's Nyerere and Kenya's Kenyatta, both implacably opposed to Amin, the OAU was forced to move the meeting to Rabat.

Field Marshall Idi Amin, President of Uganda

In July, Amin decided that he needed jet fighters and flew to Israel to ask for their help. They had, after all, provided Uganda with material and technical support for several years. Golda Meir was surprised to be asked for Phantom jets to 'attack Tanzania', according to her visitor. The Israelis refused to supply him with any advanced weaponry but they did agree to work on improvements to Entebbe Airport and to start the development of the small airport in Arua to 'international' standards with a long new runway. From Israel, Amin travelled to London, uninvited, to ask the British Government for military aid. He was hastily welcomed by the Queen at Buckingham palace as a visiting Head of State, but the British also turned down his request for arms just as the Israelis had done. They did agree to send an army training mission to Uganda instead.

*

We hurried back to West Nile in late August 1971 at the end of my nineteen days of leave and were met by Dison Aneco as we drove into the school.

'I'm sorry, John,' he said. 'I've asked the Ministry to transfer you from Mvara.'

While we were away, he had been down to Kampala to discuss the future of the school with the CEO. They had decided that it would be easier for him if I was no longer his Deputy. There was too much history involved. We were to pack our things, leave the house and garden that I had planned to bring Jenny back to and go we knew not where. Mvara no longer had a use for me. I was very angry that all this had been decided while we were away in England. It was both a bitter disappointment and a shock to both of us but I could see Dison's point of view. If the school was to have a stable future, as we all hoped that it would, it would be better to have a fresh team. That meant I had to go somewhere else.

The next morning, as we sadly packed up our things, the telegrams began to arrive. 'Two science teachers needed Fort Portal Nyakasura come immediately.' 'Hadens expected 25$^{th}$ Mbale SS.' 'Budo has posts for Chemists and RK teachers, advise availability.' 'Trinity College Nabbingo, two chemists expected.' It was good to be so badly needed but I wanted to get to Kampala to talk to the advisers at the Ministry before I agreed to anything. We said our sad farewells to Erinesti and Onessimo, the two 'house-boys' who had served each of us so well, to Wendy, Val and the Corkers, to the friends at Kuluva, and to our Ugandan colleagues. We drove away from Mvara in a state of shock. In spite of all that had happened in Arua, we were very sad that we had to go.

Staying in Kampala with Margaret and Peter Childs, I went to see Colin Brown, the senior British civil servant who was there to support ODA contract officers. He did his best to be helpful.

'You just have to accept that the Ministry makes the decisions, John, and there may be advantages for you both to being in or around Kampala.'

By the end of that week we had sorted out where we wanted to be from the dozen or so offers that still came chasing after us. Makerere College School, on the campus of Makerere University in the heart of Kampala, needed an A level Chemistry teacher to run their Chemistry Department and to work part-time on the University teacher training course. Margaret Childs was already teaching there so we knew something of the school. There was a house on campus and our advisor was sure that Jenny would be able to find a post in one of the Kampala schools. So we agreed and arranged for a Ministry lorry to collect all the belongings left in Arua and bring them down to our new home. There was just one more task for me before starting the new job. Angus Mackay had been charged with the manslaughter of the Mvara S3 boy who had died from his gun-shot wounds in Arua hospital. Angus' trial was moved to Gulu to ensure that the local anger in Arua did not influence the outcome. I had to drive up to Gulu, stay with friends at Sir Samuel Baker School and appear as a witness in the Gulu court room. I tried to answer as honestly as I could but as Angus had admitted firing the gun twice, there was little I could do to help him. No-one asked me about Betty's attitude to Africans, which was what had contributed to her panic. Nor did they ask me what I thought about the fact that the Mackays had left another teacher alone in the house with the doors open when they drove off in their car to 'escape from danger'. To me and to Jenny that fact condemned the Mackays in our eyes almost as much as the shooting. Angus was convicted of manslaughter, subject to appeal, and sentenced to seven years imprisonment in Uganda's appalling jails.

*

Our married life in Kampala started in a house with very little furniture. Without a double bed, we had to make do with two single metal bedsteads with sagging wire springs. I borrowed a row of G-clamps from the school's Physics store to hold the two beds safely together. To get from one side to the other involved a climb up to the edge and a very cosy sharing on the other side.

Colin Brown was right. There were advantages to being in Kampala. For a start, we had a large house and could share it with visitors from all over Uganda who soon discovered that we had a very convenient base for their shopping and business trips. This was fine by us as it kept us in touch with many friends, especially from West Nile. When Wendy Moore broke her hip badly and was brought down to Kampala for surgery, we could visit her in Mulago Hospital and provide her with a room for the weeks of convalescence. Janet Watford had moved to Busoga College, Mwiri, and would call in on her visits to Kampala. Other friends from Gulu, Kabale and Nairobi would arrive, partly to see us and mainly to do the things they had to do in the city.

It was also a good base for visitors from overseas, although we were not near enough to Entebbe to meet flights very easily. A group of young people from the Bible Institute of Los Angeles, the BIOLA Players, flew in to hold a series of evangelistic meetings for Ugandan young people based on a drama they had prepared. Churches were asked to host them. We were happy to offer hospitality to two of them and were just getting to know them when newcomers kept coming to our meals. On enquiring, we discovered that they had devised a scale of food quality in which Jenny's cooking was the clear leader. It seemed only fair to the BIOLA team that they should take turns to enjoy this, hence the new faces at our table each evening. That was fine although it would have been good to be asked. Less easy to accept was the request one day to Jenny from one young American to be shown our 'laundry facility'. 'You're talking to her,' was the response. The local community of house-girls roared with laughter when our washing line suddenly sported dozens of pairs of shorts of a brightness and length never before seen in Kampala. On their last night in the city, the BIOLA players kindly took us out to a very good dinner and we all went up to the roof of the building. Looking out over the busy streets below, one of our guests said, 'Isn't it great to be bringing the gospel to Kampala.' I could not help thinking that the CMS had been doing just that for almost a hundred years.

Professionally, Makerere College School with its strong team of British and Ugandan graduate teachers was a good place to work. The Nuffield based School Science Project was well established and 'learning by discovery' was easy to encourage amongst bright young pupils whose homes were largely amongst the professional and academic families of the university and government. The work with students from the University Department of Education was also stimulating and I very much enjoyed teaching on their PGCE course. Sometimes my school lessons would have a full class of thirty five pupils, half a dozen student teachers and the occasional visitor from overseas or from the Ministry, all working together in the large and well equipped labs.

For Jenny, teaching was less easy. She found a job at the Aga Khan School, an Asian day school not far from where we lived. The almost exclusively Asian pupils were not so able, tended to avoid hard work and tried to cut corners wherever possible. She found that supervising tests and exams was a nightmare as they had developed a wide range of cheating skills, from passing information between them to concealing cribs under their clothes and even between their feet and flip-flop sandals. She never really felt comfortable in the school but it was a job and, although the pay was half that of a Contract Officer, it was better than being at home all day.

But we never really settled in Kampala. For three years, I had lived in West Nile amongst non-Bantu people regarded as 'primitive' and 'uncivilised' by their fellow Ugandans around Kampala. Yet, once I had got used to the direct nature of their speech, I found the Lugbara, Madi and other West Nile peoples to be warm and welcoming most of the time, if lacking the sophistication of Southerners. Jenny shared that view. We also found that our Baganda students' love of formal obsequious greetings to men as 'my Lord', but not to Jenny as 'my Lady', ultimately irritating. It reminded me too much of D H Lawrence's comment on the irritating 'Oxford Voice', 'so seductively superior, so seductively, self-effacingly, deprecatingly, superior. '

\*

We both found that there were many opportunities in Kampala to get involved in the life of the church, in our case, All Saints in the city. Bible study groups, music groups, student Scripture Union groups all helped to convince us that this was where God wanted us to be for the moment in spite of the traumatic route we had followed to get there. In the school, the Scripture Union group was lead by a committee of students who were keen to go to the national conferences and weekend courses which we could take them to. This helped us to get to know the leaders well. Two of the most enthusiastic were Samuel Turyagyenda from Kigezi and Willie Kaddu from Kampala, both members of my S6 A level Chemistry set. We helped Willie and Sam to organise 'picnic' trips for the students down to the Entebbe Botanical Gardens where Peter and Margaret Childs would join us for the day.

Amin's move against the Uganda Asian community may have been presented to the outside world as a sudden decision in August 1992 prompted by a dream, but he had prepared his ground well. He knew that all the leaders of East Africa, Kenyatta in Kenya, Nyerere in Tanzania and Obote in Uganda, had been negotiating with the British for some time for the repatriation of Asians who held British passports. In 1969, Obote had said that they would 'just have to leave' but had not implemented this policy. Having delighted the Baganda by arranging for the return of the Kabaka's body, Amin knew how popular he would become in all parts of Uganda if he implemented Obote's plan for the exclusion of Asians with British passports. He started by ordering a census of Asians resident in Uganda in October 1971. By December, when over twelve thousand Asians had decided to apply for Ugandan citizenship, he abruptly cancelled these applications and bluntly told an assembly of Asian representatives that their own social exclusiveness had caused the bad feeling against them, which we knew to be all too true.

\*

In January 1972, Amin declared a week's national holiday to celebrate the anniversary of the Coup, the start of his $2^{nd}$ Republic of Uganda. For most rural boarding schools, this was a nightmare with hundreds of bored students unable to go to class and looking for local beer with which to join the celebrations. At Makerere, many of the students were able to go home so we set up a skeleton supervision staff leaving most of us free to do other things. I decided to try to get a job lined up for our return to England, due at the end of my contract in August 1972. With the Times Educational Supplement flown in to Entebbe only one day old, I could apply for all the UK Chemistry posts advertised - about a dozen that week.

I had discovered from Colin Brown that there was an obscure clause in my contract that would provide a free flight to London for any ODA officer who could get an interview for a post at a higher scale than his or her last post in England but no-one seemed to know how one did this. I invented an impressive form for Heads sufficiently interested in my application to want to interview me and sent these off, with an airmail reply form for them to send to me. The ruse paid off. Three weeks later I was on a plane to London with two interview invitations, both for promoted posts. Once landed, I rapidly applied for another job in Morpeth, Northumberland, which looked interesting. I borrowed my mother's car and set off around a freezing and dark England. It was then in the grip of power cuts, one of the crippling effects of the national miners' strike. Having failed at the first interview, I drove up to Morpeth, where my parents then lived, to be told by the Head that he wanted to offer me the job but had to find someone else to interview first.

'When you get to the airport on your way back to Uganda, give me a ring and I'll offer you the job.' he assured me.

On the strength of this verbal agreement, I drove to the south coast to attend a third interview which I was determined to fail. If I was offered that job, and then turned it down, I would have to refund the full cost of the air-fare. That was the deal with ODA. After a very poor interview, I left the car with a friend in London for my mother to pick up later, reached Gatwick in good time, 'phoned Morpeth and was offered a job.

Idi Amin had also been on his travels. Having failed to get significant military help from the Israelis or the British, he flew to Libya to ask Colonel Gaddafi as a fellow Muslim for help.

The visit was a great success. Libya offered US$10 million aid and military support. Amin's courting of the Libyans brought about the sudden expulsion of the Israelis and his pro-Arab support for the Palestinian cause. Unemployed young men in Kampala were even recruited for a new Middle Eastern War and the Christian majority in Uganda were surprised to hear that their President had told Gaddafi that his country was 'mainly Muslim'.

With a job to return to and a home in Kampala within the secure University campus, Jenny and I enjoyed most of our last few months in Uganda although we had little opportunity to get to know Baganda people really well. There were also anxieties about the rising number of *kondos* carrying out armed robberies in the city. No-one seemed to know whether these were disaffected soldiers wanting to deprive the affluent classes, known as the *Wabenzi*, of their smart cars, or whether the increasingly violent incidents were caused by criminal gangs. To most of us, trying to get on with the jobs we had to do, it made little difference.

Towards the end of the school term, Amin invited the King of Saudi Arabia to make a state visit. King Feisal and his entourage, with all their strict Saudi views on women and appropriate dress, were appalled to be entertained by a scantily clad Baganda dance troupe. The relaxed Amin thought that the semi-naked girls were very attractive but the King was deeply offended. The lengths of women's skirts suddenly became a national concern. A new law proclaimed that all skirts must be no shorter than three inches below the knee. That evening, girls going home in school uniform through the city streets were arrested by the Army. The length of their skirt was marked with a brutal *panga* slash across the thighs. Several of the girls had to be stitched up, literally, in Mulago Hospital. Our students wisely used long wrap-arounds over their uniform.

A few days after these horrors had become well known, Jenny and I were walking down to the Wandegaya Post Office to pick up our letters, now coming regularly from England. As we reached the P.O. Box racks, there was a sound of shooting. Two cars raced past, one hotly pursued by the other, with men hanging out of its windows and firing at each other. It was like a scene from an Italian gangster movie. Jenny was wearing a relatively short skirt. Convinced that they were firing at her and terrified that she might also be *pangered*, she grabbed my hand and dashed into the shelter of the Post Office. She was still shaking when we crept out a few minutes later to see the taxi drivers calmly plugging the bullet holes in their petrol tanks with chewing gum, as life got back to normal.

After that, it could never be normal again for us in Kampala. It was time to go. We found that we could not take Uganda Shillings out of the country but my contract covered a generous air baggage allowance. So, we invested in attractive Elgon Olive furniture made by a Danish company who arranged for it to be air-freighted to England. Matilda was next to go, sold in Kampala for more than we paid for her in Kenya two years before. Vehicles which could masquerade as Army officers' transport had a certain mark-up in Amin's Uganda. Our remaining shillings could, we thought, be invested in a new car to be delivered in England. The only company prepared to do such a deal was Renault so we ordered a small R4 and hoped that we, and it, would eventually get to London. We booked our flights just as the President had his dream and told the world that God had advised him to expel all the Asians from Uganda without delay. We left Entebbe just ahead of the panic-stricken escape of forty-five thousand British passport holders of Asian origin from Uganda. About four thousand British citizens with paler skins stayed, but wondered for how long.

Just before we left, we heard that Angus Mackay's appeal against his manslaughter conviction and sentence was to be heard in the East African Court of Appeal in Nairobi. His English barrister made much of the 'anarchy' at Mvara Secondary School. Chief Justice Kiwanuka, for the Uganda Republic, argued for the justice of the conviction and the need for a seven year sentence. The appeal was allowed on the grounds that 'the appellant was in such a position of danger that he could justifiably have fired his gun', according to the President and Vice President, both British. The Kenyan member of the Appeal Court dissented. The conviction was set aside and Angus freed to fly home to Scotland.

### 4.3 Amin's Tyranny

While we were getting used to the cold and wet of a Northumberland summer, General Idi Amin Dada set a deadline of three months for the departure of the Uganda Asians with British citizenship. He then included those with Indian, Pakistani or Bangladeshi nationality. Finally, even those who had become Ugandan citizens were told they had to leave, taking no more than US$100 each with them. All their considerable assets, houses, cars, businesses and belongings were taken by the Army and distributed to their fellow soldiers.

Perhaps we should all have seen this act of blatant racial discrimination coming. Had not Amin praised Hitler twelve months before and commended him for sending the Jews to the gas-chambers of Nazi Germany. Then Amin changed his mind again and announced that those Asians who could prove that they had Ugandan citizenship would after all be allowed to stay. Some six thousand out of a total of about forty five thousand managed to convince Amin's officials of their citizenship by the November deadline. By then, many of those who had citizenship had decided to join the mass exodus. The once rich Asian community of Uganda simply ceased to exist. Their businesses were taken, from small up-country *dukas* to massive industrial corporations such as the Madhvani Sugar Refinery and the Nytil Cotton Mills at Jinja, and given to Amin's friends. When they packed their belongings and left them at Entebbe to be shipped to England, the Army broke into the crates as their owners struggled to get out of Uganda by Amin's deadline.

In England, they were given a less than friendly welcome. Leicester City Council went to the lengths of advertising in the Kampala papers that the UK Uganda Resettlement Board's advice was that Asians 'should not settle in the city' as there was no space for them. They ignored the advice and went to that city and to other centres of Asian population. Temporary housing in disused military camps was provided for some. Churches and charities did their best to provide teachers and medical support but most of the homeless Asians found succour amongst their extended family members already in England, the USA or Canada. Those for whom there was no other help turned to the Red Cross who flew them out of England to refugee centres scattered across the world.

Several accounts of the Asian expulsion have been written from their own point of view. The most interesting is by one who was very successful in England. Manzoor Moghal[5], well-known writer and commentator who was born in Pakistan, grew up in Uganda and was a leader of the Asian community at the time of Amin. He knew Amin as an affable and shrewd soldier whose public buffoonery hid a subtle charm in private meetings. Manzoor believed that the British were wrong to ridicule Amin even if he seemed to them to be beyond the pale of civilisation. As a well-connected businessman, Manzoor knew all the key leaders of Uganda before the coup in 1971, the

Kabaka, Fancis Walugembe, his one-time Katakiro or Chief Minister, Benedicto Kiwanuka, the leader of the Democratic Party and later Amin's Chief Justice. As each of them died or disappeared, Manzoor learnt that he too was on Amin's hit list. He and his immediate family held full British passports and he was assured that entry to Britain would be no problem. In the middle of the night of 9$^{th}$ September 1972, he and his wife and their three young sons managed to buy seats on a flight to Frankfurt. His wife lost all her jewellery at the customs desk and they left all their belongings including all their photos in Uganda.

Yet Mansoor developed a respect for, perhaps even something of an admiration, for Idi Amin. When he decided to re-write his 1970s account of their experience and publish it as a book in 2009, he chose the title '*Idi Amin – Lion of Africa*'. From his new base in Leicester, Manzoor built a new business for his family and became a respected community leader. He chaired Leicestershire County Council's Race-relations Committee, work that was recognised in the award of a MBE. Unique perhaps amongst the British Asian community, he even managed to meet Idi Amin again while on a pilgrimage to Mecca in 1986. After dining together, they ended up having a long and interesting conversation. Mazoor clearly had a grudging admiration for Idi, the man, who was living in Saudi Arabia as a sprightly eighty year old without ever having been brought to justice for the crimes he committed. Mansoor found that he neither hated Amin for what he did to his family, nor felt any joy when he died in a Saudi hospital in 2003.

*

In the midst of the huge upheaval of the expulsion of the Asians in September 1972, an abortive attempt was made by pro-Obote forces to invade Uganda from Tanzania. The plan involved flying a plane-load of guerrillas from Kilimanjaro Airport to Entebbe to capture the Airport. They would then link up with a land attack from the south-west. This ill-conceived strategy soon turned into a shambles. The plane they hijacked to take soldiers to Entebbe crash-landed at Kilimanjaro Airport when the Ugandan pilot failed to get the undercarriage down. The army lorries carrying men across the Uganda border from Tanzania were delayed because no-one had thought to fill their tanks with petrol. When the invading troops eventually got into Uganda, they met stiff resistance from Amin's soldiers. Most of the invaders were killed, captured or fled, although a young guerrilla leader by the name of Museveni managed to get his lorry and his men back to Tanzania. He was one of the few who could drive. Amin was the hero of the hour. Not only had he rid Uganda of the hated Asians, he had seen off an attack from Obote and had a number of captives to parade around Ugandan towns. They were publically executed. Tanzania was forced to sign a non-aggression agreement and to close the training camps for Obote's guerrillas.

Within Uganda, leading citizens were disappearing. The Chief Justice, Ben Kiwanuka, was dragged from his car and not seen again. Others fled into exile in Kenya. The elimination of thousands of Acholi and Langi soldiers in the Army continued. At the end of 1972, all new British aid to Uganda had ceased and Amin had nationalised the larger British firms still operating in Uganda. Through 1973, the disappearances and killings continued. Chiefs and sub-chiefs were replaced with soldiers, some of relatively low rank. Libya sent more aid to Uganda, including Mirage jets and armoured personnel carriers purchased from France with Libyan dollars. The Cold War competition for African support hotted up, with Russia and America both offering training opportunities for Ugandan personnel. Then the Americans decided to stop all direct aid to Uganda and, by the end of 1973, advised all US citizens to leave Uganda before closing their Kampala embassy.

By this time, Jenny and I had settled in our Morpeth semi-detached house and were worshipping at the local Methodist Church. After a world without evenings and full of children following us wherever we went, we enjoyed the empty spaces, open skies and wide beaches of Northumberland. In October 1973 our first son, Peter, was born and although we still kept in touch with friends in Uganda, that period of our lives seemed a long way away.

A year after getting home, we received an airmail letter from Samuel Turyagyenda, one of the SU leaders from Makerere College School, then living in Russia. He had completed his A levels and been sent by the Amin regime to be trained as a helicopter pilot in the Ukraine. He was very lonely, missing the fellowship of other Christians, and, as he had our address, he thought he would write to ask us to send him tapes and books of Christian songs. Then at least, in the isolation of his Russian Air Force barrack room, he would be able to sing on Sundays of the faith he still held. We sent a parcel of books and tapes and heard no more. I wondered if Sam would get into trouble importing such Christian material into the Soviet Union.

Samuel Turyagyenda in the uniform of a Russian cadet pilot

*

For the first two years of Amin's regime, the purges of Acholi and Langi in the Army continued. To fill the gaps and expand the Army with people whose loyalty he could rely on, Amin recruited new soldiers from the Lugbara, Kakwa and Madi people of West Nile. There was little other material benefit to West Nile from having Amin as President. More and more recruits were from the Islamic Nubi group and from Sudanese soldiers who had formerly fought with the Anyanya, the rebels fighting the Sudanese government. By 1977, the senior ranks of the Army, the Police and the General Service Units, were all in the hands of a small inner core of Kakwas and Nubians. Similarly, nearl all the Battalion Commanders and all the specialist unit commanders were from West Nile or Southern Sudan. Amin's Cabinet of Ministers was made up by 1977 of eleven senior military officers from his own area and just seven civilians.

Amongst these Amin henchmen, the head of the Public Safety Unit, Ali Towili, a Sudanese Moslem, and Isaac Muliyamungu, a Kakwa from the Congo, were particularly feared. It was they who were believed to be responsible for the disappearance of numerous leading individuals from all over Uganda. What had started with the killing of large numbers of Acholi and Langi soldiers had become a campaign of terror against any individual who opposed the regime. Thousands of leading individuals simply 'disappeared' between 1971 and 1979.

*

When the OAU agreed to hold their Heads of State conference in Kampala in May 1975, and when Amin became the Chairman of the OAU at the end of the Conference, there was a howl of protest from the Liberal West, but nothing was done. Everyone agreed that to have a ruthless dictator at the helm of the OAU was a disaster, but, to all but Nyerere and a few others, he was still a hero. In the event, Amin's year as OAU Chairman passed without a major crisis. Julius Nyerere in Tanzania harboured Obote, and many of those who had left when Amin took power. The Kenyans learnt to live with their new neighbour for as long as he remained at peace with them.

But after the expulsion of the Uganda Asians and the increasing evidence of loss of life amongst his enemies in Uganda, the world's view began to change. British Army officers, who were initially proud to call ex-Sergeant Amin their friend, soon found that they were needed. His former Company Commander, Major Ian Grahame, and Lt General Sir Chandos Blair, a former Commanding Officer of $4^{th}$ KAR, were sent in June 1974 to try to save a British lecturer, Dennis Hills, from execution. Hills had come to Uganda in 1964 to teach English at the National Teachers College, Kyambogo. He was working on the manuscript of a new book in 1975 when he carelessly let it fall into the hands of Amin's army. They took exception to his description of their President as a 'black Nero' and a 'village tyrant'. Hill was arrested, tried by military tribunal and found guilty of treason. His execution by firing squad was set for June $21^{st}$ 1975.

This prompted pleas for clemency from the British Prime Minister, the Archbishop of Canterbury, the Pope and the Heads of State of numerous countries. All were ignored but Amin intimated that he respected Queen Elizabeth II. She was persuaded to write personally to him pleading for clemency and the letter was taken out to Kampala by the two British officers who knew him best, Blair and Chandos[6]. As a result, Amin first postponed the execution and then agreed that Hills should be released into the hands of the British Foreign Secretary. This forced James Callaghan to fly to Entebbe to collect Hills, prompting Julius Nyerere of Tanzania to comment on the contrasting efforts to save the life of one white man, when tens of thousands of black men were being killed in Uganda.

\*

Just before our second son, Timothy, was born in November 1975, I had a phone call from the Dover immigration officer. He said he had a young man at the cross-Channel ferry terminal who claimed to know me. It was Sam. Since he had a month of leave from his helicopter training school, he had decided to visit the only people he knew living in the Northern Hemisphere. After many adventures, including having most of his money stolen in Poland, he had reached England. I assured the Immigration Officer that I did know him and that we would be pleased to look after him while he was in England. When Jenny heard this news, she was less enthusiastic.

Sam got to Morpeth just after Jenny came home after Tim was born. We found a bed for our visitor and a cot for our new baby, and Sam did his best to be helpful, baby-sitting Peter, while I was at school. When Jenny's mother and father came to help, we had to find a temporary home for Sam with friends down the road but he proved to be a very welcome guest. He even played basketball for the Morpeth school team, the first and probably last Ugandan to do so. When it was time for him to set off back to Russia, I took him down to spend a couple of days with Richard and Liz Inwood in Sheffield on his way to Dover, a visit which both sides still remember with pleasure. Then he went back to continue his training and we heard nothing more from him for several years.

*

In the following year, 1976, after Amin and the Palestinian PLO had signed an agreement for technical and scientific co-operation, an Air France plane was hijacked by Palestinian guerrillas. They forced the pilot to fly to Entebbe. Amin announced that he had taken charge of negotiations and the mainly Israeli hostages were moved to the old Airport Terminal. In a very short time, the Israelis planned a commando raid on this building for which they had full plans from their up-grading work for Uganda not long before. In what came to be recognised as one of the most daring and successful raids ever, the Israelis flew into Entebbe, captured the building, rescued the hostages and blew up a number of Russian MIG jets on their way out. They made the Ugandan Armed Forces and their President look very silly. Fortunately for Amin, the Russians soon arrived to replace the planes lost in the raid.

*

The world's fascination with Amin continued. In London, Punch entertained the British public by publishing his more outrageous pronouncements, turning a terrifying dictator into a figure of fun. Numerous books were published. Amongst the non-fiction accounts of Amin's regime, David Martin's *'General Amin'* was written as *'the most shocking exposé yet of the Seventies' bloodiest dictator'*. Henry Kyemba's *'A State of Blood'* was very much an 'inside story'. Kyemba was a Minister under Amin and was able to leave the country with his wife in circumstances very different from those faced by the Uganda Asians.

A handful of British individuals stayed in Uganda throughout the Amin years including Peter Allen, initially a District Police Officer who rose to be a judge and finally Chief Justice. Our friends, Peter and Margaret Childs, stayed for as long as they could at Makerere teaching in the University Chemistry Department. Many of those who were working with AIM, like Maureen Moore at Kuluva, the Maclures at Mvara, Joy Grindey at Koboko and the eye doctor Keith Waddell, stayed in quiet corners of the country and got on with their jobs.

*

Bishop Janani Luwum, of Northern Uganda, was based in Gulu and well aware of the suffering of the Acholi and Langi in the Army during the early Amin years. In 1974, he was elected by the Uganda House of Bishops to be Archbishop of Uganda, Ruanda, Burundi and Boga-Zaire. Luwum became the leading voice in criticizing the excesses of the Idi Amin regime as he came to know more and more of its brutality. In February 1977, Luwum and fellow bishops of the Church of Uganda issued a pastoral letter addressed to His Excellency Al-Haji, Field Marshall Dr Idi Amin Dada, VC, DSO, MC, CBE, President of Uganda. They were protesting against the increasingly marginalised position of the Christian church and against the behaviour of the security forces, who were using *'the gun in their hands to destroy instead of protecting civilians'*. Luwum delivered the letter to Amin and Amin called a conference of all religious leaders.

Luwum attended, accompanied by Bishop Wani of West Nile and Bishop Kivengere of Kigezi. Displayed to the guests at the conference were arms said to have been found at Luwum's house. These arms, it was alleged, had been supplied by Obote. Amin's Vice-President invited the troops on duty to decide what should be done with the Bishops. 'Kill them!' came the reply.

Janani Luwum, Archbishop of Uganda

Shortly afterwards, the Archbishop was told that the President wanted to see him. The other Bishops tried to accompany Luwum but were turned away. They never saw Luwum again, alive or dead. Luwum and two Ministers from Amin's cabinet were said to have been killed in a car crash which was so blatantly faked that even the Army could not conceal the truth. The bodies were not released to the families and the church. Amin had arranged for Luwum's body to be taken to a quiet corner of Acholi District and buried there in an unmarked grave.

Luwum's funeral service and burial had been planned by the Church of Uganda for Namirembe Cathedral at Easter 1977. But the grave outside the Cathedral remained empty and open as the Christians gathered. They turned what had been planned as a funeral into a celebration of the first Easter. Their grief at the loss of their Archbishop became a commemoration of the empty tomb of Jesus. When the Bishops met to elect a successor to Luwum, several of the Bishops had fled including the charismatic Festo Kivengere. Silvanus Wani, of West Nile, stayed and was elected to succeed Luwum. 'Someone must care for the sheep,' was his comment.

\*

One Ugandan who left his country at that time was John Sentamu. He was born the sixth of thirteen children in his family in a Baganda village not far from Kampala. He tells of his gratitude to a British teacher who helped him to get to school by providing a bicycle. Sentamu was a very good student and got to Makerere University to study law before becoming an advocate in the High Court. Amin made him a High Court Judge at the very early age of twenty four but he incurred Amin's wrath because of his judicial independence and was locked up for ninety days, just after he had got married. After being, in his own words '*kicked around like a football and beaten terribly*' he was tempted to give up hope of release.

Sentamu fled to England in 1974. There, he believed he was called to the Anglican ministry. After studying Theology and training for the ministry at Cambridge, Sentamu was ordained in 1979.

Archbishop John Sentamu outside York Minster

He served as Assistant Chaplain at Selwyn College, as Chaplain at a Remand Centre and as a curate and vicar in London before being consecrated Bishop of Stepney in 1996. He was an advisor to the Stephen Lawrence Enquiry and chaired the Damilola Taylor review before being appointed Bishop of Birmingham. In 2005, John Sentamu became the 97th Archbishop of York, after a long journey from the Baganda village where he was born and the prison cell he occupied in Idi Amin's Uganda.

Amin's tyranny continued through 1978, which he had declared 'a year of peace and reconciliation' for Uganda. As plans to remove him were debated outside Uganda, the killings inside the country went on. In July, the US Congress and Senate voted to stop all trade with Uganda except for food aid. Seeking to unite his increasingly restless army, Amin then decided to attack Tanzania, bombing border towns, on the pretext that Tanzania had attacked Ugandan territory. The Uganda Army crossed into the Kagera Salient, an area of Tanzanian territory across the border. They went on a wild orgy of looting, raping and killing Tanzanians. Nyerere responded by mobilizing the Tanzanian Peoples' Defence Force and moved them up to the border.

On January 21$^{st}$, four days short of the eighth anniversary of the Amin Coup, the Tanzanians invaded, supported by units of Ugandan guerrillas. This force steadily advanced into Uganda, capturing Mbarara and Masaka. As they did so, Colonel Gadaffi sent troops to support the Uganda Army, but it was clear that Amin's forces were being forced back. In Moshi, Tanzania, a conference was convened to decide who would lead Uganda once the Tanzanians had liberated the country. A retired Makarere Professor with no political experience, Yusuf Lule, emerged as the compromise candidate and the Ugandans fighting with the Tanzanians were reformed into the Uganda National Liberation Army (UNLA). In April 1979, Kampala fell to the Tanzanians, and Yusuf Lule was sworn in as Uganda's third President.

As the Tanzanians steadily pushed through Western Uganda to Entebbe and beyond, they mopped up elements of Amin's forces but most of these followed Amin's example and ran away to the north. In Entebbe, a young Police helicopter pilot, Samuel Turyagyenda, recently returned from Russia, was captured by the Tanzanians. He wrote to us to tell us what happened. He was about to be placed against the wall of his house and shot as a member of Amin's Armed Forces when the doctor living next door ran out and told the Tanzanians that he is not Army but Police, so saving Sam's life.

## Part 5: Enduring Obote II and the coming of the NRM
## 5.1 Living with trouble in West Nile

If the 1970s were for many Ugandans a decade of tyranny, for some in West Nile, life went on much as before. When we left Arua in 1971, our student Kezzy Dombio, a Madi girl from Inde, was in S3. She is the grand-daughter of the Madi Chief Ajai whose land had been given to the nation as the Ajai Rhino Reserve. Chief Ajai had been one of Ted Williams' early surgical patients and the success of that surgery had helped the church hospital to become established. Kezzy completed her S4 at Mvara in spite of all the problems at the school and did well enough to take her A levels. She went on to gain a place on a BA degree at Makerere in 1975. That same year, John Ondoma was also studying at Makerere. He had remained as a class teacher at Arua Demonstration Primary School just across the valley from the Mvara New Site right through the time of our troubles at Mvara. He had worked his way through part-time O and A levels and the Mature Student entry examinations to gain a place on the BA course in 1974. John takes up the story:

*'As we went to start the second year at University in 1975, new students, commonly called 'freshers', went along with us to start their first year. Among them was a beautiful young lady from Arua District called Kezzy Dombio. Her subjects, apart from Sociology, coincided with mine. She was, and still is, saved and loves to sing in the choir. I shared many things with her as we went to the same fellowship, sang in the same choir and often travelled together on the same bus to and from Arua. Besides being friendly, she was kind and considerate. We drew closer and closer together until it dawned upon both of us that the relationship could be carried to the higher and desirable plain of marriage.*

*Before I declared my intentions to her I had to battle with myself and asked my two closest prayer partners, Columbus Kyohere and Manuel Muranga to join me in earnest prayer that it was not just passion but real love that was driving me towards Kezzy and that it was according to God's will.*

*Earlier on, many brothers and sisters had acted out of sheer emotion and passion and gone to declare their intentions to one sister, only to move on to another, all in the name of God. But God does not confuse people, and He is consistent. The sisters had their own network. Whatever happened at one end with any of them would be known at the other. Such* brothers were often called 'jumpy types'. I dreaded being labelled one of the 'jumpy type'.

When all indications were that all was according to God's plan, I took courage to go and declare my intentions. I had prayed that if it were not God's will for me to marry her, I should not find her where I intended to meet her. So I set off, and when I arrived at her door, I knocked, expecting no answer. But when somebody answered 'come in' I knew all was well so far. I announced my mission, which she received with surprise because we had shared our lives in such a way that we were like brother and sister to one another. However, she requested (as all good and respectful girls would) to be given time to seek God's face for an answer. She promised that whatever answer she got, she would let me know. The days before her verdict was declared to me were full of anxiety. Thank God, when the right day came, I received my 'YES' with emphasis. I felt like flying with wings. I had never felt lighter even as a sportsman. This happened in March 1977 after I completed my final examinations for my BA degree.

We came home to Arua and I was immediately employed to teach at Mvara Senior Secondary School. But my teaching at Mvara had to be halted for a while with effect from October 1977 because I needed to be trained as a graduate teacher before confidently settling down to teach. Consequently, I went back to Makerere to pursue a Postgraduate Diploma in Education (PGDE) which I completed in June 1978. By then, Kezzy had already been employed as a Labour Officer in Arua District. Since my position at Mvara was already assured, I came back to resume teaching at the school from July 1978. This coincided with the departure of the Rev Canon Lusania Kasamba to go to be the Chaplain at Makerere University. He was the Mvara School Chaplain and patron of the Scripture Union group. His departure left a vacuum with these roles needing to be filled at the school. Since I had just arrived and was in need of a house, the school authorities asked me to occupy the house Rev Kasamba was vacating. The only credential I had for the three bed-roomed house, although I was single, was my integrity as a Christian. The house was the nearest to the girls' dormitory and strategically 'convenient' for anybody interested in some mischief with the school girls. The Bishop asked me to be his emissary and acting chaplain in the school, jobs which God enabled me to do very well by His grace.

My inheriting that house brought contention against me from some teachers who believed they were more qualified than I was to get it. Instead of fighting the school authority which had the prerogative to evict me, they placed their anger against me. Later on, in 1980, when a full Chaplain was appointed, he nursed bitterness towards me on the grounds that I had refused to leave the 'Chaplain's' house for him and his family to occupy. This bitterness seemed to have a negative influence on this person's subsequent attitude towards me. I asked God to forgive me if that was a wrong interpretation of his feelings towards me.

It was not long after settling down to teach as a graduate teacher at Mvara that my father and I decided to go and settle marriage arrangements for me and my then fiancée, Kezzy. She was still working at Arua Labour Office and this definitely made it easier for us to visit and be with each other to get to know each other more and more. The more time we had together, the more we felt convinced that we needed to get married. The negotiations were done in July 1978, the bulk of the bride wealth was paid at the end of August that same year and permission was granted by my father-in-law for us to be together.

We did not start living together immediately because we needed God's blessing in church first. There were no 'wedding committees' of the type we have today to contribute things like money and other necessary items needed towards wedding expenses. All depended on what those intending to wed and their relatives could do. Thank God, we had loving friends who encouraged us and made financial and material contributions which made it possible for us to plan to wed in the church on 20$^{th}$ October 1978. Kezzy and her team of ladies had it rough with red ants disturbing them in the night before. They woke late and had to travel quickly to the place where they would get dressed. Not until we were in church did I remember photography for the wedding. Thank God, Johnson Lulua and Dr Aniku were able to take some photographs which we later had to keep. The band of trumpeters led by our brother in Christ late Crispo Uzelle provided the entertainment in church and at the reception at Arua TTC. We were honoured to have the Archbishop of Uganda His Grace Rt. Rev. Silvanus Wani wed us in what was to us a colourful ceremony, still fresh in our memory.

Kezzy and I come from humble backgrounds. We did not inherit a lot of property from our families but we are grateful that they could sacrifice so much for our education. We therefore decided to engage in extra work such as growing our own food crops in order to augment our salaries so that we could afford things we could not grow ourselves. God was very faithful to us and blessed our sweat so much that we sometimes sold our food from our gardens. To some people it was strange, if not obnoxious, to see two graduates dig and soil their hands with dirt. To us there was nothing to boast about, 'I want to know Christ – yes, to know the power of his resurrection….'(Philippians 3:10). As the Seventies drew to a close, they also saw the exit of the monstrous Dictator, Idi Amin. The liberation war jointly mounted by Uganda National Liberation Front (UNLF) and the Tanzanian Peoples Defence Forces (TPDF) drove Amin and his forces from power and ushered in a new coalition of forces to rule and administer Uganda.

The negative effects of the liberation war did not spare us. We lost quite a lot of property due to indiscriminate looting by both retreating and advancing forces. This forced many people to flee their homes for safety where they thought best. Beside threat of death, the threat of 'saba saba' created wild fears, especially for pregnant women of whom Kezzy was one. She and my mother had to walk over twenty miles in search of safety. By God's grace they stayed safe at our home in Maracha, a long way north of Arua town, although amidst constant harassment and threats of looting and killing. As soon as relative calm returned, I took the earliest opportunity to ride and bring her back to Arua on a bicycle. A malaria attack on her in May 1979 nearly caused the premature birth of our first child. Thank God, Canon Seton Maclure rushed her to Maracha hospital where she received full treatment and was cured. Two months later, on July 29$^{th}$ 1979 she had a normal delivery. We call him Grace Feta owing to those circumstances which surround his birth. Later, he was baptised Simon.'

\*

In Kampala, once the Tanzanians had established control over the city. Joseph Lule[1] was sworn in as President but he did not last long. Weak and inexperienced, he was surrounded by much stronger forces. In June 1979, Lule was removed from power by a group of politicians and Army men, Paulo Muwanga, the leader of the UPC, with Tito Okello and David Oyite-Oyok, the Commander and Deputy Commander of the Uganda National Liberation Army (UNLA), the Acholi/Langi army which had fought alongside the Tanzanians. Milton Obote remained hovering in the wings. Lule was in power for just sixty eight days. In his place, the effective leaders of Uganda placed Godfrey Binaisa, the Baganda lawyer who had been Obote's close associate in the 1960s and had drafted the 1967 Republican constitution. Binaisa lasted a little longer, about eight months, before he was replaced in May 1980 by two of the power-brokers, Paulo Muwanga and David Oyite-Ojok, in an attempt to provide a balance between Baganda and the North. They set a date for elections in December 1980, to be contested by the old Democratic Party (DP) and the Uganda Peoples Congress (UPC) still led by Milton Obote. Yoweri Museveni formed a new party, the Uganda Patriotic Movement, to contest the election.

Throughout this period, the UNLA were recruiting militias in Acholi and Lango with one aim, to avenge the massacres of their tribal groups in the Army at the start of Amin's rule. When elements of Amin's forces who had escaped into the Sudan came back into West Nile to attack the Tanzanians and the UNLA, they provided the perfect excuse for revenge. The UNLA and the Acholi Militias moved into West Nile in October 1980. When they had swept through Nebbi District, largely leaving the Alur alone, they moved north, burning villages and killing those who did not run away. There were many massacres that went unreported outside Uganda but, at Church centres near main roads where there were still ex-patriate missionaries, reports of what happened filtered back to the world media. At the Church of Uganda training Centre at Ringili, near Kuluva, south of Arua, the students who were living there were taken out of their houses and lined up. The Lugbara, Madi and Kakwa were shot. Laura Belle Barr[2], one of the AIM translators of the Lugbara Bible, witnessed these killings. When a young British TEAR Fund worker, Paul Dean, drove from the Congo and arrived at Ringili shortly after the shooting, he was able to rescue Laura Belle and they both escaped in his car back over the border.

North of Arua, at the Catholic Ombachi Mission, there was an even larger massacre witnessed by the Catholic fathers working there. Again, those who had Lugbara, Kakwa or Madi names were killed, as were all Moslems. In Arua, much of the town was destroyed. It was as if the Lugbara living there were personally responsible for the killing of Acholi soldiers years before. All household and personal property found in houses and shops was looted by the Acholi and Langi soldiers and militias, and the town was systematically destroyed. The Catholic Cathedral out to the west was said to be the only building left standing. The UNLA and Militias then moved north and did the same thing to Koboko and Moyo towns. Tanzanian forces were still occupying West Nile and it is said that they did try to intervene. But the UNLA was completely out of control. One local resident who had witnessed the killings of Acholi soldiers by Amin's men in the 1970s said that Amin had at least been able to control his army.

John Ondoma wrote: *'The UNLA process of driving the remnants of Amin's soldiers out of West Nile caused untold suffering and death in Arua and another mass exodus to Sudan and Congo. 30,000 people fled into the Sudan and over 100,000 went into Congo. Many families, including mine, took refuge within and around Arua. God covered us by His grace and we were not killed, although we lost nearly all our property again. Survival was reckoned not as an individual effort but by Divine Providence because even in those countries where people took refuge, suffering and death followed them. People sang:*

*'Pari 'bani'ba zizu ri eri Yesu alia,*
*Ama zi ama opilenia.'*

*This literally means that the only safe place for hiding is in Jesus and we should therefore hide under His wings.'*

With the refugees fleeing to the Congo were Ted and Muriel Williams, from Kuluva Hospital. Ted wrote at this time in the Uganda Church Association Newsletter:

*'We thank God that Zaire (Congo) and Sudan were so near, otherwise the slaughter might have been far worse than it was'.*

By the following year, almost three quarters of the population of the area had fled across the borders into the Congo and the Sudan, where they were able to survive by growing food much as they had done in Uganda and with help from the UNHCR.

In December 1980, the promised national elections took place although they were a travesty of democracy. Some DP candidates were prevented from standing, leaving some UPC candidates elected 'unopposed'. When, in spite of this, it looked as if the DP might still have an overall majority, a decree announced that all election results had to be passed to the two Presidents before being announced. It was hardly surprising that they announced a victory for the UPC, with Obote heading for a second run as President. Uganda had escaped from the one tyranny, only to fall into another[3].

\*

When the Tanzanians had marched into West Nile in 1979, Mvara Secondary School was taken over as a barracks for the soldiers and much damage was done. When the comparatively well disciplined Tanzanians withdrew at the end of 1980, the school was again used by the soldiers of the UNLA with further destruction. They stole anything that could be removed and used anything that would burn as firewood. John Ondoma and his family continued to hide in a deep valley north of Arua away from any roads, and at this very difficult time, their second son, Emanuel was born.

'His name is a testament to what God had done for us through those tumultuous and turbulent times. My family was given shelter in the home of Mr Yosia Olea of Wandi Oluko village in the Aca valley east of Arua town. He, together with his wife Julia, their children and kinsmen treated us very kindly and made us feel at home for the whole time we were there. That good relationship has continued to this day. But there were no medical services and no immunization programmes for young children. All essential infrastructures had been run down or destroyed. We were almost in what a political analyst would call a 'State of Nature'. The whole of 1981 was spent in fear and anxiety due to the insecurity that loomed so high. The only medical facilities were the most basic ones for those who could get to Kuluva Hospital and the normal immunisation programme broke down.

We came out of Aca at the beginning of 1982. By then the elders of Mvara Mission had met and decided that Mvara Secondary School should open in earnest. They further recommended to the Ministry of Education through their Member of Parliament that Mr Semei Adutia and John Ondoma be Acting Headmaster and Acting Deputy Headmaster. The Ministry issued letters of appointment to us in that regard. We managed to open the school within the first quarter of 1982 but this administrative arrangement met with opposition from some members of the community including some Mvara teachers. They argued that I did not deserve that post because I had not worked long enough in the secondary school. Of course there were other teachers who had come to the school before me, but I suppose those who took those decisions considered there to be more crucial factors involved other than the simple chronology of arrival to the school.

In May 1982, Emanuel was attacked by what we thought first was high fever and malaria. He had already learnt to walk and sometimes ran faster than his elder brother. After administering injectable chloroquine to him, he seemed to have rested quite well the following day, which was Sunday. Early on Monday morning, I left for school as usual at 7 am for the routine boarding duties which needed my attention as Deputy Headmaster. Our two boys used to like to compete against each other to see who could reach the school lorry, often parked on our compound, first. On this fateful day, it was Emanuel's last attempt to run. All his efforts came to nothing because, we were told later, he had been attacked by polio. It did not take long before his whole body was paralysed. Around the same time, many other children in the neighbourhood got similar attacks and quite a number died.

Before we knew it was polio, we rushed him to Kuluva Hospital. Dr Lulua's first impression was that some of his nerves could have been affected by the injection. If that was so, he would out-grow it gradually. But when we travelled back to school, Emanuel's condition deteriorated rapidly and by Tuesday evening, his body became so inflexible that he could not even sit up by himself. We decided to rush him to Arua Hospital although it was the May 1st Labour Day Celebrations where Kezzy's attention was badly needed as the District Labour Officer. From the Doctor's body language, he had given up hope that Emanuel would live and we took him back home. The only thing we could do was to try to give him milk in small amounts with a tea-spoon. Praise the Lord, he survived that night and when we took him to the Hospital again in the morning, Dr Yossa, the District Medical Officer, was able to diagnose that he was suffering from polio. He advised that there was no cure for it but that we should take care to have all side effects, like coughs and fevers treated early enough. By God's own mercy and tender love, He spared Emanuel's life, but now we had to learn to cope with the paralysis.

Before long, our village in Tara Parish in Maracha County north of Arua was attacked by more remnants of Amin's soldiers from over the border. In the process, they abducted and later brutally killed my father and a younger brother, Dramuke. Many houses with their granaries were burnt down on June 29$^{th}$ 1982. 'What a tragedy!' I thought. It nearly drove me to start arguing with God about why all these things happened to us, one after another. I felt bitter to those who were said to be responsible for the carnage and devastation. Through it all, God told me to remain hopeful despite the adversity that had afflicted us. We leant painfully to hear God speak to us as he did to St Paul. "My grace is sufficient for you."

*God, in His own way, enabled us to cope with Emanuel's paralysis in ways we cannot understand or explain. We were visited by one physiotherapist after another, who introduced Emanuel to learning to walk on callipers and crutches. We had to make frequent, regular visits to Mulago Hospital in Kampala and later to Aru Mission Hospital in the Congo. This was in 1986, when Arua District had just been liberated by the National Resistance Army (NRA). Crossing into Congo was still not safe as fleeing forces might be lurking around the border. We thank God for help from Joy Grindey, an AIM Missionary in West Nile, who took the risk of driving us to Aru in Congo in her car. Emanuel learnt to stand alone on his crutches and callipers and develop the courage to learn to walk afresh.*

*When our daughter was born on August 13$^{th}$ 1982, I did not hesitate to give her the name Hope. My aunt gave her the name 'Mindreru' because many events preceding her birth had brought tears to our eyes, 'mindre' meaning tears in Lugbara. As she learnt to sit, walk and stand, this was a challenge and encouragement for Emanuel to follow. They became and have remained close friends who are very fond of each other. She supported him in all his endeavours to walk in his callipers and crutches, struggled to lift him whenever he fell down and walked patiently with him whenever he wished to get some exercise. Our prayer had always been that when he was ready to go to school, God should enable him to move on his own. His learning to walk on the callipers by himself was an answer to this prayer. For all his Primary education at Muni, he moved by himself. One amazing thing was how God made people feel for him and love him enough to care for him to and from school. We could not be everywhere to care for him because we are not God'*

\*

While John and Kezzy Ondoma were struggling to survive in West Nile, with the added challenge of a child with polio, Jenny and I were living in North Yorkshire. I had become one of three Deputy Heads of Northallerton Grammar School, a 14-18 comprehensive of over a thousand boys and girls. Our contacts with Uganda continued by letter and through meeting friends on leave from their jobs there, and we heard again from Sam Turyagyenda. A postcard from the USA told us that he was being re-trained as a pilot on American helicopters and was enjoying his stay at the Jolly Roger Motel in Texas

Early in 1981, Yoweri Museveni[4], whose partnership with the leaders of the UNLA had been deteriorating for some time, decided that he could not continue to support Obote. He would 'go to the bush', forming a small guerrilla force, initially of just twenty six fighters. Museveni had spent some time in Mozambique in the 1970s with the FRELIMO guerrillas in their liberation war against the Portuguese. He decided that this approach was the only way that Uganda could be freed from Obote's oppression which was turning out to be every bit as bad as Amin's. The main area for Museveni's initial operations was the 'Luwero triangle', the lightly populated zone of the Baganda heartland to the north of Kampala between the main roads north to Hoima and to Masindi. To try to eliminate Museveni's guerrillas, Obote's UNLA launched a massive punitive campaign in this area, code-named LL (Locate and Liquidate). From May 1982 to July 1985, the Baganda population of the Luwero Triangle were caught between the hammer of the UNLA and the elusive rock of the NRA guerrillas.

Unlike the West Nile population, they had no international boundary across which to escape. As the numbers of Baganda killed by the UNLA grew, their orphaned families, sometimes boys as young as ten, joined Museveni's fighters. The fighting intensified to a full scale war and the casualties mounted. One estimate was that 350,000 were killed, many more than died across all of Uganda in the Amin years. When the UNLA found that Museveni's forces were being supplied with food and information by the Baganda population, they herded 500,000 of them into 'displacement camps', just as the British had herded Afrikaans speaking women and children into camps during the Boer War. They were really concentration camps in which thousands died of hunger and disease. It was in the Luwero triangle that grizzly monuments of piles of human skulls were erected and yet the outside world continued to do nothing. Obote maintained that he was waging a campaign against 'bandits'. Only the Roman Catholic Church in Uganda condemned what was happening.

By the end of 1983, Museveni's forces had extended their operations west into Mubende and Bunyoro and the unity of Obote's government was beginning to break down. In 1984, the guerrillas attacked Masindi and captured arms and equipment. They developed a Mobile Brigade led by Museveni's brother, Salim Saleh, which had further successes. After a particularly appalling UNLA massacre at Namugongo, the world finally woke up and the American Assistant Secretary of State condemned what the Obote regimes had been doing. The London Times of 3$^{rd}$ May 1985 carried a long article by the British journalist, Richard Dowden. It was headlined: 'Uganda: Britain's blind eye to terror' and it reported that the situation under Obote was much worse than it had been under Amin. Whereas about 25,000 Ugandans had left their country as refugees under Amin, about 280,000 became refugees from Uganda under Obote's second term.

Jenny and I had moved to Louth in 1982 and the struggle for the control of Uganda went on. Museveni's guerrilla operations grew more and more effective. The young Acholi soldiers in the Army under General Tito Okello were taking most of the casualties in the war in the Luwero Triangle and their Achoil commanders were increasingly dissatisfied with the favouritism Obote showed to his own Langi senior officers. Unrest within Obote's regime threatened to break out into open conflict. Disagreement over strategy turned into refusal to obey orders. In July 1985, Lt General Basilio Olara-Okello, another senior Acholi Army commander, led a successful military coup against Obote. When Obote was deposed, Tito Okello became President of Uganda with Basilio Okello commanding the UNLA armed forces.

By this stage, Museveni's NRA had gained control of much of Western and Southern Uganda. Peace talks were started between the NRA and the Okellos but these soon ran into difficulties. Each armed group tried to consolidate its control over as much of the population as possible. In spite of the terrible revenge that the Acholis had brought to West Nile in the early 1980s, West Nile rebel groups opposed to Obote, joined the Okello side of the peace talks. One of these groups, the Uganda National Rescue Front (UNRF) led by Brigadier Moses Ali brought a significant number of fighters to the negotiating table. Their Deputy Commander, representing them in Kampala, was said to be a Major Onzi. I wondered whether this was the same Onzi we knew all too well.

The Presidents of Kenya and Tanzania brought the leaders of the NRA and the UNLA together for more peace talks in Nairobi and an agreement was signed. But this broke down again as the NRA pushed ahead towards Kampala. In January 1986, they captured the city and Yoweri Museveni was sworn in as President of Uganda. When the Acholis in the UNLA retreated north and east to their home areas, Museveni's NRA pursued them. They took the Acholi towns of Gulu and Kitgum by force and reached the Nile. By March 1986, they were ready to move into the only area of Uganda not under NRA control, West Nile.

With the NRA on the east side of Pakwach Bridge ready to cross the river into West Nile, a delegation of West Nile elders assembled to meet them. These men had persuaded what fighting men were still left in West Nile to lay down their arms and offer no resistance. The elders then welcomed the NRA over the river and Museveni's forces took over the whole district. There was no fighting. Alur, Lugbara, Kakwa and Madi, people who had survived by becoming refugees and receiving help from outside agencies, returned to their homes to settle again. But economic activity in the area above the level of subsistence agriculture had all but ceased. In the 1960s and early 70s, the West Nile economy had produced significant quantities of cash crops like coffee, cotton and tobacco, sent down to Kampala to be exported through National Marketing Boards.

By 1986, production of these had almost ceased. There was little incentive to grow coffee, cotton and tobacco if it was not possible to transport these economically to the south. The roads from West Nile to Kampala had been difficult to use for much of the early 1980s because they ran through the areas of fighting in the Luwero Triangle. Within West Nile, people earned what they could from selling the food crops they grew in the local markets and smuggling coffee and other goods across the Congo border. Some got jobs with the many Aid Agencies there to support refugees. What became known as the *magendo* or 'informal' economy enabled some to become rich but did little to re-establish the infrastructure of schools, roads and civil administration.

In Kampala, Yoweri Museveni formed a broad-based government based on the Resistance Council system. This new form of democracy, which was first introduced into each of the areas captured by the NRM as they moved east towards Kampala, established five levels of participation, the village, the parish, the sub-county, the county and the District. Every Ugandan was expected to attend the meetings of, and participate actively in, at least one level, usually the village or urban ward in which he or she lived. In these meetings, nine officials would be elected to form a Resistance Council (RC) and any matters which affected the community could be discussed. Marginalised groups like women, those who were disabled and young people were all given allocations of places on RCs at each level. At the national level, the National Resistance Council formed the equivalent of a parliament and was made up of members from the original Council formed during the war, representatives of women, youth and the Armed Services and members representing counties and urban areas. The whole system was to be reviewed by referendum every four years. In the event, the NRC voted in October 1989 to extend the NRM's term of office by a further five years to 1994.

The RC system did not have any provision for conventional party politics and such parties were in fact banned, but Museveni's first and subsequent governments included ministers drawn from all political parties. Former members of the UPC, the DP, Museveni's own Uganda People's Movement (UPM) and the small Conservative Party (CP) served together to achieve a national consensus on issues which affected the whole country. After the fall of Kampala, Museveni even came to an agreement with the UNRF, fighters based mainly in West Nile, and brought their leader Moses Ali into the Government as a Minister for Tourism and Wildlife.

Ali had been a Brigadier in Amin's army and Finance Minister in Amin's administration. He had joined the Okellos in fighting Museveni and was a man of whom the southerners were deeply suspicious. Yet, once the war was over, Museveni managed to use Ali's organisational talents in the national administration until April 1990 when Ali, then Minister of Youth, Culture and Sports, was arrested and charged with plotting a coup.

President Museveni of Uganda

The new government was committed to the ten point priorities for national reconstruction which had been developed while they were still fighting in the bush. These were: democracy, security for people and property, national unity, defence of independence, building an independent, integrated and self-sustaining national economy, restoring society and rehabilitating war-ravaged areas, eliminating corruption and abuse of power, redressing errors leading to the dislocation of sections of the community, co-operation with other African countries and establishing a mixed economy. These were in no order of priority as there was much to be done on all fronts. In 1986, the key indicators of social and economic life in Uganda were still going down. According to the United Nations, between 1970 and 1990, life expectancy in Uganda had gone down from 50 years to 47 years. This reflected the cruel impact of HIV/AIDS (the first Uganda cases were reported in 1984). Infant mortality, largely due to malaria and water born disease, had risen. The provision of clean water supplies, effective sanitation (usually long-drop latrines) and per-capita income all went down in the twenty years from 1970 to 1990.

In West Nile, as conditions became more settled, the people began to return from the Congo and Sudan, ready to leave again should the need arise. Harassment by the Congolese army encouraged many Lugbara to return to Uganda, although there were still over 60,000 in UNHCR camps in the Congo in mid-1984. The north of the District was still being infiltrated by rebels from the Sudan and very few Kakwa returned to Uganda. As the Arua area became more secure, the Church of Uganda in West Nile opened more secondary schools including a new girls' school at Muni, south of the town. The church had included girls in Mvara Secondary School from the 1960s, but there was a feeling that girls would do better if they were educated on their own, as they were in some of the best schools. So Muni Girls Secondary School was started and had been going for a year when John Ondoma was asked to transfer from Mvara to be the Headteacher. Thirty pioneering girls had reached S2, but John was not at all sure that he wanted to go:

*'The only thing you could call Muni Girls S. S. were those thirty girls and new ones trickling in to ask for S1 vacancies. I seriously considered turning the offer down. It looked to me more like a punishment than a promotion, not remembering my earlier commitment to 'hope despite adversity'. Before I decided, I consulted my long-time mentor, Mr Baranaba Avinyia, who had also been seconded to the Muni*

Teachers' College nearby, which was no less discouraging for him. He counselled me wisely, to face the challenge valiantly as a man and a Christian, trusting that God would enable me to overcome all obstacles. Not doing so would also be detrimental to my future prospects of Headship. I reluctantly accepted it, praying that God would see me through because nothing is impossible for Him. But those who had opposed my becoming a Deputy 'prematurely' at Mvara rejoiced that I would go and languish in the bush school and possibly get crushed in it.

Before I actually joined Muni Girls, God invited me to preach a sermon to them during their Sunday service. The theme was 'Moses' call' and God spoke to me directly through this sermon as He has always done when He wanted to prepare me for something. I learnt that God had sent Moses to learn the desert situation in order to be able to lead the Israelites through the desert. Fortunately, the Acting Headmaster showed me the compound of the school and shared with me what they were doing, little knowing that I would soon take over from him. Having been convinced to stay and work at Muni, I put God to task. I asked Him, 'God if this is your plan that I should work at Muni and endure adversity as preparation for where you want me to serve next, make what I do prosper to give glory to you.'

The challenge was formidable. There was nowhere for me to live, no office, no books, no equipment and no teachers. Suffering, discouragement and heartache were never in short supply, but God was ever present in every situation and fully in charge. I started by sharing an office with the Headmaster of the Primary School. I rode to work from Mvara SS while I was winding up my Senior 5 class for the whole of the first term. At the beginning of May 1984, we moved to live in a house lent to the school by Mr Sulumani Awua. It was not as spacious as our Mvara house but we learnt to fit in, although this was a nightmare for our children. Besides being small, the roof beams had been eaten by termites and were dangerously loose, threatening to be blown off by any storm however light. But God held that roof on as long as we were there and not long after we had settled in, our fourth child, Moses, was born. My young daughter challenged me about the need to have our own house to move into, I helped her to realise that none of these houses belonged to us, we were merely using them.

I soon realised that any meaningful work in that school would only be done by God leading the way and because He is always faithful, He opened ways for partnerships, first through

Canon Maclure offering textbooks and arranging for short-term AIM personnel to come to teach at Muni Girls. Later, AIM sent long-term workers, the Martin family, who did a very commendable job at the school. They lived simply with us and carried out their tasks with full dedication and exemplary diligence which won for them admiration and friendship among the Muni community. God also sent an experienced lady teacher with a fine reputation, Milcah Avinyia, to be my Deputy at the school. The two of us upheld one another in prayer and in work. We literally had a staff meeting every single day because there were only two of us from the beginning as full-time teachers. God also gave us a Board of Governors who were very caring and thorough at their job and it gave a solid foundation to the school.

When it came to deciding on the motto and the uniform for the school, the pioneer students, led by the Head Girl, Florence Buzu, were very instrumental in shaping and deciding their destiny. They quickly suggested the motto 'I WILL TRY' which was accepted and adopted by the Board. Milcah helped them to design the uniform and to choose the colour. The rules were also agreed and adopted. Milcah worked hard to develop a model girls' school which should be the pride of Arua District if not the whole country. Sadly, she died just before the Higher School Certificate classes started in 1988, but her legacy has remained in the school till this day. In her generosity she made a sweater for our youngest child, Francis Ozimati, born in October 1987. I called him Francis because Francis of Assisi had called every adversity his little sister or brother. He was never discouraged and prayed that God should make him an instrument of His peace. I adopted this prayer for myself:

'Lord, make me an instrument of your peace, where there is hatred, let us sow love, where there is injury, let there be pardon………………'

The whole school community at Muni, from the Board of Governors to the teaching and non-teaching staff, the parents and the students worked with dedication and diligence. Our commitment to God and our prayers helped us to forge ahead as a unit at home and school This unity caused jealousy and envy, even from members of the community around the school. There was even a plan to kill me and my wife which God brought to light through a small boy from the family where the plot was being hatched. When this plot was exposed at a fellowship meeting in Muni Church, the perpetrators called a parish meeting hoping that the informers were from another clan. When it dawned on them that my information came from *their own home, they did not know what to say. They sent one of their family to beg for forgiveness from me. I told them that I was ready to forgive them provided that they accepted that they were under the yoke of Satan and did not know what they were doing. They should be truly penitent and be led to inherit the kingdom of God in heaven. After that, I spent the rest of my time at Muni Girls peacefully and even today, I can go back there freely and as a friend. Praise the Lord!'*

John Ondoma spent ten years leading Muni Girls and it did become the leading girls' school in the District. He discovered a talent for attracting grants from a range of sources including the Church of Sweden Aid, USAID, the Uganda Ministry of Education, the World Food Program, UNHCR, and CARE. He mobilized a team of parents to draw up site plans, give advice on building projects and to give their time, energy, money and talents to improve the school. The girls themselves made a big contribution by making and burning the bricks for their dormitories and classrooms, a project which attracted a Swedish TV company to make a film and so persuaded other donors to support the school.

From the start, the school had a Christian ethos and helped girls to find a faith of their own. Many committed their lives to Jesus and went on in faith for years after leaving the school. One of these was a Muslim girl, who began to read the Bible while she was at the school. The other girls prayed for her and encouraged her and she received Christ as her Saviour and Lord. When this news reached her family, they came to the school with a Muslim cleric to confront John, saying that he was converting Muslim girls to become Christians. He told them that it was not him but Jesus Christ, whom he could not control in any way. They wanted to take the girl home but John persuaded them to let her stay until the following Saturday so she could attend her classes. When the day came, they had an answer to prayer in that it rained so hard that the family arrived very late and John was able to walk with her to the car and encourage her to trust in God's unfailing love. When they got the girl home, she was shunned by her family, left alone without anyone saying anything to her. She decided to return on foot to the school and was baptised as 'Hope'. Although her parents disowned her completely, hoping that the hardship she would face would make her renounce her faith, she found a new home and family in the Church. They supported her with school-fees and everything she needed to complete her education successfully. She trained as a secondary school teacher and when she was qualified, God gave her a school to teach in, a husband to whom she is happily married and a family of her own.

*

Meanwhile, in England, I moved from the Headship of King Edward VI School, Louth to Wymondham College in Norfolk. Wymondham is unique in the UK state sector in that it was set up after the war by a visionary Norfolk County Education Officer to provide technical grammar opportunities for the children of a very rural County. Norfolk had grammar schools in Norwich and the market towns. The elementary schools became Secondary Moderns and those children from all over Norfolk who were deemed suitable at the 11+ for a technical grammar education were sent to Wymondham College as boarders. They were housed from 1951 in the Nissen Huts left after World War II on a former golf course near Wymondham. These huts had been the wards, operating theatres and offices of the US Army Air Force Hospital serving the $2^{nd}$ Air Division, the fourteen heavy bomber stations spread across South Norfolk. The College therefore had strong links with a community which had 'triumphed over adversity'. That became part of the ethos of the school, with young people learning to live with each other as boarders in a community which strove for excellence in all that they did, from the science labs to the sports fields.

When Jenny and I were asked to go to Norfolk to meet the Governors and first saw the College, with its rows of rusting corrugated iron huts, we could not imagine that it had a future. Although the boarding houses were based in good 1970s permanent buildings, most of the teaching and all the administration were still in the huts. The place seemed almost to celebrate dereliction. I could not see how I would persuade the loving parents of eleven year old boys and girls to leave their children in such depressing surroundings. At the interview, I told the Governors that it would take 'ten years and ten million pounds' to turn round the then rapidly declining boarding numbers. A day later I was surprised to be 'phoned by their Chairman and invited to take over the leadership of the College.

We had eight very challenging, and for me, immensely rewarding years at Wymondham. In the event, it took eight years and eight million pounds of capital grants from a range of sources, but mainly the Department for Education, to create a very impressive and attractive campus. Boarding numbers bottomed out and started to rise. Our team of very good teachers pushed up academic standards and the College became more attractive to parents. At first, Norfolk County Council supported about a hundred students who could show that they were in need of boarding places with generous boarding grants. Many of our students came from RAF and Army families and the rest of the boarders came to us a matter of choice. It helped that our fees were about a third of comparable opportunities in the region's independent schools. Our sporting success had always been a strength and that continued. By the end of our time there, all but one of the Nissen huts had been swept away to be replaced by a collection of modern, attractive specialist facilities, particularly for Technology and Design, and for the first time, we had to open a waiting list for boarding places. Day places were always popular and we struggled to devise a fair way of allocating them while making sure that the College remained a majority boarding community.

If the College was an exciting place to be for me, Jenny had a more difficult time. As the Principal's wife, it was difficult for her to simply join the staff-room as a teacher and some of our classes were more challenging than she was comfortable with. She found a role in the local Methodist Church and did some science teaching but it was always difficult for her to feel fully at home. Losing one of our sons to university and the other to a boarding place in Louth did not help, but she loyally supported the College and me in all the struggles that we faced during the eight years we were at Wymondham.

*

In 1992, John Ondoma was still the Headmaster of Muni Girls when Yoseri Museveni, as President, invited Asian businessmen to return to the country. Many did return, rebuilding their businesses and even being allowed to reclaim the property which they had to leave behind in 1972. By 1997, there were about six thousand in the Asian community resident in Uganda. They brought with them much needed business expertise and capital investment which helped to re-establish some of the rapidly developing sectors of the Ugandan economy. In most of the country, they were welcomed, as they provided desperately needed jobs for the many young people leaving school and university. Only in the rural areas, where many still remembered the attitudes of the *duka* owners of the pre-Amin era, was there much resentment when they returned.

In Arua, the battered buildings of Mvara Secondary School buildings, which had been new in 1970, were still standing, an empty shell of a school. The school did re-start as soon as possible in the early 1980s under the leadership of Mr Semei Adutia but he sadly died at the end of 1982. The school then had a succession of short-term Heads until the start of 1994, when the Governors decided to appoint John Ondoma, transferring him from one Church of Uganda School, Muni Girls, to another, Mvara Senior Secondary.

## 5.2 Taking over Mvara – again.

John had been Head of Muni Girls School for ten years and had established a reputation for insisting on high standards of personal and professional behaviour for both staff and students. Although this did not endear him to everyone at Muni, he was able to count on the support of his Governors and the Diocese. It was a time when there was still a legacy of violence and instability in much of West Nile. When he was moved to Mvara, on paper a promotion to a mixed A level boarding school considerably larger than Muni Girls, he faced a wealth of new challenges.

The staff were less than welcoming. Some had got used to working with 'co-operative' Headteachers, who joined the staff in drinking sprees and provided school money for staff trips to Kampala accounted for as 'school business'. As the general lack of security in the area deteriorated, staff commitment, good teaching and lesson preparation became very difficult to maintain. Salaries were not always paid and staff had been able to 'borrow' school property for use in their homes or even to sell to raise funds to augment their meagre incomes. The District Education Officer (DEO) resented the fact that secondary schools remained under the control of the Ministry in Kampala although the DEO had direct control over all Primary Schools and their Headteachers. This led to potential conflicts of interest as some DEOs saw Secondary Heads as rivals. It was easy for the DEO to intimidate and embarrass Secondary Heads by siding with their staff or students in disputes which could make leading a school like Mvara very difficult.

When the news of John Ondoma's transfer from Muni to Mvara was confirmed by the Ministry of Education and made public, there was a strong reaction from some teachers and students. They clearly did not want such an 'uncooperative' Headteacher to take over. They even tried to stop him moving on to the site and tried to incite the students to strike on his first day at the school. In the event, John was accompanied to Mvara by a group of Muni girls who helped him and Kezzy to move into the Head's house. The school was formally handed over to him by the Governors, Parents and the District Education Officer.

Mvara had a thousand students, sixty teachers and fifty non-teaching staff. Rather than going on strike, the students agreed at least to listen to what their new Headmaster had to say to them before deciding what they would do. They all met in the school hall on the first Saturday of term and John was introduced by the retiring Acting Headteacher. It was a critical moment and John described what happened:

*'I began by greeting them as a former member of staff of the school coming back home. I told them that I had come to help them to succeed as they had left their homes to come and endure the conditions they found in the school. I told them that I would not bring new rules from Muni Girls or anywhere else but use the rules that Mvara Secondary already had. They would be my guide and I reminded them that one of their rules said 'Attendance of all school programmes is compulsory'. I explained that this rule would be enforced. If I found one of them absent from lessons and going to the town without permission, I would have to punish that student as a result. Would they say that this was harsh? In being absent, they would miss lessons and the teaching which was the very reason for their coming to school.*

*I praise the Lord very much that these words touched the students and those staff who had come to listen. They took them to be words of encouragement rather than the brutality and dictatorship which had been preached by my accusers. One of the girls, who was saved, quickly ran to thank me for what I had said and wished me well. Many of the students resolved to cooperate with me for the sake of their own academic success and even on that Saturday decided not to go into town without a good cause. I learnt that what I had said was debated by the students in their dormitories and the positive reaction frustrated the hopes of those who had schemed for a strike, at least on this occasion.*

*I decided to meet different groups of the school community to hear what they had to say, starting with the Heads of Department, and then the rest of the Staff. I met*

Prefects, non-teaching staff, the Parents and Teachers Association Executive and the Board of Governors. These meetings became a regular pattern of my administration throughout the time I had at Mvara S.S. During the welcome party organised for me, the teachers' spokesperson informed me that Mvara teachers were frank people and they would talk with me frankly too. I responded by informing them that perhaps I was more frank than them. If I had a fault in some people's eyes, it was my frankness, which many did not like. I also asked those who were not at ease with my coming back to Mvara, to forgive me for any of my previous mistakes. They should start loving me in earnest. I told them this was imperative because if rooms in heaven were shared between two persons, and I happened to be any one of their room mates, they should start loving me while here on earth in order for us to enjoy our eternity.

At the time of my arrival, teacher-pupil relationships had deteriorated into mutual distrust and suspicion. General discipline at the school was characterised by personal chaos and recklessness. School programmes were not followed as laid down. Everyone was his or her own master and decided what to do at will, without regard for any authority at all. Students would choose whether or not to attend a particular lesson and no teacher dared to raise a finger against them. Similarly, it was up to each of them to decide when to get out of bed. No teacher dared to check dormitories, particularly at night, lest he or she be stoned. Drunkenness by students and staff was not restrained and various forms of immorality were practised without restraint. After 10 pm at night, many girls would change into trousers and ties for nocturnal duties. The school was like a disorganised market. I had inherited a 'leaking pot'.

The task looked overwhelming. Some of my friends warned me that the task was so awful it was unbearable. However, I had taken up the challenge and trusted that God would not leave me alone to be crushed by the weight of what I faced. The only logical thing for me to do was to look to Him, if I wanted to make any order out of the chaos in Mvara S.S. Had He not brought order out of chaos, the same thing, in the beginning of creation? I prayed for His help in giving me wisdom, good health and patience, to be able to cope with what was expected of me. I was convinced beyond doubt that God alone was able to accomplish any positive thing in that situation. To remind me constantly, that it was only God who was able to succeed, I asked my Fine Art teacher to print for me a motto which read 'GOD IS ABLE' and hung it conspicuously on the wall in the Headmaster's office. It would be there for anyone to read and, more importantly, to remind me of God's constant care and love. God spoke to my heart to create a friendly atmosphere with everyone, especially members of the school community, rather than resort to harshness. Such an atmosphere made it possible for many students to draw closer to me and to confide in me as a friend. In that way, many students began to un-learn the practices they had got into. It was easier to counsel them and help them adjust to taking their studies more seriously than they had been doing. By this means, a more cordial atmosphere was created between me and the school, although, when there were difficulties in the school, some of these students came to be called my 'spies'.

One evening after supper, a student was so ill in one of the dormitories that his friends were scared he might die. They had no way of taking the sick boy to hospital. A few gathered up their courage to try and see if I would respond differently to what they had known of other teachers' attitude toward students' welfare. I offered to go with them to the dormitory to see the patient. From there, they led me to Mr Onzima's house to borrow his bicycle so that they could carry the sick boy to hospital that night. By the time we got to Mr Onzima's house, I had a swarm of students walking behind me but we did not find him at home. As we came back to the school gates, we met Mr Arigawuzia coming from the town on a bicycle. He kindly allowed us to borrow it and the students were able to take the sick boy to the hospital that night. Fortunately, he recovered. After that experience I decided to purchase a bicycle for the students to use for such hospital trips. This was from the third term of 1994. This concern for their welfare created a more healthy relationship between me and the students.

During staff meetings I encouraged the teachers to regard the students as their own children, to be loved and helped to develop in the proper way. I became convinced, just as I was at Muni G. S., that students are never prone to doing wrong things because it is in their nature, but rather that it is adults, be they teachers or parents or any other influential person, whose bad example misleads them. Otherwise, they are capable of learning to do desirable and beneficial things for themselves and society. Because God who called me is faithful, He began to guide and bless our work in the school mightily and He caused the students to settle down in His own way. As many students confided in me, I tried to counsel as many as I could on careers and other social matters and encouraged them to see other members of staff for the relevant advice they needed. To help them to settle down, I put up a notice in the dining hall written boldly that 'FREEDOM WITHOUT LIMIT RUINS'. This notice stirred up a lot of discussion and challenge amongst the students.'

Staff-pupil relationships were John's first priority. If the pupils were to be convinced that he was serious in his concern for their education and well-being, he needed to overcome the lack of books and equipment. He applied to the local UNHCR office for help with projects which would meet one of their priorities, to provide benefits with a 'quick impact for returning refugees'. The school received funds for refurbishing, furnishing and restocking the library, which had been completely stripped of anything useful. The only parts to survive the destruction of army occupation were the walls of reinforced concrete and the aluminium sheets on the roof. John also applied for help through the local office of the Dutch Community Action Programme (CAP) who put him in touch with the Netherlands Embassy in Kampala. They provided more books and furniture for the library which could then be used as a reading room for all students, rather than an exclusive corner for HSC (A level) students to use.

There were other vested interests to break down. The junior laboratory had been turned into a mosque for Muslim students and was out of bounds for all non-Muslims throughout the week. This became available for others in the school, including acting as a classroom for teaching S6 Arts classes, although it reverted to Muslim use on Fridays when the Muslim students held their 'Jumaa' prayers there. The Kampala Ministry of Education gave the school a grant to re-install the laboratory plumbing and wiring. More equipment was added with grants, savings from the school budget and gifts from the school's well-wishers. As so much time was wasted by students looking for medical treatment when they felt sick, an on-site dispensary was opened at the school through the co-operation of the District Medical Director, the Medical Superintendent of Arua Hospital and the Doctors of Kuluva Hospital. Equipment, drugs and seconded staff were provided by all three sources and this helped the students to concentrate on their studies.

In the school office, the accounts system was improved with numbered receipts to provide a good audit trail, and a petty cash safe installed with two different keys. This ensured that both the Headmaster and the Bursar had to be present before any monies could be used. Most of the school-fee income was banked as soon as it was received. Teachers' salaries were checked and any which showed that a teacher was still receiving two salaries, but only able to do one job, were corrected. These changes inevitably produced complaints from the staff affected, including an anonymous allegation addressed to the DEO and the District Commissioner that the new Headmaster was creating suffering for the teachers' families. The letter contained threats against John. When John invited the teacher whom he suspected of making the threats to meet with him, he asked his Deputies and another colleague to join the meeting. He asked the teacher what his reaction had been to the moves to rectify salary anomalies. He was frank enough to admit that he did not like it, and then admitted that the letters had been from him, for which he apologised. John agreed that the matter should be closed and his apology accepted.

Other improvements included having the school accounts audited annually from his arrival in May 1994, the first time this had been done since 1978. A system of stock control was introduced for food taken into the school store, with a record kept of what food had been stored and what was issued to the cooks. This was very unpopular with all those who had been thriving on the 'fluid' situation which had been going on for years. Fees paid in for private entries for examinations had been received by a teacher who paid them into his personal account. This was stopped and all fees were paid in through the school office and bank. This created another aggrieved colleague who had lost a useful source of income. But the school was beginning to benefit from firm leadership and support from outside. John could show that his 'God is able' conviction was not just a religious theory but could help to encourage everyone to work together to improve the school.

\*

After seven years of relative peace in Uganda, Uganda's Museveni government was also making great progress. The President had travelled to Europe in 1986 and secured $125 million of aid from the EEC. The growing threat of HIV/AIDS was being addressed with a vigour which impressed the rest of the world, to the point at which Uganda became an exemplar for effective AIDS limitation policies. But there were still major problems in the Acholi and Langi areas of the country. When the Museveni's NRA ousted Okello's UNLA from Kampala, the defeated elements of the UNLA refused to accept Museveni's victory. They went home to organise resistance in the Acholi and Langi areas and came under the influence of Alice Lakwena. She was an Acholi woman who had met Tito Okello before the UNLA's defeat and had formed the 'Holy Spirit Movement'. She encouraged the Acholi and Langi ex-soldiers to join her movement and to fight on against the NRA. She told them that a commitment to a curious range of spiritual and secular 'commandments', together with the smearing of their bodies with the butter of the *shea* nut, would protect them from NRA bullets. Thousands of her followers initially defeated NRA forces in a series of battles across the north, from Kitgum to Soroti and even as far south as Mbale and Tororo, but the NRA stopped them at Jinja. Alice Lakwena escaped to Kenya but the movement was taken over by a ruthless former soldier from Acholi, Joseph Kony. His Lord's Resistance Army (LRA) of about twenty thousand rebels continued to terrorise Northern Uganda for nearly twenty years.

Joseph Kony, the leader of the Lord's Resistance Army

These strange 'Holy Spirit' and Lord's Resistance' movements were not unique to Northern Uganda, or to those associated with Christianity or to the last decades of the Twentieth Century. As long ago as 1905, there was a 'Maji-Maji' rebellion in German East Africa. This was prompted by a man said to be possessed by a powerful snake spirit, who convinced his followers that special water ('maji' in Kiswahili) would be strong enough to turn away German bullets if they were anointed with it. The rebels were mown down by German machine guns in an awful precursor to the slaughter of British and French infantry in the Flanders fields of World War I. In West Nile, at the time of Weatherhead in 1919, there was a similar uprising amongst the Lugbara. Rebels who did not wish to pay their taxes were encouraged to drink 'Yakan Water' or 'Allah Water'. Their leaders convinced them that when the

British fired at them, water not bullets would come out of the rifles. Those who drank 'Allah Water' died discovering that it was no match for the rifle fire of Weatherhead's askaris. The survivors paid their taxes.

But the Lord's Resistance Army of the 1990s brought terror to great swathes of Acholi towns and villages. Huts were burnt, men and women killed and children abducted. Operating out of the Southern Sudan and supported by the Islamic Sudan Government from 1993 to 2002, Kony and his Acholi followers attacked their own people. The 'Kony rebels' of the LRA laid waste to their own homeland for decades until they were finally driven out of Uganda[5].

\*

Of all our friends who had been at Mvara with us, only Gordon and Grace McCullough went back to West Nile in the 1980s. After a time teaching at home and bringing up their two young daughters, Jenny and Rosie, in Kilkeel, County Down, they both felt the call to serve God through AIM again. They were accepted by the Mission and in 1984 were invited by the Church of Uganda to go back to Kuluva Hospital. Gordon became the Hospital Administrator and representative of AIM in West Nile, Grace was involved in the local church and looking after Jenny and Rosie. When the girls were 11 and 13, they went to Rift Valley Academy. This AIM boarding school in Kenya supported many Mission families, from the USA and Europe, by providing their children with a high quality secondary education, following an American curriculum. Although the girls settled at RVA, this was a very hard time for Gordon and Grace, being so far from their girls at an important stage of their lives, when travel to and from West Nile was very difficult.

They were there when the NRA crossed the Nile and they were there when Museveni's Government established a Human Rights Commission to investigate atrocities and abuses of power during and since the time of Amin. They were there when the NRM Government passed an Amnesty Act requiring all rebels since 1986 to surrender without fear of retribution, and they were there when the Lord's Resistance Army began to terrorise Northern Uganda, from the Acholi country west of Gulu right down to the edge of the Lango territory south of Lira.

Throughout this time, Gordon and Grace lived at Kuluva and Gordon had the challenging task of keeping the hospital supplied. Lorries could not use the main road to Kampala even when hostilities in the Luwero Triangle ended, because the LRA attacked vehicles driven along the main road from Pakwach to Karuma. The only way through was to use the narrow Tangi track through Murchison Game Park. What had been a game-viewing path, used by a few Land Rovers and their tourist passengers, became the main road from West Nile to the rest of the country.

After three years at Kuluva, Gordon was asked by AIM to move to Lubowa[6], just south of Kampala and to become the AIM representative for Uganda. This involved setting up a new home, learning a new language and making new friends. Their house at Lubowa became the hub for AIM Uganda activity and the guest house for all visitors from other parts of Uganda needing to come to Kampala. In many ways it was a challenging time as the need to build new Mission – Church relationships took up much of Gordon's time.

Whenever they could they travelled together to the centres of AIM activity around Uganda, to the hospital at Kagando in the far west, to the work in the huge refugee settlements at Nakasongola in the centre and at Adjumani in the north. They needed to collect Jenny and Rosie from RVA at the end of each term and then take them back to Kenya for the start of the new term and all this travelling was hazardous on Uganda's rough roads in a country recovering from decades of war. Yet it was also a rewarding time as they saw the Ugandan Church grow in numbers and in service to the people. For a time, Gordon was asked to go back to Kuluva to help the Hospital get through a difficult time when the administration broke down. When that was sorted out, they were able to go back to Lubowa.

By early 1994, Jenny and I were established at Wymondham College, Peter was enjoying life at Pembroke College, Oxford and Tim got a place to do the same Physics and Philosophy course at St Anne's College. We wanted to take them both to Uganda over three weeks in the summer holiday to show them the places that we had known so well. Gordon and Grace were pleased that we were coming to see them and suggested that Simon and Clare Martin up in Arua would be happy to put us up for a few days.

So we planned what Gordon called the 'ultimate Uganda trip', to Entebbe via Ethiopian Airways, the cheapest carrier, and then three weeks in Uganda. Friends warned us that Uganda had changed and that we should not go back to Mvara – it would be too depressing to see the state it had got into. The Foreign Office was equally discouraging. Armed robberies were said to be continuing throughout Uganda and the North was particularly dangerous. But friends, Ugandan and British, with whom we had kept in touch for all those years of Uganda's suffering, encouraged us to go.

We spent some time with Gordon and Grace at Lubowa, while Peter and Tim linked up with an International School in Kampala and did some painting work for them. We were able to hire a 4WD vehicle for a trip up to Murchison Falls and camped at the Falls on the south side of the river. Travel north of the Nile was said to be very dangerous but we did sneak across the ferry at Paraa. We saw some of the animals which had survived Amin's army and twenty years of poaching, many giraffe, some Uganda cob and hartebeest. No elephants or buffalo were visible. Driving past the shell of Pakuba Lodge by Lake Albert was sad. Nothing remained except for a few lizards scuttling around in what had once been a swimming pool. Paraa Lodge, the splendid hotel where we had slaked our thirst so many times on the long hot drive up to Arua, was home to hundreds of baboons They were running across the roofs and in and out of the rooms where tourists from America, Europe and Japan had once brought Dollars, Euros and Pounds into Uganda's economy.

We did manage to get a trip on a boat along the Nile, from the ferry at Paraa to the foot of Murchison Falls. The crocodiles were still lying on the mud banks, and the many birds were as colourful as they had been back in 1971. There were lots of hippos but very few elephants left by the river. We returned to Kampala and joined Gordon and Grace at Lubowa, to be visited by Samuel Turyagyenda and his wife Ann. They invited us to their house at Entebbe where we met all their family and another former student, Ezati, from Mvara. Peter and Tim then joined some friends in Kampala for a few days while Jenny and I went up to Arua. Travel to West Nile by public bus or minibus was not possible because of the rebel activity on the road between Karuma and Pachwach so the only way was to fly. Fortunately, the Missionary Aviation Fellowship, the air life-line which supplies Mission stations in even the most remote corners of East Africa was sending a 6-seater plan up to Arua via Ajumani and they were prepared to take the two of us.

Entebbe at that time was full of American military pilots. It was just after the Ruanda Genocide and they were manning an air supply route taking aid to the large numbers of refugees in the Goma area of the Congo. These flights shipped tons of food-aid in enormous Galaxy jet transports to be airdropped to the camps. We joined two other MAF passengers, climbed into the tiny single-engined MAF plane on the Entebbe tarmac and waited for our pilot to finish praying for safety. Our flight followed a fully laden Galaxy down the Entebbe runway, like a gnat in the wake of an airborne elephant, and took off for the North with the pilot reading a map spread across his knees. Adjumani airfield was just a grass strip in the middle of no-where but we found it and rushed down between the walls of elephant grass before coming to a bumpy halt. As there was no terminal building, in fact no buildings at all, those who needed a 'comfort stop' hopped out of the plane and walked into the long grass. Then we were off again, across the Nile valley, to Arua.

From six thousand feet, the countryside of West Nile looked green, fertile and very peaceful. Clusters of grass-roofed huts, small fields of millet and cassava, winding footpaths feeding into red roads by the iron roofs of village schools, it all looked unchanged from the early 1970s. The people had come back. Although there was very little evidence of development, the signs of war-damage were largely gone except the occasional empty shell of a brick house where the roof had been burnt out.

In 1971, we had left a District with just four secondary schools. By 1973, the whole of the country had about half of the secondary teachers it needed as the British left and the Asians were evicted. Although the economy and the rule of law had collapsed under Amin, the school system had struggled on throughout his eight years in power and on through the chaos of the Obote II period. Every year, the Primary Leaving Examination, Uganda's equivalent of the 11+, had been administered promptly at 7.30 am on one set date in December in 400 different centres across West Nile. After the 'auction', Mvara Secondary School continued to receive its allocation of the successful S1 pupils.

Thanks to the fact that many graduates in government posts fled from Kampala in the Amin and Obote II years, preferring the safety of their home areas even if this meant accepting a low paid teaching job, West Nile's secondary schools were fully staffed by 1975. By 1980, new secondary schools had opened all over the District. These were then forced to close by the events of 1979 to 1981 when the teachers fled with the rest of the population, but most of the schools had re-opened under Museveni and were growing again. By 1994 when we landed at Arua Airport, a very long grass landing strip built by the Israelis with a small terminal building, the school system was obviously expanding again with new private schools springing up along the road into Arua.

Arua town was busy, full of the smart new 4WD vehicles of innumerable Aid Agencies, from the well-known UNHCR, USAID and OXFAM to the obscure, a Swiss Civil Service Charity for Well-Drilling and Finish Food Relief. Simon and Clare Martin were living near Mvara and very kindly found space for visitors. They were working with the Church of Uganda supporting Pastors and their wives. Simon took us to see Mvara Secondary School and its new Headmaster, John Ondoma. He had only been there for three months and we knew nothing of the challenges he had already faced. It was the first week of the school holiday and so the thousand students who would have been there in term-time were replaced by the enthusiastic members of a residential conference on the 'Challenge of Christian Living' run by the Scripture Union. Their joyful singing and keen studying reminded us of similar conferences we had run in other schools all those years ago.

Mvara Secondary School still functioned although the buildings bore the scars of war. Earth paths with neat flowering hedges and tall shade trees had replaced the earth and elephant grass of the 'New Site'. Washrooms and toilets, designed to depend on a mains water system, had ceased to function when we were there and had not improved since. There was now no piped water at all – most of the pipes had been stolen. The school of a thousand boys and girls and all the surrounding villages depended for water on just two boreholes, both equipped with hand pumps. Two long queues of patient women, with their yellow plastic jerry cans, formed every morning and evening. In the classrooms, there were a few desks but no chairs. The conference members had brought their own stools.

In the Science Laboratories, which we had left fully equipped for A level teaching, all that was left for students to use were a few test-tubes, a row of chemical bottles and a few pieces of dusty Physics apparatus. On the display board at the back of the Chemistry Laboratory, the poster which Jenny had drawn in 1970 to show the blast furnace production of iron was still there, with the same four rusting drawing pins holding it to the cork surface. On the shelf beside the poster, the polystyrene molecular models of carbon dioxide and oxygen and the model of the sodium chloride structure, teaching aids I had made in 1970, sat deep in dust. These sole survivors of our personal contribution to Ugandan chemistry teaching were of so little use that no-one had bothered to steal or destroy them. They could not be eaten, sold or burnt for fuel so they had survived.

We walked down to the edge of the site, to the pair of bungalows in which the McCulloughs and I had lived, wondering whether they were still there. They were and both were occupied by teachers' families with many children running around the bare earth next to the houses. Behind what had been 'my' house, a very large fig tree spread its branches right over the roof giving welcome shade. I realised that I had 'planted' it in 1970. Needing a washing line, John Martin and I had cut two rough poles off a wild fig tree and pushed them into the earth to rig up a line just behind our kitchen. The two poles took root and one had survived as this impressive tree. The house itself was sad. All the furniture, the cooker and refrigerator, most of the pipe-work and even most of the louvered glass window panes had been stripped out. Twenty five years of the use of charcoal burners in the kitchen had left a thick layer of black soot on the walls. Only the garden area showed any improvement. Where the elephant grass had been, there were neatly cultivated patches of beans and maize. Teachers now grew as much food as they could to supplement their tiny salaries.

Peter Ogani, the Okebu student who had led the iron smelting project, heard that we were in Arua and cycled in from Ringili to see us. He and his wife were training for the Church of Uganda ministry. He came across the school site to greet us, sporting a fine new set of stainless steel teeth. He was delighted to see us again. One evening, we were able to meet up with John Ondoma and Kezzy his wife, when they entertained us in the Headmaster's house – the same house that Lewis and Angela Stephenson had once occupied. John told us a little about the realities of life for his teaching staff, trying to survive on a government salary of about U Sh 40,000/- per month, the equivalent of £28. This did not even meet the basic living expenses of a small family. Many tried to do two teaching jobs quite legitimately. It was only those who were paid two salaries for doing one job that John had stopped. He explained that the Government had devalued the Uganda Shilling some years ago to try to bring inflation under control. Although basic salaries had been re-valued at the new level, the allowances teachers were paid for extra responsibilities had not yet been increased. Heads of Department earned an extra Sh 400/- per month, about 28p, the price of an airmail stamp or ten small bananas. For doing boarding duties, teachers were paid an additional monthly allowance of Sh. 285/-, the wholesale cost of the bottle of Pepsi which they so generously had offered us.

All schools, whether boarding or day, received the same capitation allowance per student which was supposed to pay for books and equipment they had, nothing more. The only other source of funding was the school fee, paid by parents and guardians and agreed between the PTA and the Governors. Mvara charged Sh.55,000/- per term (about £40), which was low compared to the Sh.200,000/- charged by the leading schools in the south. Yet, the great majority of students' families found it very difficult to pay their fees and schools increasingly had to accept payment in kind in lieu of cash, sacks of beans or cassava flour for the school kitchen, or work on the school compound. For a village pastor, on a monthly salary of about Sh. 6,000/-, with two children at Primary school and two at Secondary, the cost of school fees alone was almost twice his total church income. To survive, he and his wife had to find some other source of income by growing food. It was a salutary reminder that most Ugandans in 1994 did not have any salary at all.

Three forms, each of forty three students, were still admitted to Mvara in S1 each year. By the time they reached S4, the class size would have risen to sixty. They still followed much the same curriculum that we had used, modelled on a post-war UK grammar school. 'Romeo and Juliet' was the O level set book, alongside Achebe's 'Things Fall Apart'. The system was still ruthlessly selective with progress to A level dependent on O level results aggregated over eight subjects. Entry to University was limited to perhaps twenty or thirty of the one hundred and thirty young people who had started in S1 at the school. Once at Makerere, the degree course was free so it was no wonder that the focus on academic success was brutal and unforgiving. Uganda's schools had survived twenty five years of tyranny and chaos, but the Museveni Government still faced huge challenges. They took over the lowest levels of school attendance, adult literacy and life expectancy in all East Africa, in spite of the huge injections of World Bank Funding for new buildings between 1970 and 1990. As these buildings were destroyed and schools forced to start again in the wreckage of the past, the burden of national debt had grown.

Walking around the school site in 1994, we had to accept that it was a miracle that the school still functioned at all. When we left in 1971, all the new buildings were complete, all the equipment, books, and furniture had been delivered and we were about to take the first 6$^{th}$ Form group through to A levels in Science and Arts subjects. The investment had been provided by the World Bank as a Development Loan to the Uganda Government and would have to be paid for. Even before we left, we knew how inappropriate some of this investment had been. The cooking facilities could not be supported by the town's power supply. The inadequate water supply made most of the washing and sewerage facilities unusable. Over the twenty three years that followed, neither of these problems had been overcome and the school's furniture, books and equipment had disappeared. Yet it still functioned, students lived in the dormitories and teachers taught in the classrooms.

While we were in Uganda, the British Overseas Development Minister, Linda Chalker, was also in the country discussing British Aid projects. Uganda was a workshop for overseas aid. The majority of cars on the road were the 4WDs of every conceivable aid organisation, many focused on the needs of refugees or returned refugees. Few contributed to the needs of schools. It was much easier to persuade Swiss Civil Servants to give a Leprosy Project Land Rover or an HIV/Aids Clinic Building than to contribute to a teacher's salary or a supply of text books. Yet John Ondoma had managed to persuade donors to help Mvara. In spite of all the damage done to the school and in spite of all the opposition of staff and students to the introduction of higher standards of teaching and learning, he had made a start. We wanted to help if we could.

Well-intentioned individuals and organisations had collected books no longer needed in UK schools and sent them out to Uganda. Mvara had a sad library of such books of little use to one thousand students desperate for information. They queued each evening for their turn to read one of the few modern textbooks kept locked in a metal cabinet. They had an hour each. As one frustrated science teacher told us, 'we too live in 1994, not 1964, so please send us the cost of the postage and put your out-of-date books into your recycling bin.' British Aid had started a programme of Secondary Science In-service Training for Uganda's teachers which had been well received. They especially liked the kit of modern text-books which went to all participants on the course.

Some schools in the UK had revived the links which had been established in the 1960s, sending the product of parental and school fund-raising to the link school. Bristol Cathedral School had raised money for a computer block and library at their link school in Jinja and sent GAP students out for six months of teaching. Sherborne Girls School had re-established their link with Gayaza High School. We learnt about this when we met a lorry full of enthusiastic Gayaza 6$^{th}$ Form Biologists in Queen Elizabeth Game Park. They were studying an exotic food chain, from hartebeest to lion, thanks to funds raised by the Sherborne girls and their parents.

Jenny and I wondered what we could do to help Mvara. Perhaps we could find a similar small-scale project which might be funded by a link between Wymondham College in Norfolk and Mvara Secondary School in Arua. We talked to John about this and learnt that what his school would really value was some way of breaking down the sense of isolation which so many Uganda teachers felt. All that they had been able to do for twenty five years was to survive. Those who were not killed in wars, eliminated by despots or died of HIV/AIDS were now hoping to look outside their small world and to share that sense of being part of a wider world with their students.

Before we left Uganda, we drove with Gordon and Grace down to Kagando Hospital and Queen Elizabeth Park in the south-west. These areas had come through the years of Amin and Obote II with much less damage than West Nile and the Luwero Triangle. Even the game park was rapidly recovering. Camping at Mweya Lodge surrounded by hippo and listening to the roaring of lions in the night reminded us of a Uganda we had known so well.

We flew back to London and read in the Sunday paper of events in Arua the day after we had left. Where we had been sitting in the grounds of the White Rhino Hotel enjoying a cool drink, hand grenades had been thrown by WNBF rebels at a party of tourists. They had been camping in the hotel garden while travelling through West Nile on an overland expedition. One tourist had been killed in the attack and several other injured. The casualties were being treated in Kuluva Hospital. 'One day later, and that could have been us,' we thought, as we read the reports.

### 5.3 Uganda Link

John Ondoma wrote: *'God, in his own time, opened a link between Mvara Secondary School and Wymondham College from the United Kingdom through her Principal, John*

Haden. He had taught at Mvara from 1968 to 1971 and visited us in 1994. After discussion with most of the stakeholders at Mvara, it was hoped that this link would benefit the two sister schools through exchange visits and other activities to enhance teaching and learning in both schools. We hoped also to use these cultural experiences to benefit students and staff in an era of globalisation. God, in His own way, arranged a trip for me to the UK in 1995 to attend Margaret Lloyd's funeral. She was the founder Headmistress of Mvara S.S. when it started as a Junior Secondary School in 1949 and developed into a Senior Secondary in 1960. During this trip, I visited Wymondham College briefly, stayed with the Hadens and discussed how we might develop the relationship between our schools with College officials. When this began to develop, a project proposal had to be written to try to solve a major school problem. Wymondham College students and staff decided to address our problem of water at Mvara S.S. Students wasted a lot of valuable study time in searching for water from local wells or from the two bore holes we shared with the communities around the school.

At that time, donors were more willing to support projects involving girls. So the Mvara S5 girls carried out an investigation into alternative water supplies and planned and costed a project, working with my second deputy headmaster, Mr Luke Onzima. This project was then used to solicit funds from the British High Commission in Kampala and they offered to supply three water tanks for collecting rain-water, one for the labs, one for the dining hall and one for the girls' dormitory.'

\*

While this project was being developed at Mvara, the Wymondham College community set about raising funds in the UK. I encouraged a team of staff and students to plan a visit Arua in July 1996, to work at Mvara on the Water Project and then spend a further week travelling with some Mvara students in the South-West of Uganda. We planned to fly out via Nairobi to Entebbe by Kenya Airways and to travel up to Arua by Eagle Airways, as the road to the north from Kampala was still said to be dangerous. By May 1996, our efforts to raise £15,000 to finance the Mvara Water Project were making progress even if we had not yet reached our target. Staff and student members of the exchange group were all signed up to go, and our flights were booked.

Then we heard further bad news from West Nile. A group of WNBF rebels led by Juma Oris, a Madi Muslim from the Sudan with links to the Lord's Resistance Army and to elements of ex-Amin forces in the Sudan, had come across the border into Uganda in April of that year and had attacked refugee camps in the Koboko area. Oris had once been a Minister under Amin and the WNBF had operated inside Sudan against the Sudan People's Liberation Army, who were then fighting the Sudanese Government.

In the light of these reports and remembering what had happened just after we left West Nile in 1994, we realised that to take a school party into what was said to be a war zone would not be possible. We were dependent on grants from the Commonwealth Youth Exchange Council and had the endorsement of the Young Explorers Trust. Both advised cancellation of the visit. But we also heard from the Martins and others living in Arua, that things were not as bad as had been suggested. Travel by air to Arua was still possible and relatively safe. The town itself was peaceful after the initial anxiety about the grenade attack. Provided one avoided going north from Arua, where roads were said to be mined and attacks still happening, we were told that it was perfectly possible to visit Arua safely. We were advised by Kenya Airways that cancellation at such short notice would mean losing our large deposit, but that if we took up some of the tickets, and agreed to re-book for 1997, they would honour our agreement. So the 1996 school visit became a 'planning visit', with Jenny and me, and our younger son Timothy, travelling to Uganda in July 1996 for four weeks, again travelling up to Arua by the MAF flight. We were once more very grateful for the kind hospitality of Gordon and Grace McCullough at Lubowa and Simon and Clare Martin at Mvara. This time, we had an opportunity to plan the 1997 school visit in detail. Tim also joined the teaching staff of Mvara for a time, teaching A level Maths to some VI Form students!

Arua seemed very peaceful and there was little evidence in the town of the recent disturbances. We stayed with the Martins at Mvara and called on friends at Kuluva and in Arua with no difficulties. At the school, although the term had finished, there were more staff and students still there. They gave us a wonderful welcome party and a present of a batik painting to commemorate the start of the link between our schools. We spent some time discussing with John Ondoma and his staff the details of the Water Project and how the school link might develop in the future, with plans for a visit by Mvara Staff and Students to Wymondham in 1998.

We managed to hire a 4WD car in Kampala to take us down to the south-west to see whether Tim and I could get permits to visit the gorillas in the Virunga Mountains on the Ruanda border. We bought our permits and spent an exhausting day in the Mgahinga Gorilla National Park, climbing the slopes of Mount Sabinyo only to be told that the gorillas had gone, first to Zaire (Congo), then to Ruanda and finally back to Uganda. Each crossing of the border involved more $20 bills changing hands, more steep mountain climbing and more rain. I was so exhausted that it took the persuasive effect of one of our guides prodding me in the backside with his 303 rifle to keep me going upwards. But we did see the gorillas, a small family of silverback and females half hidden in the undergrowth and not particularly interested in our arrival.

'If they show signs of aggression, adopt a submissive pose,' we were advised. 'Avoid eye contact, turn away and crouch with your rear in the air.'

When the silverback turned to look at us, we were so busy being submissive that we forgot to get a good picture, which explains why all my gorilla pictures are of parts of a gorilla with the rest well hidden by the foliage.

\*

By delaying the school trip and taking Jenny and Tim with me in 1996, we had at least secured the flights for 1997. With hindsight it seemed that we had taken far too many risks. Yet it had not seemed like that. We agonised over the decision whether we should go ahead or cancel and we prayed for wisdom and guidance.

In the end it was the Wymondham staff and students who helped us to make up our minds. They were still keen to go in July 1997 and had been preparing for the venture for almost two years. We held meetings for students and parents and explained what we could of the risks. They all knew that Arua might be dangerous and that it would be safest to stay in Norfolk. The students and their parents were prepared to wait until May 1997 before we made a final decision and fully understood that this might involve losing our deposits. For the rest of 1996, there were sporadic attacks on refugee camps in the north of West Nile and, at one point, the relief agencies withdrew nearly all their staff. Road travel was restricted to the middle of the day and it was still dangerous to travel to the northern areas.

But, by the start of 1997, the Museveni government had moved more of the Uganda Peoples Defence Force into the District, linking up with increased activity by the SPLA in the Sudan and even into Zaire. In March, the UPDF and SPLA swept through the border areas of West Nile and the Congo, driving out the WNBF and other rebels and restoring peace and security to West Nile. By April, the Uganda government claimed to be in full control and even the cautious experts of the Foreign Office were saying that it was now safe to travel to Arua.

While all this was going on, we were trying to raise more money for the Mvara Water Project. I was fascinated by the parallel problems faced by Mvara and Wymondham College over water supply, two boarding schools in very different contexts sharing a problem. I wrote an article for the local paper, for which I was paid, another contribution to the Water Project fund! In the east of England, successive dry summers, leaking mains and escalating use of water, had dried out the river beds and village ponds, forced the introduction of hose-pipe bans and raised everyone's awareness that we had a major water problem. At the College, the cost of water was escalating. In spite of all the ingenious devices to reduce consumption, such as using spray taps and limiting flushing, our water charges were over £25,000 each year.

We learnt that most people in the UK used about 200 litres of water a day. If they had to get it from stand-pipes, as was happening in some places when the drought really hit supplies, they would carry home about 20 litres a day per person. In those parts of the world where everyone had to walk at least 5 km to fetch water, they made do with 2 litres a day each, carried back on the heads of women. Our problem in the College was that we appeared to be using much more than 200 litres each every day however much we tried to persuade staff and students to save water. The problem was waste, not use. Thousands of litres were being lost from our 1940s war-time water system. The storage tanks, pipe-work, drains and sewage farm had been hurriedly put in to accommodate the 1000-bed military hospital. We were still using their Nissen huts and their drains. For as long as the County Council paid our water bill, it was their problem but, once the College became a Grant Maintained school, the Governors' budget took the strain. A significant proportion of the £25,000 charge was going, literally, straight down the drain.

For the students and staff of Mvara in Uganda, the problem was not wastage but supply. They had the use of relatively recent good buildings; all equipped with flushing toilets, showers, and septic tank drains, none of which were in use. The connecting pipes within the site had long since been stolen, the supply to the large storage tank from the town was cut off, and the whole system lacked any piped water. All their needs had to be met from two bore-holes with hand pumps. And yet, although little rain fell in Arua from December to March, for most of the rest of the year, there was rain in abundance. The heavy clouds came up from the Nile valley and thunder storms deposited curtains of water all over Arua. All that fell on the school ran to waste. None of the buildings had gutters and there were no storage tanks.

The S5 girls proposed an initial effort to put up gutters and install a small number of rain-water tanks as conveniently sited as possible. These would provide washing water for the community, from April to November, which would be a start. The £15,000 estimated cost of four such tanks and guttering would also include the first stage of providing piped water, by re-establishing the link between the town mains supply and the school storage tank. It did seem that the Mvara Water Project, using the combined fund-raising of the two schools and the labour of a team of students, could actually make a difference. Meanwhile, our efforts to help a linked school in Uganda might draw attention to our own water problems and perhaps encourage capital funding for our own major need for new mains and drains!

By the end of the July term, the five staff and six students of Uganda Link 1997 were fully immunised against a range of tropical diseases, as fully briefed about life in Uganda as possible and trained to build water tanks out of chicken wire and cement. We built a prototype in the school garden, a concrete and steel structure which held enough water for the summer watering of tomatoes.

Our student group had been reduced by the year's delay and, in the event, all the students would be leaving the College shortly after getting back from Uganda. This made continuity difficult to manage, but the staff team was strong, two young teachers keen on outdoor activities, one of the matrons who had worked in Kenya who persuaded her doctor husband to come too, and the College Principal, me. We flew to Entebbe via Nairobi and stayed at a cheap guest house to give the students a chance to get used to being in Uganda before they faced too many challenges. It also gave us a day to visit the British High Commission to thank them for their support and to complete our arrangements for supplies before flying up to Arua.

Eagle Air ran a daily flight to Arua from Entebbe by 30-seater twin-engined turbo-prop plane, by far the easiest and safest way of covering the three hundred miles to the north as the main road was still subject to occasional attack by the Lord's Resistance Army. We reached Arua to be greeted by a welcome party from the school and were taken to Mvara by *matatu,* overloaded minibus. To our delight, the school had decided that two new teachers' houses, not yet quite finished and still unoccupied, could be our base at the school. They were on the edge of the site, with a papyrus matting fence and clean, bare rooms easy to use as sleeping quarters for students and staff. We had brought our own sleeping mats and bags so were relatively comfortable on the concrete floors.

As Arua is a high risk area for malaria, we all had mosquito nets to sleep under and a plentiful supply of DEET based repellent. We had been advised to take Larium as a weekly anti-malaria tablet, which was fine for all but one of us. She reacted by going blue and having exotic dreams, but even these interesting symptoms disappeared after a week. The new 'long-drop' latrines behind the houses were brought into rapid use by those of the party who had been hanging on from Entebbe!

Mvara School Assembly in 1997: Emanuel is in his adapted tricycle.

We spent seventeen days at Mvara Senior Secondary School, starting with a programme of formal welcomes from everyone, Governors, PTA executive, District Officers, Staff and Students. We attended their Assemblies, sang their National Anthem and our own College song, attended their lessons and ate lunch with them in the Dining Hall. For most of our other meals, we had decided to cook for ourselves. This was partly to avoid being a burden to our hosts and partly because we were sure that a diet of repetitive *enya* and beans would soon undermine morale, no matter how willing our students were. We split the party into duty teams whose first task each morning was to walk the two miles into Arua town to buy food for the day from the market. This proved to be the most popular activity.

Arua is a great place to buy almost anything. The market had fruit and vegetables in abundance; meat and fish were sold on stalls by the road. You could buy fresh bread and rolls, chose from a huge range of printed cotton fabrics and find everything you needed for the home, from knives to water-containers. Each day, our foraging party would set off in the cool of the morning, spend a couple of hours bargaining for what they wanted and stagger back with full baskets and bowls. The braver ones tried to carry them on their heads. One shopper was amazed to be overtaken along the road by a Ugandan lady carrying a huge basket of sweet potatoes on her head with a large bunch of sweet bananas balanced on top, all the while breast-feeding her baby as she strode along. Multi-tasking by women is nothing new.

Getting sand in the school lorry and a coffee break for the women

We ate well; *posho* (maize porridge) for breakfast with bread, 'Blue Band' (margarine) and local honey, washed down with gallons of tea, lunch with the school and a cooked evening meal with lots of fruit. Most of our time was spent working with the Mvara students on the water-tank project.

To our surprise, the 'experts' at Mvara had decided that the large black plastic water tanks donated by the British High Commission should each be installed on a concrete base and then clad with a layer of brickwork right up to the top. This was to prevent the expensive tanks being 'penetrated' by some enemy armed with a sharp knife or spear. To us, this seemed unlikely to happen, but who were we to argue. So a team of bricklayers joined the students and there was much passing of bricks from the rough pile by the gate to the site of each tank! This was declared to be 'men's work' by the boys in the school, because it was fun, and there was much hilarity when the ladies in our party joined in. Also designated as 'men's work' were all the more interesting tasks such as brick-laying, fixing guttering and taps, and actually building our one Ferro-Crete water tank. Digging holes for the concrete bases, fetching water and other menial tasks were designated 'women's work', although both the Doctor and the Principal enjoyed joining the ladies.

On Sunday, most of the party joined in a worship service in the school, led by John Ondoma with the help of his students. I was asked to preach to the small Catholic group meeting for Mass with their Priest from the Arua Catholic Diocese. It was the first time that I had the opportunity to preach in such a service and it was a very moving experience. When we came to the Mass, I was unsure as to whether I, as a confirmed member of the Church of England and practising Methodist Local Preacher, would be allowed to share in fellowship in the Mass. I asked the Priest.

'Are we not all brothers in Christ?' he said and invited me to receive the elements with all his Catholic students. In the heart of Africa, it seemed, the brotherhood of the Christian Church could reach out across all our differences.

*

By splitting the UK party into two and cramming half of us, with some Mvara staff and students, into a *matatu* taxi, we were able to take everybody for a day trip to the Murchison Falls Game Park, including a boat trip to the Falls and a game-watching drive around the Buligi Circuit. None of our Ugandan hosts had ever been to the game park and were as excited as our students at this opportunity. We saw the Falls at close quarters and the many crocodiles and hippos along the river banks. There were signs of increased numbers of cob and buffalo on the north side of the Park, but nothing like the numbers that were there in the 1960s.

On the second trip, we took John Ondoma's family with us, again their first opportunity to do something that we had regularly done while at Mvara. To our delight, we spotted a Shoe-billed Stork on the river bank, perhaps the ugliest bird in all creation, slate grey and five feet tall, standing as motionless as a prehistoric fossil until its head moved, and the extraordinary bird fixed us in its inscrutable gaze. On both days, we left Mvara early and got back to Arua late in the evening but we had no problems with road-blocks or any disturbances along the road. West Nile seemed to be as peaceful as we had always known it, but this was an illusion.

The completed water tank for the Mvara girls' domitories

One evening, as we sat in the twilight enjoying our post-supper coffee, we heard gun-fire near to the school.

'I expect it's just someone firing at a jackal,' I said reassuringly.

But it wasn't. In the morning, John Ondoma explained to me quietly that the Army had caught some men nearby, including the District Security Officer. His home had been searched and he was found with arms to be smuggled to rebels over in Zaire. After a fire-fight in which two had died, the DSO had been captured and was now on his way to Kampala in an

Army lorry, in hand-cuffs, dressed only in his underpants. We did not tell the UK students what we knew and prayed that there would be no more trouble before we left Arua. Our students were invited to visit the homes of their Mvara friends and given a meal. All were touched by this, knowing how little the local people had to live on and that it was only the more affluent homes that could invite them. Before we left the school, we had a handover ceremony for the water-tanks, planted a mahogany tree in the centre of the site and were formally thanked by the Bishop and the Board of Governors.

We then took four Mvara students with us on a trip down to Kampala and Entebbe where we camped by Lake Victoria and entertained Gordon and Grace Mc Cullough and Sam Turyangyenda and his wife to dinner. It was a happy reunion only slightly marred by the swarms of lake flies which got into our tents, our mouths and even our eyes as we vainly tried to fend them off.

The whole party travelled down to the far south-west by *matatu*, beyond Kabale to the high pass at the Kanaba Gap. The sun was setting behind the chain of Virunga volcanoes, a magnificent set of cones running west right into the Congo. We camped on the lower slopes of Mount Mgahinga. The following day, one group climbed Mount Sabinio, another visited iron-age caves on the mountain and a third went into the nearest town to forage for supplies for a celebration party to mark the the end of our expedition and the Principal's birthday. That evening, we feasted on rice and beans, seven tins of tuna, four bars of Cadbury's whole-nut milk chocolate and one tube of Smarties, washed down with two bottles of wine of dubious origin – the total stock of the only shop selling food in Kisoro. We promised to invite a party of staff and students from Mvara to come to Norfolk in the summer of 1998.

The last few days were spent camping in the Queen Elizabeth Park at Mweya, where a hyena decided to share one sleeping girl's tent and removed her day-sack in which she had stashed a packet of biscuits. When the remains were found in a nearby bush, the deep teeth marks in her water bottle convinced everyone of the wisdom of making sure you had no food in your tent. We reached Kampala in time to visit the British High Commissioner to give him a report on the successful completion of our Water Project and to enjoy his beer and sodas. We flew home from Entebbe on August 11th in time for the release of the A level results. Welcoming us at Heathrow was a very relieved party of parents and friends. As one of our students said, we had spent a month on the adventure of our lives, with the most friendly and hospitable people that we had ever met.

\*

Later that year, John Ondoma became the chairman of the local Head Teachers' Association, a role in which he had to work with the District Office to try to sort out school problems including delays in paying student grants. Uganda has sadly established a world-wide reputation for corruption within government and trying to find out where the money had gone did not endear John to the local officials. They responded by mounting a rumour campaign that he was about to be transferred from Mvara. The clear aim was to discourage him not just from pursuing the lost funds but also from implementing the development plans that he had started at the school.

By February 1998, he was in Kampala on the S1 selection conference when he heard a voice telling him, '*Satan is planning to attack you.*' He heard the same message again on the following day with the additional advice that he should not '*lash out at the people Satan is going to use, but rather imitate God and love them.*' A friend told him that evening he had heard from an education official that his name was at the top of a list of transfers from Arua. When John checked this with the Ministry he found that his file had not been tampered with.

One school, Ombaci, north of Arua went on strike early in 1998 and the indiscipline spread to many other secondary schools in the District. At Mvara, the S6 students organised a strike, but firm action by the Head and the Board of Governors avoided major trouble. A dispute grew between the District Education Officer and the Heads of the Secondary Schools who felt that they were not being supported over matters of school discipline. These Heads asked John to be their spokesman for discussions with the DEO but, while John was away in Kampala, a number of allegations were made against him.

When he got back to Arua, he heard that some of the Mvara teachers had vowed to have him removed from the school, spreading rumours that he was anti-government. In April, Kezzy had a dream that they had been walking through a swampy place with him in front. When she followed him, they looked round and saw that those who followed them were struggling and drowning in the flood. They had stood and praised God for saving them but wondered what the dream meant. Shortly afterwards, the Mvara S6 students refused to take their end of term examinations and went on strike again, demanding to meet with John. They did have a grievance, as the Uganda Ministry of Education had decided to move the A level Exams back for their year group, from the normal March 1999 to December 1998. To compensate students for three months loss of teaching time, the January – March 1998 term was extended until May, but the students had to pay extra fees to cover their food costs at school. He was told that their grievance was that they wanted to continue at school for part of the holiday but be refunded the extra fees which they had paid. John told them that their request would be considered but first, they must sit their examinations. They refused and decided to march to the District Offices in Arua to meet with the DEO.

John was sure that the strike was orchestrated by those S6 students who had not been selected for the party for the UK trip and who felt seriously aggrieved. The students returned to the school but met later that night with some of the teachers who advised them to drop their earlier demands and to focus on the allegations that their Headmaster was guilty of corruption, dictatorship and nepotism. They should demand his removal. Fortunately, when the NRM District Commissioner, the highest government official in the District, heard of this on the following day, he commented 'Ondoma is not a mountain to be moved.' The matter was put into the hands of the Board of Governors and the PTA. Both committees found that there was no evidence to support the allegations. When the District Inspector reported later to the Commissioner for Education, it was said that the Board of Governors had examined the alleged problems one by one in a joint meeting with the Parents and Teachers Association and found the Headmaster innocent. It was decided that the UK trip should go ahead.

All this was going on against a background of local elections in Arua, when the NRM won most of the seats, the first time that the area had shown unequivocal support for the Museveni government. The President flew up to Arua on a state visit, accompanied by President Moi of Kenya and announced the decision to build a new tarmac road from Karuma to Pakwach, providing West Nile with a reliable link to the south at last, provided that it was not broken by the LRA rebels on the Acholi side of the river. The President's personal helicopter pilot for the flight up to Arua was Major Samuel Turyagyenda, the Sam we knew so well.

In May, there were further small scale disturbances in the Koboko area and it was very difficult for John and Kezzy to visit their family home not far from the town. The Koboko–Moyo road was again closed but by July, Arua itself was peaceful again. The party visiting England came down to Kampala to catch their flight from Entebbe. With them came the student who was the Chairman of the school branch of the Uganda National Students Association. Before the party left Arua, the Governors had decided that this student should forfeit his place on the trip as he had been identified as a ringleader in the strike. He was not told until they got to Entebbe. On the night before they flew to London, John had to tell him that he was not going to England. Although he was given the money to get home, the UK party left behind a very angry and influential young man. He started to make trouble as soon as he got back to Arua. Clandestine meetings were held to plan how John would be destroyed. They planned to attack his house, burning it with Kezzy and the children inside. Kezzy heard that John would be in danger although she knew no details of what was planned. She arranged for a friend to meet John at Entebbe to warn him. None of us in the UK were aware of any of these problems when we met the party at Heathrow in July 1998.

Cutting the welcome cake and emailing home

The visit of the Uganda staff and students to Wymondham College was a great success. We welcomed them formally to the College and introduced them to the students and staff who would host them while they were with us. All the students stayed in the boarding houses, sharing rooms with College students and the members of staff were put up by College families. We hosted John in the Principal's house. For the first few days of settling in, the Ugandan students joined lessons and this in fact proved so popular that it was difficult to restrain them. Those taking A level English Literature at Mvara wanted to attend all the Wymondham Y12 and Y13 classes, on the set books which they were studying, and then to spend the evenings watching videos of the same texts. The girls played netball with College teams and the boys, all of whom were good runners, took part in athletics matches against other schools, running in bare feet.

We all took part in the regular College Boarders' Sunday morning service, with the Ugandan *udungu* band playing for some of the songs they loved to sing. The students had brought their instruments with them, a full set of stringed lyres from a bass on which the player sat to a set of trebles held in the hand. They captivated their audience with their playing and singing.

John had agreed to preach and I was concerned that he might not be able to hold the attention of a chapel full of teenage boarders. They could get restless with visiting preachers but I need not have worried.

John preaching at Wymondham and the Mvara *udungu* players

From the moment he started, talking quietly and simply about the nature of love and describing the predicament of the young Ugandan woman who had come to him and Kezzy seeking advice, they listened and heard what he said. 'Was that love?' he repeated at each crisis the young woman faced in her relationship with a young man who wanted her to please him but showed her little consideration. They knew what he was talking about and he was able to explain to them what Christian love and forgiveness meant.

When we visited Mvara in 1997, we had been able to carry out a practical project with the work on the water tanks. John and I were keen to find a similar project to complete while the Ugandan students were with us. Fortunately, the crumbling buildings of the old USAAF hospital came to our aid. The site still had the remains of the mortuary building, the place where the bodies of those whose lives could not be saved rested before being taken to Madingley US Cemetery for burial. It was a small brick structure with an asbestos roof next to the College pond, a peaceful and quiet place to sit in the summer time. As it was unsafe, we had planned to demolish it but felt that what it represented was worth trying to preserve.

The idea developed to turn the base of the building into a garden which would remain as a memorial to all those who had died.

The completed Memorial Garden at Wymondham College

This would provide a peaceful corner of the College for students who wanted to talk, read a book or just relax in the summer sunshine. The asbestos roof was removed by a professional team and we demolished the walls, retaining as many of the bricks as possible to create small wind-breaks and places for hardwood seats. Much of the work was simple manual labour and a team of College students joined our visitors in completing the project in five working days, even planting up the garden with a range of old-fashioned English shrub roses and herbs to make an attractive scented space for students to use. The Memorial Garden has been maintained at the College ever since and is visited by the remaining USAAF veterans who had been at the hospital in WWII and their families. They maintain strong links with the Norfolk community.

Over the Half Term holiday, the Uganda party and some of the College students joined us at our home in Lincolnshire, camping on the lawn. They shared in visits to York and the Lincolnshire coast. The weather was cold and wet but that hardly mattered. None of the Ugandans had seen the sea before and enjoyed the novelty of playing the curious game of cricket on the beach at low tide. Swimming in the very cold sea was less popular! We returned to the College for a farewell party and service and took our visitors back to Heathrow for their flight back to Entebbe, back to Mvara and the situation which John, his colleagues and the students found when they landed.

In Kampala, John got a message from Kezzy warning him of the threats against him. Writing about this later, he described remembering the story of the prophet Elisha, how he had been '*besieged by his enemies, and how his servant had quaked with fear. Elisha had prayed that God would open his servant's eyes to see that the army fighting for them, God's army, was far more formidable in strength and numbers to that of the enemy.*' John decided to travel up to Arua, where Kezzy and the rest of the family were amazed to see him. They welcomed him home and together they prayed for God's protection and peace that night. They also prayed for forgiveness for all those who had been working against him, through slander, hatred, intimidation, insults and persecution. Convinced of God's protection, they slept very soundly until the morning.

But the intimidation went on. The local FM Radio stations and even the national newspapers portrayed how bad, corrupt and wicked he had been. He was said to have been possessed by a fanatical desire to evangelise people for Christ. Muslims were said to be afraid of his influence on their children, which they thought would corrupt their minds, citing the case of the girl at Muni. Others alleged that he had been very harsh by insisting on collecting school fees even from very poor families, although this was what he was required to do by the school regulations. As the campaign against him grew, even those who knew the good things that he had done for Mvara began to drift away and to shun him. They were afraid of being labelled his 'spies'.

In spite of all this opposition, John tried to start work at school, meeting with the teachers and with S5 students. The meetings went well and a meeting with S4 was planned for the following day. Some of the disaffected teachers persuaded the S4 students to lock John out of their classrooms and to daub 'no classes unless Ondoma leaves the school' on the door. A crowd from the town gathered at the school to see what would happen. John found some comfort from the sign in his office 'God is Able' but realised that he could do nothing but wait at home even though the house was surrounded by rowdy students, shouting for his removal. The DEO, who had sided with the students in much of the dispute, decided to send John on leave, although he had no authority to do so. The people of the town were convinced that he had been dismissed from his post. All John could do was to sit at home and wait.

Others who had come to England with the Mvara party suffered also. Two of the S6 students were threatened with violence and decided to stay in Kampala, completing their S6 year at another school. One of the teachers was assaulted by students at Mvara and forced to leave the staff. Two other teachers left for posts in other schools. John's children, living in the Head's house in the middle of all this anger and violence, tried to continue as students at Mvara. They were ridiculed, intimidated and threatened with eviction from the school. Two of them had to have hospital treatment for stomach ulcers as a result. An Acting Headteacher was appointed to run the school and he arranged for security guards to watch the Ondoma's house, especially at night. After a while, the guards were withdrawn on the grounds of expense and as John put it *'God then took over and brought fierce dogs from all over the neighbourhood to guard us at night'*.

One of the most distressing aspects of all this opposition was the fact that at no time did anyone ask what John had done for Mvara. They were all so busy working out ways to engineer his leaving the school that no-one commended his honesty, commitment and frankness as Head. Nor did they welcome the support for Mvara that had been a direct result of his links with the UK or look forward to the assurances of future support which he had received. The Governors, Staff and Students of Wymondham College and the Lions Club of Norfolk had all promised to help Mvara Secondary School. The College was in fact planning another visit in 1999 to continue their support for Mvara. Other UK support had been pledged by a group of West Nile ex-patriates in London to try to help improve science teaching and a study had already been made of what was needed. Former Mvara students living in England had also set up the 'Margaret Lloyd Memorial Foundation', through Margaret's home church in Rugby to support teaching and learning at Mvara. All this was forgotten in the drive to get rid of John.

He did have some support. His sister arrived from Koboko to tell him of a dream she had in which God spoke to her and told her that His grace would be sufficient for him. He should not worry but sing the Lugbara hymn: '*Asi ndriza mini mavu, Ma eyo ni ega, ti…*' '*I cannot imagine your grace to me. Let the grace bind me to you. Let me walk with you so that I do not leave you. Lead me by your power so that I walk straight.*' He found much encouragement too in the words of Jesus:

'*Blessed are you who are persecuted because of righteousness, for theirs is the kingdom of heaven. Blessed are you when people insult you, persecute you and falsely say all kinds of evil against you because of me. Rejoice and be glad, because great is your reward in heaven, for in the same way they persecuted the prophets who were before you.*' (Matthew 5:10-12)

'*I have told you these things, so that in me you may have peace. In this world you will have trouble. But take heart! I have overcome the world.*' (John 16:33)

One of the hardest things for John to face at this very difficult time was the fact that even those in the Church began to turn against him. Local clergy who had led services which John and Kezzy had attended, lay people who had shared 'Praise the Lord' greetings with them, now joined the critics. Even the Christian Radio station 'Voice of Life' provided his detractors with air-time to voice their opposition to him. John was reminded again of the story of Joseph whose own brothers were so filled with envy, jealousy and malice that they sold him into slavery. When he met with the Christian friend who ran 'Voice of Life' and received his apology, John had to learn to forgive. He was helped by a book he bought in Kampala called 'Struggling to forgive' which he took home to read. Kezzy too was struggling with anger and a desire for revenge against those who were attacking John. In a dream, she saw a girl student throwing an unripe mango at her, which missed her, but prompted Kezzy to throw a lump of soil back at the girl. But she heard a voice telling her: 'vengeance is mine, I will repay.' The lump of earth crumbled in her hand.

John was torn between wanting to attack his enemies and knowing that his faith told him to forgive them. He remembered what Peter had done when his Lord was threatened. He had chopped off someone's ear. Jesus had healed the ear. Peter had to learn that taking up the cross and following Jesus means taking insults, intimidation and misunderstandings just as Jesus had done. John felt that God was insisting that if he was to find peace again, with Him and with his fellow men, he had to leave revenge to Him and obey the one key command, to forgive those who planned and executed evil against us for Christ's sake. If he was to overcome evil with good, the way forward was to forgive. Paul had encouraged the Colossians to:

'*Bear with each other and forgive one another if any of you has a grievance against someone. Forgive as the Lord forgave you. And over all these virtues put on love, which binds them all together in perfect unity.*' (Colossians 3:12-15)

In the midst of these problems, while John and Kezzy were still living in the Headmaster's house in the centre of a school which had apparently rejected him, the Uganda Scripture Union team had arranged a student conference and invited speakers from the UK, who needed somewhere to stay. The Ondomas put them up and John learnt from both speakers that they too had faced false accusations in the past and had learnt to forgive. It was possible with God's help. Armed with this encouragement, John went to see the Resident District Commissioner in Arua, the senior representative of the Government, and the Local Government Chairman, to tell them both that he would make no apologies for doing anything wrong at Mvara S. S., but that he forgave everyone who had planned and carried out the campaign of malicious lies against him and his family.

John and Kezzy decided to go away for a time, to a place of peace and spiritual renewal and chose to go to the retreat centre or 'prayer mountain', at Biko in Nebbi diocese in the south of West Nile. There they were encouraged to keep listening to God's voice. They were joined by Bishop Henry Orombi and his wife as they sought God's face and listened to Him. They came back from Nebbi much encouraged and resolved to forgive those who had hurt them and their pride. They knew that they would never find peace unless they followed this path. But the authorities in Arua were still determined to get rid of John and decided that the allegation that he had taken money from the school during his time as Head there should be investigated. A full audit of the school accounts was ordered. The Auditors examined all the school books from 1994 and reported that there was no financial mismanagement. John thanked God for the wise decision to make sure that the school accounts were straight. He wrote about the next stage of the challenges he faced:

'The only allegation left was that I was hiding the money that had been given to Mvara Secondary School from the UK. In response to this accusation, John Haden wrote from England to the Chairman of Governors at Mvara, the Bishop of Madi and West Nile, the Rt. Rev. Enock Lee Drati, copied to the DEO, informing them what money had been given to me during our visit to the UK and his opinion of me, which was contrary to the popular thinking in the Arua District official circles at that time. Then the DEO invited me to his office to tell me, in the presence of his top officials, to go back to work, become the head of another school and forget what had happened. After all, I was their 'good headmaster', or so they said. All the things that had been done to me had been instigated from somewhere else, not by them.

I asked them to write another report to that effect and to publish it through all the media, the national newspapers and local FM radio stations, which had been used in the campaign against me. I told them that I forgave them for Christ's sake and asked them to leave me alone. God, who had created me and, cared enough for me to die for my sins, would sort out my future which lay secure in his hands. When the new Acting Headmaster came to take over the school, we were still living in the Head's house and, although I was not invited to the hand-over ceremony, I joined some of those who had campaigned against me and witnessed the hand-over with them. I told them that I had forgiven them for what they had done and asked them never to do to the new headmaster what they had done to me.

There remained the problem of the members of our church who had spread rumours against me. We were members of the same worshipping community at St Philip's in Arua Town. One Sunday morning, just before the service started, I stood with Kezzy and my family at the front of the church and said this:

'I would like to say to visitors, fellow worshippers, ladies and gentlemen, Satan attacked us fiercely for the greater part of this year (1998). It wanted us to be crushed beyond recognition. But God never left us alone. He urged us to love even those who persecuted us and to pray for them. We should not be revenged, but leave revenge to God, who will do it better. We should not let evil defeat us; instead we should conquer evil with good. Consequently, our faith and our souls *have been drawn closer to God, the Father of our Lord Jesus Christ, our Refuge and our Comforter! That is why we want to sing with you 'It is well with my soul'.*

*Everyone in the church then sang 'When peace like a river attends my soul, when sorrow like billows roll; whatever my lot, You have taught me to say, It is well, it is well with my soul'.*

*Nobody got up to ask forgiveness from us. Rather I was later informed that some had grumbled about why we were given a platform to speak to the congregation. But we walked away from Church that morning feeling confident that our God reigns and He is in control of all our circumstances, bitter or sweet and we were very grateful to the Vicar of St Philips' Church for having given us the opportunity to speak.'*

\*

In Norfolk, when we heard of all the problems that John had faced, we had to decide about the future of the link between our schools. Sadly, we decided that in the circumstances the link could not continue and I wrote to all those who were interested:

'As some of us know, the situation at Mvara Secondary School, Arua, is not good. When the Mvara group left Arua to come here in May, the school was already in difficulties. It is also sadly true that many in Arua have become jealous of the opportunities which those who came to visit us were given. These allegations, of 'corruption', are, as far as I am aware, without foundation. It is certainly true that anyone who has heavy responsibilities and who tries to root out misuse of school funds, as John Ondoma has done, will be very unpopular with some staff. This is particularly true of those who have not served the school well and have been recommended by the Governors for removal from their posts.

Although the Ministry in Kampala has not substantiated the allegations in any way, the Ondoma family have had a very difficult three months, with threats against them and considerable hardship. The DEO has tried to persuade the Mvara governors to allow him to transfer John from the Mvara Headship to a small rural secondary school, although this does not have the support of the Ministry.

Faced with all these difficulties, John has decided to resign from the Teaching Service and to move to their own house near to Arua. This is a brave step to take as he now has to find another job. Kezzy, his wife, is still working as the

District Labour Officer in Arua and their children are still in school. Emanuel is at Mvara. John is very sad to be leaving Mvara and teaching, but he feels that this is the only way forward for the family.

He is particularly sad that the link with Wymondham will not now be easy to maintain. The Mvara Governors have appointed a successor, but the school is not yet back to normal, with a lot of confusion and lack of discipline. We have heard from other members of staff who hope that the link may be able to continue, but this will be difficult. The Mvara Deputy Head, Mr Augustine Juruga, has also been moved, to take over the Headship of Ombaci School, which will be a challenge for him.

I have written to the Bishop who is their Chairman of Governors to express our sadness at all these developments and to say that the Link between our schools will be suspended for the moment. It clearly will not be possible for a group from the College to visit Arua next summer, which is very disappointing. The security situation generally in the Arua area is not good at the moment as the breakdown of government in the Congo to the west has enabled dissident groups to use the border area for raids into the north west of Uganda. The war to the north in the Sudan has also caused continuing instability.

All this is very sad, but we can look back on two very successful exchange visits, to Arua and to Wymondham, and reflect that both schools have benefited from the contact, from the friendships established and from the opportunities to learn from each other. The good news is that the four Mvara students who came with us in 1997 to the south west of Uganda and who took their A levels in March 1998, all passed their exams. Their year group achieved the best grades ever awarded to Mvara students.

To all those who have been involved over the past four years, I can only thank you for your support and hope that we shall find other ways of expressing our interest in, concern for and support for the people of West Nile now that the formal phase of our Uganda Link has come to an end.'

\*

John and Kezzy Ondoma still had their faith and their family. They were also still living in the Headmaster's house at Mvara Secondary School, in the middle of a hostile community. They prayed together that God would help them to endure the continuing slights and snubs that they all experienced. John assured the children that their needs would be met somehow. Their school fees would be paid and they would be encouraged to go as far as they wished in their schooling. He went to see his doctor, as his blood pressure had been very high. He was amazed to be told that it had returned to normal. It seemed that he had experienced both physical and spiritual healing.

By October 1998, he was sure that the Arua authorities would not change their position. They would offer him any other Headship in the District but not that of Mvara Senior Secondary School. He and the family prayed over the options open to him and they were sure that God would honour his stand against what he believed to be wrong. He decided to resign from public service and to apply for early retirement as he had completed the minimum thirty years of service. Many of his friends advised him against this as he still had children at school but he was sure that their future would be secure in God's hands and that He would both guide them and provide for them. They read the words of Paul together:

'*I know what it is to be in need, and I know it is to have plenty. I have learned the secret of being content in any and every situation, whether well fed or hungry, whether living in plenty or in want. I can do all this through him who gives me strength.*' (Philippians 4:12-13).

John described what happened:

'*Realising that I would need another job sooner or later, and that the requirements of such a job would include computer literacy and a valid driving licence, I enrolled in a computer school to learn the basic packages to make me computer literate. I thank God for the services of DESCOM systems, particularly of Charles Asiki, the proprietor, for having devoted time and energy to teach me and time to practise the skills I learned. As a result, I quickly mastered word-processing and using spreadsheets, when God gave me a job using these skills.*

*One Sunday morning, I was coming to Church for the service when I met a man who asked me if I was free to see him the following Monday. When we met, he asked me what packages I had learnt on the computer course he had heard that I had taken. I explained what I knew and he told me about his wish for me to work with SIL part-time, to perform tasks which needed computer literacy. I readily said yes and, in this job, I was able to learn further skills, handling emails, radios for communication and meeting people from different cultures. After a few months, members of the organisation asked me if I would work full time with them. Again, I said that if it was God's will, I would and this led to exposure to many more things, including attending work-shops in relevant fields.'*

John had found a new job, or as he believed, God had found it for him. SIL (formerly the Summer Institute of Linguistics) is a world-wide NGO involved in literacy support particularly in indigenous languages and is a partner organisation of the Wycliffe Bible Translators. John's role was to run an office for SIL in Arua and to work with Wycliffe personnel based in the area. He found this hugely encouraging and felt that through the support of SIL/Wycliffe staff, he had experienced a strong friendship and a sense of being valued. It was such a positive experience that he decided to celebrate by putting up a notice on his office door 'MUNGU AZA KU', Lugbara for 'God does not make blunders'.

While working for SIL part-time, he and a group of friends began to plan for a new venture. Unhappy with the low quality of education and the lax moral framework in government schools, they decided to set up a new private Christian School. They decided to call the school 'Ushindi', Kiswahili for 'Victory'. The school motto would be 'Victory in Christ'. The founding group was eight Christian families in Arua, six Lugbara, one with both British and Lugbara members and one British. They became the Governors of the Ushindi Schools.

They knew that the Uganda government attached great importance to education and had a strong commitment to Universal Primary Education (UPE) followed by Universal Secondary Education (USE). But their own experience as parents and teachers over the previous decade had led them to seriously doubt that these policies could deliver what parents wanted. Families were encouraged to think that Primary Education should be free and for all, but in reality, there were simply not enough classrooms to accommodate all the eligible pupils and not enough teachers to teach them. Under UPE, in their view, quality teaching and learning was no longer possible. The teacher-pupil ratio had rocketed, until teachers were trying to teach seventy or even a hundred pupils in each primary class. Standards had fallen and were getting worse. Although primary school education was still geared towards academic excellence, pupils could not be prepared adequately to compete in the national examinations, in spite of their natural talents.

From the start, the founding families wanted Ushindi School to have high standards and to recruit only qualified and dedicated teachers of high moral integrity. They planned that the school should be as sustainable as possible, that all income, from fees, from donations and grants and from community contributions would be properly used and accounted for, with a focus on reinvestment so that the school could develop. Wherever possible, the school would grow its own food, raise poultry and keep cows to reduce food costs. Administrative costs would also be kept as low as possible although better salaries would be paid to teachers who made an effective contribution to the school.

This was a brave venture when they set out in 1999 and started to build Ushindi Primary on a leased site near to the Mvara Diocesan headquarters. The school opened in 2000 with the first primary classes and plans were soon under way to provide a secondary school. John was able to use his experience at Muni and at Mvara to approach a Dutch NGO, ZOA Refugee Care, for financial help. Through this NGO, they approached a Christian College in the Netherlands, Driestar College, for their support. The funds received enabled a start to be made on a Secondary School building programme. The site chosen was well away from Arua town. John knew how difficult it was to run a mixed secondary boarding school right next to all the temptations of a large town. Land was available behind Kuluva Hospital to the south of the main road to the Congo border at Vurra. It was a long way from any mains supply of water, drainage or electricity but this fitted the ethos of sustainability and there was space to grow food. A site so close to the Uganda/Congo border may not have seemed sensible, until one remembers the experience of many of those who had to flee across international borders or into extremely rural areas to save their lives in times of great trouble.

The school started with a block of four classrooms, two dormitories, an administration block, a kitchen block and housing for seven teachers. There was enough money left to buy the minimum needed of books, furniture, science equipment and chemicals, games facilities and a few solar lighting panels. Senior 1 opened at the beginning of 2002 with forty nine students, all boarders. In the following year, the school grew to ninety four pupils, again all boarding. Reflecting on how their plans had come to fruition, John wrote:

*'Our plan is to offer education with a Christian ethos and global outlook so that the graduates of the school are able to fit into society as responsible citizens, ready to make a contribution to the development of our country. They should be people who are morally responsive to God's ideals and mindful of their fellow men and women. We are grateful for the way the*

*school had taken off. The character of the pupils should demonstrate the Christian ideal, which was the desire of the founders. It is our prayer that God will continue to bless the school and all those who come to pass through it and that, through them, our whole country will be blessed.'*

## Part 6: God does not make blunders
### 6.1 Going back to West Nile

I resigned from Wymondham College in 2000 and spent three years working full time for the Cambridge company which won the contracts for administering the UK Government's Teacher Appraisal plans. They offered me a job co-ordinating the introduction of their schemes in all the schools in Lincolnshire, Norfolk and Peterborough. I worked from home and supported the implementation of these new schemes in the areas around the Wash. It was professionally rewarding and gave me opportunities to work with the Heads and Governors of Primary and Special schools, a privilege rarely open to Secondary Heads. Throughout this time, we kept in touch with John and Kezzy Ondoma in Arua and with Sam Turyagyenda in Entebbe. Through them and others still working in Uganda, we learnt of the progress which the Museveni Government was making towards peace in the north of Uganda and the development of Ushindi Secondary School.

Retirement came in gentle stages, until by 2011 I was free from all paid commitments and could pursue other interests in the church and in the community. In that year, Jenny and I had a very happy Ruby Wedding summer, a succession of parties for local friends, family and those we had known for forty years since our time together in Uganda. Our eldest son, Peter, found that he had a lot of 'air miles' which had to be used by the end of the year, and some free time in November or December. He asked me where I would like to go. I contacted our Ugandan friends, especially the Ondomas and the Turyagyendas, and enquired whether it might be possible for us to visit them. They were very encouraging – so we planned a visit to Uganda, to include a visit to the gorillas of the Impenetrable Forest and a school reunion in West Nile.

The week before we left, I met a friend in Oakham High Street and he asked me if I was doing anything interesting.

'Going to Uganda,' I said, 'planning to have a school reunion almost on the Congo border.'

He looked anxious. 'Have you seen the BBC programme – about child sacrifice in Uganda?' He was warning me that Uganda might not be as welcoming as we had hoped.

I saw the programme before I left. It described a community around Kampala 'living in fear'. It was claimed that the practice of abducting and killing children for the purposes of ritual sacrifice to ensure success in business had been growing for the past few years as the Uganda economy grew. Mutilated bodies of children had been found lying by roadsides. A Church Pastor was interviewed as he had taught local children a new song: '*Heal our land, end child sacrifice.*'

The report claimed that it was possible to buy a child for a fee. For another fee, it was possible to have the child ritually murdered by a witch doctor so that body parts could be buried in the foundations of new business premises. This would ensure the financial success of the business. Children had become a 'commodity of exchange' in the processes of business development. The UK Charity 'Jubilee Campaign' was strongly critical of the Uganda Police for failing to investigate such atrocities, claiming that there were more than nine hundred cases still waiting for police action, because of corruption and lack of resources. One victim, who had survived castration, and an attempt to behead him, had been taken to Mulago Hospital in Kampala with horrific injuries. He was just nine years old.

Watching the programme, I was reminded of the film '*Africa Addio*' which I had seen in 1968 shortly before leaving for Uganda. This new 2011 catalogue of horror was equally appalling. Yet another awful story about Uganda, I thought, even if is not about West Nile. When I met my friend again that week, I could only say that such horrors are not unknown, even in England. If we find it very difficult to prevent *muti* child murders in the UK, how much harder it must be to stop them in a country where belief in spirits is wide-spread even after over a hundred years of the presence of the Christian Church. 'Enjoy your trip,' my friend said, 'but you were warned! I'm not going to Uganda.'

\*

In the event, we had a wonderful fourteen days in Uganda, from the moment we enjoyed a full English breakfast together in the Terminal 5 Concord Lounge and slipped out of a grey November Heathrow by BA 063, heading for Entebbe. Thanks to Peter's 'Air-miles', we had Club World tickets and sipped champagne over the Alps, enjoyed our steak and Rioja over the Med and afternoon tea over the deserts of Libya and the Sud of Sudan. It was a very different return to Uganda from my first journey in 1968 and I thought how easily I could get used to travelling Club World. We carried with us Andrew Roberts' excellent revised version of the Uganda Bradt Guide and enough Malarone tablets each to keep us free of malaria.

Entebbe was very warm and welcoming and the road to Kampala crammed with cars and lorries even at just before midnight. Mobile phone adverts were plastered everywhere and there were other obvious changes. When we came back in 1994, Baganda women had set up tiny stalls all along the roadside. They were selling a few tomatoes, boxes of matches, small bags of ground-nuts, sachets of detergent, all by the light of a candle in a jar. They were running micro-businesses on a scale which would be regarded as hopelessly small in the West, making perhaps a few shillings a night to feed their families and to buy more stock. By 2011, these stalls had gone. In their place were large market stalls selling piles of fruit and vegetables, just like the greengrocers' stalls on Oakham market. Along the main road into Kampala, shops were open late into the night. Many were selling snacks to passing bus passengers on a co-operative basis. When a bus slowed down, dozens of boys ran out into the road with trays of *samuzas.* They wore a uniform, had a licence number and reported back to their 'manager' at the food stall.

The Speke Hotel Kampala, the setting of my first night in Kampala as a Government Education Officer in 1968, was again our base for two nights in the city. The Asian owners were back, with this and several other hotel businesses clearly doing well. It still had echoes of its colonial past, sepia prints and maps of Speke's journeys. An ancient fig tree grew by the same rows of spacious rooms under a tiled roof. Staying there was very good value, apart from the throb of the Congolese music from the adjacent Rock Bar and the 'affectionate but commercially motivated ladies' who frequented the bar. Peter had three offers on his way to check the football scores – I fell asleep in spite of the music.

In the morning, we wandered in the hot sunshine around the vibrant and colourful city centre of Kampala, visiting the Bookshop from which supplies of books and stationery were sent to Church schools all over Uganda in the 1960s. It was still serving schools with basic educational supplies but it was also sad to see that, in 2011, the shelves of books on Uganda offered a depressing collection. Accounts of atrocities filled more than a metre of titles, from the murder of the Uganda Martyrs, through the victims of Idi Amin's regime to the sufferings of Acholi children at the hands of the LRA. Looking at the books on offer, I vowed to try to write something positive about this beautiful country.

In the backstreets of the City, by the Nakasero Market, the buildings which could have been in Bombay or any Indian city and once housed Asian shop-keepers, now had Ugandan owners, suppliers of 'glasses for windows' and anything else you might need. We met up with our Matoke Tours driver to plan our journeys. Matoke, the green plantain banana staple food of the people of the South of Uganda, ('those brown boys' according to our 1960s West Nile students), is also the name of the small Dutch/Ugandan tour company who organised our transport and accommodation extremely efficiently.

Our first visit in Kampala was to Makerere College School and the University Campus where we had lived and worked in 1971-72. The school laboratories looked much the same, if perhaps a bit down at heel, but there was also an impressive new residential block. All over the school, the anti-HIV/Aids campaigners had put up reminders: 'true love waits', 'virginity is a virtue', and 'delay sex for your own benefit'. More enigmatic aphorisms, such as 'attitude determines altitude', accompanied gentle encouragement: 'lost time is never found'. I wondered if classes did now start on time. They never did in 1972. On our 1994 visit to Kampala, we had walked down the road past the Parliament Buildings. Men were standing on the pavement with weighing scales. For a few shillings, you could check your weight in your coffee break. Educated Ugandans were worried about losing weight because they knew that this was a sign that they had developed 'Slim', as HIV/Aids was then called. Then, there were massive hoardings along the roads, encouraging everyone with frank messages: 'Abstinence, faithfulness, but if you must, use a condom' and 'Your friend with AIDS is still your friend'.

This time, the messages were more subtle, and in Luganda. There were no scales on the pavements. But the campaign against HIV/AIDS was not yet fully won. The Saturday Vision government newspaper carried an Intimate HIV Special, a six page pull out asking such questions as 'Is Uganda losing the HIV battle?', 'What if your wife tests positive?', and 'Raising three HIV positive children.' It seemed that Uganda needed to re-launch its HIV control strategy with a new focus on using anti-retroviral drugs for those who are at risk. The positive merits of male circumcision were emphasised. HIV incidence had fallen, but it was now stuck at 6.5% of the population and began to rise again, particularly amongst young people.

From the Speke Hotel, we could look across the gardens surrounding the five-star Sheraton, Imperial Royale and Serina Hotels. It was in this park that Milton Obote had built a smart new conference centre at huge expense for the planned conference of the Organisation of African Unity. Amin's Coup prevented Obote from hosting this conference and it was moved to Rabat, but Amin hosted the next meeting in Kampala. In 2007, the Commonwealth, the world-wide association of English-speaking friends, held their 20th Heads of Government Conference (CHOGM) in the Kampala International Conference Centre. President Yoseri Museveni welcomed representatives of forty eight countries and invited Ruanda to attend as a guest. The Commonwealth admitted Ruanda's Head of State, Paul Kagame, into full Commonwealth membership in 2009. Looking across the busy Nile Avenue in the heart of Kampala, the modern hotels and conference centre were a reminder that as Uganda takes her place as a valued member of the full range of international fellowships, she particularly welcomes visitors who can afford $350 a night!

From the crowded city, we drove up to the relative peace of Namirembe Hill to walk around the Anglican Cathedral with its monuments to James Hannington, the martyred first Bishop of Uganda, and Janani Luwum, the Archbishop murdered in 1977 by order of Idi Amin. I remembered seeing Luwum's statue amongst the other 20th Century Christian Martyrs on the West Front of Westminster Abbey. Inside Namirembe Cathedral, four couples and thousands of beautifully dressed Baganda men and women were celebrating four simultaneous weddings with much joy and familiar English hymns. The Anglican Church has been at Namirembe for over a hundred years and has a strong place at the heart of Baganda society. As we walked down the hill to our car, we were caught in a cloud-burst of truly tropical rain.

That evening, we had our first reunion, with the Makerere College School 'old-boy', Sam Turyagyenda, now a Brigadier and Deputy Commanding Officer of the Uganda People's Defence Air Force. He met us, with his wife Anne and his son, Hilary, at the Kyber Pass Restaurent at the Speke where we enjoyed an excellent Indian meal. It was good to see him again. He reminded us of the time he had come to see us in Morpeth in 1975 when we were the only people he knew in the Northern Hemisphere and Peter was a two year old. Sam's training in Russia to fly helicopters had led him to join the Uganda Police Air Wing and then to transfer to the National Resistance Army's Air Force. As well as being Deputy Commander of the UPDAF, he was still the personal helicopter pilot to the President of Uganda. Sam told us that he was half-way through a Masters Degree in Air Accident Investigation at Cranfield University near Bedford, where Richard Inwood was the Anglican Bishop. Sam was planning to retire from the UPDAF in the not too distant future and to take up a new role as an Air Accident Investigator, probably the only one working in Uganda.

We had planned to do the 'high-end tourism' first, so our Matoke Tours driver took us off to the West. Once we had escaped from the chaotic Kampala traffic, we made good time on the tarmac road through the valleys of Buganda, all a deep rich green with *matoke shambas* and papyrus choked swamps. The fast main road runs for one hundred and forty km to Masaka and about the same distance again to the President's home town of Mbarara. We rushed past the sellers of fruit, papyrus mats, drums, colourful stools and fresh tilapia fish, in the same places as we had passed them along the same route when it was just a *murram* road all those years ago. Mbarara was booming, the 'land of milk and honey' according to Alfred, our driver, whose home was in the less advantaged far-west district of Kigezi.

The tarmac went on to the small town of Rukungiri on the northen edge of the Kigezi District and then we hit the *murram*, still the type of road you find in rural areas all over Uganda, good enough in the dry when freshly graded but soon corrugated and very dusty. It had been raining heavily. The bumpy, tortuous, muddy Buhoma road took three hours for one hundred and fifty km, through increasingly hilly country past the small fields of Kigezi on terraces climbing high up the steep hillsides. It was getting cooler as we rattled through the tea gardens and into the valley which leads to Bwindi, Uganda's famous 'Impenetrable Forest'. We found our up-market Mahogany Springs Lodge, a new tourist hotel booked by Matoke on a 'special offer', and enjoyed three nights there as the only off-season guests for the team of staff to look after. Uganda can now offer very comfortable accommodation to those who can afford to live in luxury but there are cheaper options all along the road into Buhoma.

We had booked two Gorilla Tracking permits for a visit to the Bwindi gorillas some months before as this is a very popular activity, even at $500 per day each! Very early the next morning, we set off for the start of our 'gorilla adventure'. Concerned about being banned if I showed any signs of a head-cold, I sucked lozenges and blew my nose well before getting to the Uganda Wildlife HQ about a mile from our accommodation, but I need not have worried. The cold was cured! We were fully briefed: 'get no nearer than seven metres, no food, no drink, no sneezing - was anyone feeling ill?' No-one dared. So we set off, Peter and I armed with heavy wooden poles as third legs. Peter carried four litres of water and our packed lunches in a day sack. 'If your pack is more than 2 kg, you should hire a porter', we were advised. Everyone felt the need of a porter!

Gorilla tracking at Bwindi is very well organised and provides employment for significant numbers of local people. 10% of the fees charged by the National Parks now goes to the local community and it is now very safe. The hard lessons have been learnt from the incident in 1999 when a murderous gang came over from the Congo and shot a party of eight tourists and four Ugandans, including the Park Warden. This tragedy halved the number of visitors to Bwindi for a time, but, as confidence returned, the numbers rose again. In 2009, over twelve thousand overseas visitors spent time at Bwindi visiting the gorillas. They come from all over the affluent world. Few Ugandans can afford to join them as visitors when they meet at the Centre for Gorilla Tracking on the edge of the Park. This has a base for holding briefings and showing a short film and then each party moves off in the rain to the entrance to the forest. Buhoma lies in a steeply sloping river valley at the eastern end of a track which goes right through to the other side of the Impenetrable Forest. We crossed a slippery foot bridge and started to climb.

Peter accused me of setting a fast pace.

'I'm trying to keep up with the guides,' I muttered between gulps of air.

Our Head Guide and his team of two rangers were armed with automatic rifles 'in case we meet elephants'. It occurred to me that they would have to be pretty athletic elephants as we clambered up a narrow zigzag path through the trees. I decided after half an hour that this was all a very bad idea. Fortunately, two of the 'porters' decided to take charge of my ascent, with one acting as puller and, at the really steep bits, the other acting as pusher. (Think: three legs good, five legs better, seven legs wonderful.)

We stopped for a breather at Africa Corner - a rock shaped a bit like the Continent - not that I was very interested at that point. Then, it was onwards and upwards. By the end of two hours of exhausting climbing, we had reached the ridge and our leader announced that he had made contact with his team of rangers. They had found the gorillas' nest from the previous night.

'They are now not far!' he announced with confidence.

Peter expressed the cheerful view that I should please delay my heart attack until we got down. Then, we slithered down the far side of the ridge into a bowl of thick vegetation. There they were, a family of gorillas lounging around in the bushes, scratching, chewing, snoozing, and utterly ignoring the arrival in their world of six *muzungu* and their escort team. We saw the young ones first, clambering around in the vegetation as if enjoying a play-school, climbing up into shrubs and falling out. Then the older females appeared, having an argument, beating their chests, and chewing the odd stick. They seemed completely disinterested in our seven metre proximity, but then I suppose we would have been if we had been visited by strangers with cameras every day for the previous fifteen years.

The silver-back, confident in his role as dominant male, was lounging under a bush, stripping shoots and chewing. With a diet of green vegetation in vast quantities, the occasional loud fart was excusable. His was a family of nineteen, each known by name to the guides. They were clearly doing well. Earlier this year they had been living within thirty minutes walk of the Park HQ for most of the time, and even enjoying eating the banana shoots of the village *matoke* gardens, so our climb to 1700 m and longish walk was a bit unusual. But, according to one of our party who had seen the other family group the day before within half an hour, we got the better experience.

After an hour we had to leave them to get on with being some of the last seven hundred mountain gorillas in the world, half of whom live in this Ugandan forest. We started back. It was raining - hard. We clambered back up to the ridge and stopped to have our packed lunch under the dripping trees. The path up had seemed steep but relatively safe. Going down in the heavy rain, it was treacherous - not the thing to do in shoes! It took us about an hour of slipping, sliding and sitting in the mud. My two supporters were superb, offering helping hands and encouragement. One of them mentioned that they had a special wicker chair to carry those who refused to go any further, which made me feel better. At least I had got up with help! We reached the bottom, were presented with our gorilla tracking certificates, exchanged email addresses and tottered back to the Lodge. We were muddy, sweaty but happy, very ready for a hot shower and a drink after an absolutely brilliant day. That evening, Peter and I celebrated with a delicious steak and bottle of wine. It was my second day with Uganda's gorillas, having been with Tim on the Virunga Mountains in 1996.

In the morning, every joint creaked, every muscle ached and the cold damp air of Buhoma was getting into my bones. But we had another good day, strolling gently along the dirt road through the forest, listening to and occasionally seeing all sorts of interesting birds. Some of them are unique to this area, the 'Albertine Endemics' of Bwindi. Our guides for this were local Bakiga experts, including our Matoke driver, Alfred. He had worked at Buhoma learning about wild life some years before. Bird-watching in dense forest is not easy but technology came to our aid. Armed with iPods on which were recorded all the likely bird calls and with a hand-held loud speaker, they could play the call of each bird. For example, a black bee-eater call produced an answering chirp from the dense forest and then the bird itself, certainly black against a bright sky. Some visitors of a more twitching nature than us have identified over a hundred exotic species on this road in just one morning; we managed forty eight, or rather, the experts did!

The other activities for visitors to Buhoma are organised by the local community, both the Bakiga who live all over Kigezi and the Batwa. These pygmy people have lived in the Albertine forests for millennia, eking out a precarious hunter-gatherer existence and pushed further and further into the forest by Bantu incursions. The designation of the Impenetrable Forest as a National Park deprived Batwa communities of their homes and their hunting grounds. They now survive at the forest edge in small sad communities willing to share what remains of their culture with visitors who will pay. Village walks include activities such as farming, brewing beer, preparing traditional medicines and ending with a display of Batwa dancing. There are opportunites to buy their handicrafts and to contribute to their school and health centre. At least these funds go direct to the local people and this growing interest in tourism provides employment for some of the poorest people in Uganda.

*

It was a long drive back to Kampala. If you want to see the Bwindi gorillas, you have no choice, unless you charter a plane and fly into Ishasha not far to the north or come in through Ruanda. We were upmarket tourists but not that upmarket. When we got back to Kampala, we spent one night at the adequately comfortable Church of Uganda Namirembe Guest House, full of Bishops and NGO workers, and set off in the morning for the north.

The good tarmac road beyong the town of Bombo runs through the Luwero triangle area, the scene of the appalling suffering when Museveni 'went to the bush' in 1982 and fought a guerrilla war against Milton Obote's second government. The towns and villages along the road are slowly recovering and there are many small-scale aid projects supported by churches and communities overseas.

We were on our way to Murchison Falls Park via Masindi, by the fast road which runs straight as a die through some pretty dull country. This clearly brings out the gladiator spirit in bus and lorry drivers. We passed mangled and overturned trucks, the product of head-on collisions between drivers unwilling to give way until they could see the whites of each others' eyes. There was even an overturned bus – probably caused by a burst tire – with its horde of excited passengers, mostly still in one piece, spilled out onto the side of the road.

On a branch off this road, an enterprising charity, Rhino Fund Uganda[1], (RFU) is trying to re-introduce these wonderful animals to Uganda. The last known Ugandan rhino was seen in 1983. All the others, both white and black, have been killed by poachers or soldiers, victims of the high prices on world markets for rhino-horn. This is now more expensive than gold pushed up by the demand for rhino horn as an ingredient in Chinese traditional medicines. As more of the Chinese middle classes can afford pills and powders laced with rhino horn, there seems little future of the world's remaining rhinos.

The RFU project leased seven thousand hectares of empty bush just north of the Kafu River and built a high electric-fence around the perimeter. Donors in Kenya, South Africa and the US provided adult white rhinos. It's a long business breeding rhino but if you start with three fit young males and three willing females, the calves do come. So far, three have been born at the Ziwa project. 'Obama', the son of an ex-Disneyland female, was the first white rhino to be born in Uganda for twenty eight years. Guarded twenty four hours a day by armed rangers and closely studied by vets, these are the pioneers of the programme. Sadly, the RFU white rhinos are all from the southern race, indigenous to Africa south of the Zambezi River. The entire Northern race, once found in areas of Africa west of the Nile including Ajai's reserve in Uganda's West Nile, have been killed. But with the birth of the first calves, the white rhino is beginning to return to Uganda. There is a long way to go before the numbers get up to thirty or forty and rhinos can be resettled in Murchison Park again.

You can track the Ziwa animals on foot, much as we tracked rhinos in the West Nile Inde/Ajai reserve in the 1960s. When I got home, I sent our thanks to the Ziwa project with an old photo of the last white rhino we saw in Murchison Park in 1971. Angie at Ziwa emailed: 'you have absolutely no idea what that photograph means to us here on the sanctuary. Thank you so very much for sending it and ….I am very happy you got to see rhino in Uganda again.' As for black rhino, the smaller, more aggressive species which once lived in Uganda's northern game parks, the project has not yet started for them.

*

We reached Paraa in time for the ferry over the Victoria Nile. The last time Peter and I saw Paraa Lodge in 1994 the roof was off and the rooms were home to troops of baboons! This time, we lived like kings in the same restored and air-conditioned rooms, with excellent meals and attentive staff. Early next morning, we set off for a game-drive with Alfred and a ranger to see what was left of the more than fourteen thousand elephants and the great herds of buffalo, hartebeest and Uganda cob we used to see in the 1960s. Through the 1970s and 1980s, the game was decimated by wars. By the 1990s, the animal populations were recovering slowly. When the Lord's Resistance Army brought murderous chaos once more to Northern Uganda in the early 2000s, game numbers fell again but are now recovering slowly. This time, we saw good herds of cob, giraffe and buffalo and some elephant. Then a lion came out of the long grass by the track, looked at us, sauntered along the track, sat down, yawned and rolled over.

After a short snooze, he got up, scent-marked a small tree and pushed off again into the grass. It's tough being a lion.

Oil has been found under the grasslands of Murchison Park and all along the west side of the Albertine Rift. Over the past five years, test drilling in the area to the east of Lake Albert and up into the Murchison Falls Park has shown that there are proven reserves of up to 2.5 billion barrels of oil in the field.

The first oil is likely to flow in 2012, although discussions between the companies involved and the Ugandan Government have delayed progress. What is clear is that Uganda has an oil bonanza with the potential to turn it into a medium range oil exporter, perhaps like Mexico, with an estimated $2 billion annual income from oil.

The economic impact is already being felt in a small way in Hoima and Masindi, the towns nearest to the test-wells. Hotels are booming as Turkish contractors, putting in a road from the oil-field to the Kampala road, need somewhere to stay. People in Hoima are already dreaming of becoming rich. The French oil company, Total, the Irish drilling company, Tullow[2], and the huge Chinese CNOOC company are all involved.

Murchison lion lying in the heart of an oil field

Uganda's oil is viscous, with high wax content, difficult to pump unless pre-heated. Some may be refined in a small way within Uganda but if the oil is to achieve its international value, it must first be transferred by pipe-line to the Kenyan or Tanzanian coast. The cost of getting Uganda's oil to world markets is said to be US$10 billion. With the focus on oil wealth comes the ongoing concern about the corruption said to be endemic in Museveni's Uganda. Meanwhile, exploration continues along the Albert Nile basin with test drillings down in the south-west around Lake Edward and up into West Nile in the area known as the Rhino Camp basin. Both are potentially very rich in oil deposits and both are today very poor regions of the country. They are also tetse-fly areas where sleeping sickness made human settlement difficult and cattle-raising impossible. As a result, both areas became Game Reserves, vast tracts of scrubby bush reserved for game because human habitation was so difficult.

The adjacent major national game parks, Queen Elizabeth Park in the south-west and Murchison Falls Park in the north, are both on the edge of tetse-fly areas and are both potentially excellent areas for oil production. There is much anxiety about the impact of oil exploration and extraction on these two prime assets for Uganda's fragile tourist industry. Tragic images of what crude oil does to wild-life are seared into the collective memories of the West after such disasters as the wreck of the Torrey Canyon and the spillage of crude from BP wells in the Gulf of Mexico. No oil is actually flowing from the Uganda wells yet and when we stopped to wait for the lion to move off the track in Murchison in November 2011, the activities of the Tulloch exploration programme were barely visible in the Park. How long this freedom from pollution will survive actual oil extraction remains to be seen.

In the afternoon, we took the boat trip up the Victoria Nile to the base of Murchison Falls, a beautiful stretch of river with interesting animals and birds along the way. We were surprised at how few crocodiles there were, just ones and twos, where there used to be dozens, large and small, hauled out onto the banks. Perhaps the rising river level has flooded the sand-banks they need for laying their eggs and forced them to move elsewhere. We landed on the rocks just below the Falls so that Peter and I could walk up the steep path. It is a stiff climb to the eastern edge of the Albertine Rift, the scarp over which the great Nile River falls with such thunderous power at Murchison, but the views of the falls are magnificent.

We had one other trip on the Nile, by boat from Paraa all the way down to the delta where the Victoria Nile slides into Lake Albert and turns south as the Albert Nile on its way through the Sudan to Egypt. With beautiful birds, some game and a lot of papyrus swamps, this peaceful setting was used for the filming the '*African Queen*'. While we were there, we went in search of another sighting of the elusive Shoe-billed Stork, that most supercilious of birds, but if they were there this time, they preferred to stay off-camera.

\*

In the afternoon, we crossed Pakwach Bridge into West Nile, bought a carved tortoise from the noisy children selling trinkets and set off up the fast tarmac road to Arua. Andrew Roberts describes this road in his guide-book as the only place in Uganda where you can you speed along a fine tarmac road lined by homes still predominately roofed with thatch instead of iron sheets. It is an unmistakeable indicator of poverty.

West Nile, the region I knew so well, seemed on the surface to have changed very little. Apart from the new tarmac road, it had, if anything, gone backwards since the 1960s. Commercial activity seemed limited to sacks of charcoal by the roadside and stalls selling small mangos, whereas before there had been fields of cotton and productive tobacco barns. The villages had some brick buildings and iron roofs but nothing compared to the affluence of towns and villages around Mbarara in the west of Uganda. West Nile was still the land of wide open spaces, great skies and extremely friendly people which we had grown to like and think of as home forty years ago. I was still drawn back by the sense of being right on the backbone of Africa at the heart of a huge continent between the great rivers of the Congo and the Nile.

If rural West Nile had hardly changed, the town of Arua was very different. It had become a bustling, busy place, probably three times the size it was when we first knew it. There were new buildings going up everywhere. If Pakwach, Nebbi and the rural areas looked very poor, Arua looked thriving. There were tarmac roads, several supermarkets, banks, filling stations and the biggest market in Northern Uganda.

For much of the 1990s, and up to 2005, NGOs and Aid Agencies were the big players in the Arua economy. They had the expert personnel, the resources and the transport. Their clear focus was supporting refugees, mainly the Lugbara and Kakwa families who had fled to Congo when the UNLA swept through West Nile. These people needed help and the NGOs supplied it. But as the people came back to West Nile, most Lugbara and Kakwa remained very poor. The more enterprising amongst them saw another benefit in an NGO occupation of their town. Western Aid experts needed housing. The market for rented accommodation in Arua had never known such a boom. Enterprising locals built houses to rent to NGOs. From the funds raised, they built bigger and better houses. NGOs also needed local individuals with appropriate skills to help administer their Aid programmes, drivers, translators, and office personnel. That was how John Ondoma got a job with SIL and it paid better than being the Headmaster of the largest secondary school in the district!

While the Lord's Resistance Army, Kony's rebels, were still terrorising much of the Acholi and Langi areas of Northern Uganda, right up to 2005, much of the supply traffic for the South Sudan and the Congo passed through Arua. The town continued to be the logistic centre for every sort of economic activity from food aid for refugees to building supplies for the development of infra-structure in both countries. The Arua route still serves Yei and the extreme south-west of the new republic of South Sudan and it remains the main highway into north-east Congo.

From all this building development, Arua now has a feature novel to us, plenty of hotel accommodation of a standard acceptable to Western travellers much of it in the houses that were built to rent to NGOs. We found our en-suite rooms (called self-contained in Uganda) at USh 53,000/- a night bed and breakfast (about US$20) at the Slumberland Hotel. We met up with John Ondoma there and found that a friendship which had started thirty years before was still as strong as ever. It was very good to see him. Peter discovered to his delight that UK Premiership football could be watched live on Saturdays on wide screen TV in the Slumberland garden. What was impossible in England was readily available in the remotest corner of Uganda. The hotel served passable steak and chips and, protected by DEET mosquito repellent, it was even possible to keep the voracious insects at bay before they took the edge off the pleasure of the evening.

Sunday morning saw us exploring the town, finding that the Chawdas, the Asian family who in the 1970s had owned the biggest general store, the bus company and most of the lorries running goods down to Kampala, had sold up and left. They had survived right through the worst of the Amin years and were one of the few families to have their Uganda citizenship respected when nearly all the other Asians had been expelled. The Chawdas made sure that they were useful to Amin's cronies and also to those who ran West Nile during the Obote II years. Joy Grindey told the story of a visit to Chawda's shop in the 1980s when she noticed that the almost empty shelves still had bottles of whisky on them.

'We have been short of many things,' Mr Chawda told her, 'but we have never been short of whisky.'

We found the Mvara School site on the edge of the town, now behind a wire fence with a gate and a sleeping watch man. He woke up when I cautiously enquired if we might have a look around and explained that I had been a teacher there. He took us to the Head's house and waited for the current Head to be summoned by one of his relatives. He recognised me not only as a former teacher but his own Science Teacher at the school in 1971! He was happy for us to look around the school but warned us that nothing had been done to carry out any repairs.

'We are not given money for repairs,' he said with a note of resigned despair.

That was all too clear. The whole site had an air of dereliction, far worse than it had been in 1997 when the Wymondham party were visitors. The rain-water tanks which we had helped to install were still in partial use, although their brick cladding had split from top to bottom. In any case, there was now less need for rain-water harvesting. Water was being pumped from a bore hole into the main water tower when the electric power was on.

The classrooms were still bare shells and the boys' dormitories a nightmare of crammed-in metal beds, rubbish and little else. It was uncared for, scruffy and depressing, and yet over a thousand young people, boys and girls, still received their secondary education here up to A level standard. The girls' dormitories, named in memory of Margaret Lloyd, looked a little better, surrounded by flowering shrubs and with panes of glass in most of the windows – perhaps the girls cared more about their surroundings than the boys did. We found the staff house where I had lived next to the McCulloughs and where we would have lived, newly married, if we had not been moved to Kampala. It too was a mess and we moved quickly on. Even the great fig tree at the back had been cut down and burnt for firewood.

I called back at the Head's house to thank him for allowing us to visit the school.

'I am pleased that you are still interested in this place,' he said. 'I may be coming to the reunion at the Slumberland, if I have the time.'

'Do you know if many from your time as a student here are coming?'

'There will some, but not very many and some will not come. Do you remember the student called Onzi, who was accused of being a ring-leader of the school strike when you were here, the boy who had to leave the school? He is now the commander of a thousand rebel soldiers in the bush in the Central African Republic far to the north-west. Once bad, always bad,' he said with a wry smile.

The Kony rebels had been driven out of Uganda in 2005 into the neighboring Garamba forests of the Congo. From there, the combined efforts of the Ugandan, Southern Sudanese and Congolese armies had driven them further north and west into the CAR where Onzi and his soldiers were still bringing fear and death to the village people of that impoverished African state. The most recent effort to find and capture Kony himself has come from a video programme posted on the Web by an American journalist who had seen the horrors of Achloliland for himself. The video 'Kony 2012' rapidly 'went viral', achieving more than seventy five million 'hits' when it was first posted on the Web and yet Kony remains at large.

John and Kezzy Ondoma and Peter Haden, Arua 2011

We had been asked to meet John Ondoma at the English Service at St Philip's Church in the town, so we went to join hundreds of worshippers at what was a very happy occasion. John was preaching at all three services, in English, in Lugbara and in English again. The singing was lively, the service moved along and the sermon was a very practical account of forgiveness in marriage. We were asked to bring our greetings from England and I told the congregation that we had heard that a man called Ondoma was preaching in Arua. I had heard him preach in England and had come all this way to hear him again – they loved it! The service was an Anglican communion in which all shared and to my surprise, the priest who helped to celebrate the Eucharist was a young woman, a Madi girl from Moyo who had been appointed two years before. Women in West Nile had come a long way in the forty years we had been away. John invited us to join him and Kezzy at their smart home not far from the church, and we had lunch together. Peter was introduced to *enya* with stewed goat, chicken in ground nut sauce and an interesting dish of fried grass-hoppers and mushy peas. Peter afterwards declared that if I could get away with an objection to onions, he was opting for an aversion to grass-hoppers

That evening, we gathered at the Slumberland for the great Reunion Party, over twenty former students and staff, from the 1960s and 1990s. We sat around long tables, chewed chicken and goat, drank sodas, and renewed friendships.

Dick Nyai was there, one of the young teachers we had worked with at Mvara. He became the MP for West Nile and had travelled all over the world on Parliamentary business. He was instrumental in saving the people of the District from further bloodshed by persuading them not to fight when Museveni's forces reached Pakwach. He was not well, suffering from HIV/AIDS and kept alive by anti-retroviral drugs, but still the same Dick. We met many former students and colleagues, including those who had come to Wymondham in 1998. All the teachers in the party had shared some of the aggression which John had faced when they got back from England and all were now teaching at other schools. The only person who sadly was not able to come was Silas Adrabo, the former colleague with whom I had clashed at Mvara and who rose to be a Headmaster at Rhino Camp on the banks of the Nile. It would have been good to see him again and to make our peace, but sadly, he was not well and sent his apologies for not being able to meet us.

Of the many others who were not there, our former colleague, George Okai, had died in the HIV/Aids epidemic of the 1980s and our Headmaster, Dison Aneco, had been killed in a violent conflict in Kampala. His widow Esther was now living in Goli. Dick Nyai gave a moving speech thanking us for coming and for keeping the people of West Nile in our hearts. I responded with the thought that West Nile had given me a rich experience of God's love, a wife and a wonderful three years and asked them to forgive the mistakes we had made. Peter thanked them for their hospitality and said that he had two reasons for being thankful to Uganda – his parents had become close there and the surgeon who helped his wife at the birth of their first child in London was Ugandan, trained at Makerere. Joy Unyuthi and Charles Dradria presented us with a long length of *kitenge* cloth to take home for Jenny to turn into a dress and a shirt, and our guests made their way home after a lovely evening.

Driving north the next day, with John and Kezzy, we first visited Ojapi, the Lugbara village at the foot of Liru Mountain where he had been born in the late 1940s and where they still have a house and *shamba*. His old primary school was also still there, tidy and well-cared for. Murals decorated the walls with everything from the map of Africa to the digestive system of a goat! The Ondomas' village was similarly well-kept, but was also a sad place as it was here that remnants of Amin's soldiers had attacked and killed John's father and younger brother in 1982. We later heard that three weeks after our visit, John and Kezzy had arranged a memorial service for his parents and his brother at Ojapi. The Bishop of Madi/West Nile led the service in the open air and two thousand people came to give thanks for the lives of his parents and his brother. At last, they could bring to a close this very sad chapter of their lives.

From Ojapi, we drove into Koboko town, now the centre of a new District with a smart new Headquarters where Kezzy worked as the District Community Development Officer. She proudly introduced us to her District Council Chairman and showed us her smart new office. She was responsible for all the community development activity in this most remote corner of Uganda by the Congo and Sudan borders. It struck me that Kezzy, a Madi from Inde, led a team of graduate area managers from all the peoples of West Nile to serve the Kakwa people of Koboko. This showed so clearly how West Nile had become a small Ugandan United Nations. From her offices, Kezzy took us into the market at Koboko where village people from all over the area bring their spare food crops, vegetables and fruit, eggs and palm oil in Pepsi bottles to sell for a few shillings. Also on sale were piles of the fried grasshoppers we had met at lunch and crude rock salt which looked more rock than salt but which Kezzy said was good enough for cooking.

There were many stalls selling second-hand clothes and plastic shoes. Right at the back of the market, a group of women were using treadle sewing machines to make shorts and skirts. In the 1960s, every Asian owned *duka* in Arua had a 'tailor' working with a similar machine and making most of the clothes which people used. Now it seemed that most Ugandans wore cheap used clothing, collected in America and Europe by charity shops, bailed up and shipped to East Africa by the ton, and sold in the huge Owino market in Kampala. From there, the clothes were distributed to the markets of Uganda, except the most remote, like Koboko. A country which once had a thriving cotton growing and ginning industry supplying the weaving mills of Jinja and exporting 'Jinja Cotton' fabric all over East Africa was now reduced to recycling the discarded clothing of the Western World.

Several of the women in the market had another item for sale piled up on the concrete floor, bundles of a green leafed plant which I did not recognise.

'That's *marungi*,' Kezzy explained. 'The women grow it as a cash-crop and sell bundles of the leaves in the market. They make quite a good living from it but many people are against it.'

'Why?' I asked.

'Because they think it is a drug which is harmful. In Ethiopia and Somalia, it's called *khat* and many people chew the leaves. They say that it gives them energy and helps them to work, but I think that they also get a good feeling from it – making them feel a bit 'high'. It's a good crop for women to grow because the bushes do well without much fertilizer or watering and they can easily carry a few bundles of leaves into market with their crops. It has to be sold 'fresh' so there is no point in sending it out of the area.'

John explained that the Church was against the growing of *marungi* because they say that it is harmful and can cause addiction. I later discovered that khat can be bought in London as selling it in the UK is not illegal, although in the USA and much of Europe it is a banned substance. How hard it is to earn a living in a country as poor as Uganda! The cash crops you can grow, like coffee and tea, are very expensive to get to market in the West. Those crops you may be tempted to grow and sell locally, like *marungi* and *tobacco*, are frowned on by the Church and bad for your health.

On our way back to Arua, we called in at the village called Wandi, in Terego County, not far from West Nile's other peak, Mt Wati. It was to this village that I had been invited in 1969 to stay overnight with the Pastor, Canon Enoka Yada, and to preach at their Easter Service in 1969. His successor as Rural Dean welcomed us to his home and gave us tea. He then explained that he held a second job as Deputy Headmaster of the village primary school. Only by doing two jobs, could he earn enough money to survive and to send his children to school. We sat in his front room, drank his tea and nibbled some 'cakes' served as always by a kneeling daughter of the house.

Peter had to fly back to UK the following morning so he set off for the airport to catch the Eagle Air flight back to Entebbe. He sent me a text a few hours later to say that he was somewhat surprised that Eagle Air had flown him to Yei in South Sudan to pick up other passengers, but eventually they all got down to Entebbe and he got back to London. Eagle Airways has maintained a vital link for Arua through the years when road transport was dangerous and difficult. Whether there will continue be a market for its flights, now that travelling to Kampala by road is so much easier, remains to be seen. With the opening up of flights to Yei and Juba in the Sothern Sudan, perhaps Arua will simply become the first stop in an Entebbe-Juba service.

Meanwhile, John and I made a courtesy call on Bishop Joel Obetia of the Madi-West Nile Diocese at Mvara, still the Headquarters of the Anglican Church in Arua. The Bishop was very welcoming and told me all about their new UK links. The Winchester Diocese had encouraged each of their Deaneries to establish links with a Diocese of the Church of Uganda. Madi/West Nile's link was with Andover Deanery. It was interesting to see that West Nile is now closely linked with the CMS (Church Missionary Society) while still having some links with AIM. This brings Madi/West Nile in line with all the other diocese of the Church of Uganda.

Paul's Letter to the Corinthians reminded his readers: 'I planted, Apollos watered, but God gave the increase.' Almost a hundred years ago, the first AIM missionaries came to West Nile from their work in the Congo. Like Paul, their prime focus was to plant Christ centred churches amongst the Lugbara, Alur, Okebu, Kakwa and Madi peoples. This they did and now the Church of Uganda and the CMS are 'watering' that seed. God has given a wonderful increase in Christians throughout the area and the church is still growing.

Bishop Obetia and other clergy had visited Andover Deanery earlier in the year and were looking forward to welcoming a party from the UK in 2012. He also talked about the need for the church to change its attitude to business, from thinking of it simply as an evil to be shunned to actively supporting the business community as much as they can. Now that the NGOs have mostly moved out of West Nile up into the South Sudan, the only way that development and prosperity was going to come to the area was through business activity. I could not but help think about the issues raised by the 'Occupy' camp then spread outside St Paul's Cathedral in the heart of the City of London. 'What would Jesus have done?' was splashed all over our television screens as the clergy of St Paul's struggled with their response to this situation. Should they welcome the protesters, effectively siding with the 'poor' against the vested interests of the City of London? Or should they insist that the camp be moved as a health and safety risk and an affront to good order? I also thought of the experience of a friend whose UK church runs the village Post Office and turned the church hall into an upmarket coffee/tea shop for the village. Business activity and the church have to find ways of working together for good.

This focus on business development has also brought a new form of Aid to Uganda, business advice through the Church. In Arua while we were there, staying with us at the Slumberland Hotel, itself a thriving Ugandan owned business, were new 'missionaries'. Two were from the UK Pentecostal Church and one was an American Episcopalian (Anglican). All were offering business advice. The American had spent his working life as a consultant with Boston Consulting, advising multinational corporations on their investment strategies and development plans. Now semi-retired, he was in Arua to hold a series of small business seminars with the full support of the pro-business Bishop of Madi/West Nile. An enthusiastic member of our reunion party who had been a teacher at Mvara Secondary School had come to the seminars for advice about a honey business. It seemed that there was a good market for West Nile honey in the south of Uganda and there were bee-keepers around Arua who could each supply small amounts of honey. But collecting the honey, processing and packing it and getting it to Kampala had not yet been organised.

Neither my former student, nor the friend with whom he planned to go into business, kept bees or knew anything about honey but they were thinking of setting up a honey business together. They needed advice about partnerships and contracts, about how to raise small amounts of capital for honey-processing equipment, how to market their product effectively and how to reinvest to help their business to grow. We left them earnestly listening to the patient advice of one who had come to West Nile because he believed his Christian faith led him to use his secular skills to support the Church in

Uganda. Strong churches need lay business people to develop a strong local economy and provide support for the church, not from 'outside' but from West Nile itself.

Slowly but surely, small business enterprises were lifting people in West Nile and all over Uganda out of extreme poverty, just as they have in other poor countries such a Bangladesh, the home of the Grameen Bank's Micro-financing initiative. The first of the United Nations Millennium Development Goal (MDG) is 'to eradicate extreme poverty and hunger, initially by halving the percentage of people whose income is less than one dollar a day, between 1990 and 2015'. In Uganda overall, by 2009, this indicator of poverty had fallen to 29% of the adult population. In Arua and Gulu Districts, it remained much higher but it was falling. And yet in the same year, 2009, Uganda received US$ 1.79 billion in 'official development assistance' i.e. Aid. Where did it all go, if not to the very poor? Some would say that it went into the pockets of the already rich.

\*

John Ondoma and I walked along the road through what had once been the Mvara Mission station, past the houses where the Coles, the Vollars, the Maclures and others used to live, now all well kept and occupied by Ugandan clergy. The Bishop lived in what was Margaret Lloyd's house, and at the end of the road, the church had built a huge new Cathedral to replace the Old Emanuel, now gently rusting away by the Arua road. The new structure was complete and inside there were chairs but very little decoration. I wondered how it had been possible for a church whose village pastors were so poor could find the resources to build and maintain such an impressive building. Perhaps that was the wrong question. How could the people of the church take their place in the modern world, even in Arua, without such a building, when the Catholics had built their own cathedral to the west of the town?

\*

From Arua the road south runs to Eruba, where a branch to the west took us towards the Congo border. Halfway down, a sign welcomed visitors to Ushindi Secondary School, the Christian private school set up by the Ondomas, Joy Unyuthi, the Martins, the Asikis and others when John lost his job at Mvara in 1998/9. The school has flourished and by the time of our visit had two hundred and twenty boys and girls including an Arts 6th Form. The projection was that when more classrooms and dormitories become available, the O level years would become double stream with at least four hundred and eighty students and A level classes would grow to over two hundred students.

The Uganda Education Standards Agency visited private schools throughout the country in 2011 and placed Ushindi SS 12th out of 2000 schools. This is a triumph of faith over adversity as the school has only existed for eight years and was only set up by the commitment and energy of the original eight families. Such recognition of success is vital to the school's future in the highly competitive world of West Nile schools where primary leaving pupils have an open choice of secondary school. The best schools can attract the best P7 leavers and thus get even better results at the equivalent of O and A level.

I was impressed with what we saw at Ushindi Secondary School. It looked well cared for and John has incorporated ideas from Wymondham, including staff flats attached to the dormitories. This was a novelty for Ugandan boarding schools where staff supervision of boarders was normally much closer to the old English public school system of 'leaving it to the prefects' for overnight control. At Ushindi, these flats were for teaching staff who accepted boarding duties. They called them 'Matrons' for the girls and 'Patrons' for the boys, an interesting new term. Their role was actually closer to UK Housemistresses and Housemasters. Although the site lacked mains electricity and was too far from any mains supply to be linked up, a German NGO had been approached for funding for the installation of more effective solar power. They have drawn up a scheme and will install what they can afford in stages, year by year.

Water was provided by an on-site borehole and large storage tanks for harvesting rain water from the roofs of the boys' and girls' dormitories. This meant that students could collect what water they needed and use the cubicles attached to their dormitories for privacy while 'showering' with a plastic mug, using a minimum of water very efficiently. They had similar arrangements for their own laundry and places to use a charcoal iron – all skills that Ugandan young people learn early in life. All sanitation was by 'long-drop' closets, requiring no running water and kept clean by regular washing down with a bucket of water. They may not be as comfortable as Western flushing toilets, but they are eminently sustainable. John

Ondoma was pleased to hear that organisations like the National Trust now install composting toilets where they need public toilets and have no mains water supply.

Ushindi's next major need is for a science laboratory as, without this, A level work in the sciences cannot be sanctioned by the Government. The school site is large (about ten hectares) and there is potential for agricultural activity, not just teaching agriculture, actually doing it. We were shown round by the keen young staff and then given a lunch of roasted chicken pieces and livers, chapattis and banana with sodas, all very hospitable. They clearly hoped to get teaching staff and resources for development from UK and American sources, and I promised to help in whatever ways I could. They were considering applying for some government grant aid as the fee income did not allow the payment of comparable salaries to those paid in government schools. Having worked with a Dutch school and a Dutch NGO, they knew of the arrangement in that country by which church schools could receive grant aid from central government for teaching staff costs, while retaining their church school status. For the moment, the Ushindi Governors have to raise capital to cover all building costs so any future development will be a challenge. In my discussions with John about the future of Ushindi, we explored the possibility of setting up a UK Trust as the Friends of the Ushindi Schools to raise some funds to support development of both the secondary and the primary schools. Any profit generated by the sales of this book in any edition will go to that trust.

\*

Sadly, I had to say farewell to John and Joy at Ushindi, but my visit had been a wonderful reunion and I had one last visit to make in West Nile. We drove back down to Nebbi and up the *murram* road to Goli to try to see Esther Aneco. Once there, high on the ridge and just before the Congo border, I bumped into other friends, Stephen and David Kasamba. They were there with a group of students from Kampala to support a local Scripture Union Children's mission. They are the sons of Canon Lusania Kasamba, one time Chaplain at Mvara and later at Makerere University. Jenny and I had met him and his sons on one of our visits to Uganda in the 1990s. Meeting them again at Goli reminded me that the last time I had been there, in the late 1960s, I had gone to support a Scripture Union conference in the same school! It was good to see that God has blessed this work and that Scripture Union is actively supporting school Christian groups all over Uganda

Sadly, I learnt that Esther Aneco was ill and in Nebbi hospital so I could not see her. The Goli Diocese Guest House offered comfortable beds and nets, adequate washing facilities and long-drop latrines, but nothing more. We enquired where we could get something to eat and were advised to try the neighbouring village of Paidha where there was said to be a 'hotel' which offered meals. When we got there, we found that the Sky Lux hotel offered chips and fried meat of unknown origin. The chips were very good. The place was full of Congolese truck drivers bringing goods back and forth across the border. When we got back to the Goli guest house, there was no light as well as no food, so we went to bed early.

Next morning, we got up without breakfast and drove down to Nebbi hoping to find a cup of coffee and some sweet bananas, but we were too early. Nowhere was open. So we drove on to Pakwach and picked up a packet of biscuits and some water which had to last us all the way to Kampala. I then had one night at the Lake Victoria Hotel in Entebbe, and just enough time to visit the Botanical Gardens by *boda-boda* (motorbike taxi) and the Wildlife Rescue Centre's small zoo. A lone shoe-billed stork, which had been saved as a chick and brought to Entebbe, was finishing its days in splendid isolation.

Before catching my flight home, I met up with Sam Turyagyenda again at the hotel, resplendent in his Brigadier's uniform. He told me that he had been chairing an investigation into an air-traffic accident. No-one had been killed or injured but one of the Air Force's new Russian SU-30MK fast jets had crash landed at Entebbe. It seemed that landing gear had not been lowered in time and the investigation was trying to establish blame – the Russian instructor or the Ugandan pilot. What interested me particularly was the thought that when Idi Amin had gone to Israel and to Britain for funds to buy jet fighters, both had turned him down. Now Uganda had the funds to buy fast jets off the shelf. Now that the nearby regimes of Ethiopia, Eritrea and the Sudan had fast jets, the Uganda military leaders could make the case that they too should have them. Was not national defence the first priority of all good goverments even if there was little obvious benefit to the rural poor?

Sam was keen for me to come back to Uganda in 2012 as in that year Uganda will be 50, he will be 60 and I will be 70 – we shall have to see. Then it was back to the Airport for the midnight BA flight to Heathrow and an end to two weeks of wonderful reunion.

## 6.2 'May God uphold thee'

What does the future hold for the people of West Nile and Uganda? Their National Anthem encourages them to leave it in the hand of God but, meanwhile, it remains in the hands of President Museveni and his NRM government. Over the past twenty six years since they came to power, no-one can doubt that Uganda has made huge advances. Many areas of the country look more affluent today, although not all are yet the 'land of milk and honey' of Museveni's western towns and villages. Museveni's NRM introduced a form of grass-roots democracy which has survived. It is not the parliamentary democracy the British tried to leave behind, but it has become the norm for generations of Ugandans. He won elections for the Presidency in 1996, 2001 and 2006. When multi-party politics was re-introduced in 2004, the country's first multi-party elections for twenty five years were generally accepted by the international community as having been free and fair. Museveni won. When he had served the maximum period allowed by the constitution as President, he promptly changed the law governing terms of office and stood again in 2011. He won again.

As President, Museveni has demonstrated a pragmatism unusual in African leaders. He encouraged Asian businessmen to return to Uganda and rebuild their economic assets. He won strong support from the Baganda when he recognised the son of Kabaka Mutesa II, Ronald Mutebi, as the 36th Kabaka of Buganda. In Bunyoro and in Toro, the traditional monarchies have also been restored. All this also ensures that the rich cultural heritage of the Bantu peoples is recognised and respected. There is a growing opposition to the NRM government led by Museveni's rival Kizza Besigye[3] and there is an increasing willingness amongst Ugandans to challenge Museveni's rule. Although Uganda has a Human Rights Commission, not everyone is convinced that this is effective in protecting citizens from abuse of power. But most Ugandans still enjoy an improving standard of living. They have an Army which does not oppress them and a Police Force which upholds the law.

Yet, in the north of Uganda, including West Nile, the daily lives of ordinary people have only improved very slowly and, amongst many Ugandans, there is still a fear of going to West Nile. Our Matoke Tours driver was prepared to drive us to Arua but very worried about his car. He made sure that each night it was parked safely in a locked compound. Many still see this part of Uganda as a land of violence and backwardness. Up in the distant corner of a relatively poor nation, next to two even poorer states, South Sudan and the Democratic Republic of the Congo, West Nile is still remote and undeveloped.

Over the last fifty years, the people of West Nile have become experts in survival and have offered to their neighbours the hope of peace and security. In the 1960s, violence in the Congo forced many to flee from that country. They found refuge in Uganda's West Nile. In the Sudan, war between the Islamic Government and southern rebel groups, from the Anyanya of the 1950s to 1970s to the SPLA of the 1980s right up to 2005, drove many to become refugees. Tens of thousands of Southern Sudanese came to the haven of Uganda's West Nile. Today, West Nile is still an island of peace in a sea of troubles.

To the west, the Congo has been, for more than a century, the Conradian 'heart of darkness' of Central Africa. When Joseph Kony's LRA were driven out of the Garamba area of the Congo into the Central African Republic, they left a region in north-eastern Congo which continued to be chaotic. After the appalling 1994 Ruanda genocide, Hutu refugees fled into the Congo. Many of them had been involved in the killing of Ruandan Tutsis and they formed Hutu militias which the Ruandan Army pursued. That Army occupied significant areas of Congolese territory, effectively controlling large parts of Kivu province, yet the killing continued.

Meanwhile, north of this Ruanda controlled area, the Uganda Army established a similar zone. Originally there to chase out the LRA, the Ugandans have been accused of using this as a pretext to profit from the rich mineral deposits in the area and especially the mining of Coltan. The Democratic Republic of the Congo is said to have 80% of the world's reserves of this mineral, an ore of Columbium (now known as Niobium) and Tantalum, hence Col-Tan. Since the 1990s, the world price of Coltan has rocketed. It is the source of an essential component of the capacitors used in micro-circuits. These drive electronic devices such as cell-phones, laptops, play stations and many others for which the world has an insatiable hunger.

In the Congo, Coltan is mined in small scale diggings and 'panned' with water, much as gold was in the Californian gold rush of the 19th century. Small scale workings of this type are intrinsically dangerous and often involve child labour. Because the product is so valuable and because there is little security in the area, armed gangs, including the LRA, can steal it to finance their murderous activities. Trade in 'Coltan' in the Congo is the equivalent of trade in 'blood diamonds' elsewhere in Africa, a trade of savagery and death.

To add to the misery of this part of the DRC, ethnic conflicts have arisen close to the border with West Nile. Two neighboring people, the Lendu and the Hema have been in conflict over land. Both Hema and Lendu have crossed into Uganda as refugees from the fighting. Both sides in this conflict, which is in some ways similar to the Hutu/Tutsi conflict in Ruanda, have accused the Uganda Government of taking sides. The Uganda People's Defence Force has occupied the area for some years, claiming to be a 'peace force' but they are also accused of recruiting and training militias for both sides. Leaders of both sides have been captured and indicted by the ICC for 'crimes against humanity', accused of recruiting and employing child soldiers in their militias.

To the north of West Nile, the new republic of the South Sudan clings to the hope of a peaceful future. With the bombers of the Khartoum government still killing Sudanese villagers and their President threatening open war against the upstart leaders of the South, the chances of a long-term peace still seem slight.

To the east of West Nile, the land of the Acholi is still only slowly recovering from the long war against Kony. Surrounded by all these conflicts, West Nile remains a haven of peace, for the moment.

\*

Back in England, I came across two very thought-provoking arguments about the role of the West in countries like Uganda. The first was from the writing of the economist Dambisa Moyo[4] of Zambia. She has argued that Africa is poor not because it has received too little Aid from the rich countries of the West, but too much. African countries are poor because of Aid. How can good things, such as Aid to build infrastructure, Aid to combat starvation, Aid to develop education and improve health care, ultimately cause an extension of poverty?

For a country like Uganda, much of the blame has been put on the succession of wars and bad leaders that the country has suffered. But poor governments and the destructive nature of civil war are not the only reasons and there is a growing movement which blames the concept of Aid itself.

Reading Moyo's ideas made me think about the Ugandan examples I knew. For example, overseas aid funds have been wasted on unused or inappropriate infrastructure. One of the best investments through Aid for West Nile District was the Pakwach Bridge, built by Mowlems in the 1960s through a loan from ODM. The bridge is a life line for West Nile, helping the remote district to keep in touch with the rest of the country. Running across that bridge, there is also a railway. The tracks are still there. They run from the Acholi side up to Gulu, then down through the eastern towns of Lira, Soroti, Mbale and Tororo, to link up with the railway into Kenya and on to the Indian Ocean at Mombasa. As far as I know, that railway has never been used to capacity and some parts have not been used at all. During all the years that the LRA terrorised the north of Uganda, the railway could not be used. But even in the years before 1985 and after 2005, few trains ran and no trains crossed over Pakwach Bridge on a regular basis. The railway was funded by aid, loans which the people of Uganda have had to pay back, and what might have provided West Nile with an effective transport link through to Mombasa seems never to have been of benefit to the people.

We were ourselves part of the British Aid programme to Uganda as employees of the Uganda Government in partnership with the Ministry of Overseas Development. Our new buildings, and all the equipment which went into them, were financed by a World Bank loan. They were not gifts. They had to be paid for in terms of interest and principal repayment. They were, by Ugandan standards, very expensive and much of what was provided was inappropriate. They certainly took far too long to build and even the jelly moulds for the Domestic Science flat had to be paid for.

By 1990, Uganda was paying 46% of its earnings from exports and services on servicing its debts, and it was not alone. The sheer impossibility of sustaining Third World debt payments led to the view in the mid and late 1990s that debt relief was the only solution. This led to the Jubilee Debt Campaign, supported by many Church lobbying groups. Huge sums of Third World debt were written down or written off – and one consequence was that countries could then afford to take out new loans and more debt!

A lot of the Aid provided for Uganda has been very appropriate. In the 1960s and 1970s, the focus of much Western Aid to Uganda was on building infrastructure, roads, bridges, airports and hydro-electric dams. Uganda received help to dam the Nile at Owen Falls to generate the power which stimulated the industrial development around Jinja but little benefit was felt in the rural areas of the north. There are still no power lines running across the Nile into West Nile.

More recently, the Museveni government has proposed that the Karuma Falls, where the main road between Masindi and Gulu crosses the Nile, should be the site for a new hydro-electric scheme. There are very few people to displace and little current tourism interest. 2016 has been suggested as a completion date for the project. It remains to be seen whether the capital investment for this scheme is ever raised and whether power from Karuma ever reaches West Nile. Meanwhile, the two major towns of Nebbi and Arua, struggle with inadequate power and numerous 'outages'. On some evenings during our stay at the Slumberland in Arua, power was only on for a brief two hours and off for much of the day.

Yet there has been a plan to provide consistent power to these towns for over a decade. The West Nile Electrification Company was set up specifically to ensure that the District had power, with a hydro plant on the Nyagak River in the south of Nebbi District, not far from the Congo border, and, as back-up, a new diesel generator in Arua. Yet 'outages' in Arua have become more frequent. This became a national scandal when Arua Hospital, the regional medical centre for a great slice of Northern Uganda, Southern Sudan and North-east Congo, was forced to use its own small back-up generator, consuming its three months allocation of funding for diesel in just one month. Operations were cancelled, patients were suffering and some fatalities were blamed on the power problem. Meanwhile, the private Church hospital at Kuluva, where a German missionary engineer had installed a small but reliable hydro scheme in the late 1980s, continues to function without power problems.

Without power, the people will continue to use wood to cook their *enya* and to make charcoal, the only significant source of cash sales along the Pakwach–Arua road. Without power, the deforestation of West Nile will accelerate. But even when the oil does start to flow and the power from Karuma does come across the Nile, will the two honey-marketing entrepreneurs in Arua benefit? The reality is that they have invested time and energy on a low-tech small-business project which needs neither oil nor electic power to start generating an income. But if it is to develop, the first essential will be a reliable source of power and the sad fact is that it will be a long time before the benefits of the oil extraction from the Albert Rift trickle back to the villages of West Nile and probably even longer before hydro-electric schemes provide reliable power for businesses in Arua.

Even with oil, the experience of other oil-rich African countries is not all encouraging. Becoming oil rich can have a human cost, as the people of Libya, Nigeria and the Sudan know all too well, and there are other players outside East Africa who are becoming increasingly interested. Since the coming to power of the NRM, co-operation with China has increased. Museveni had visited China four times and Chinese leaders from three generations had visited Uganda. From 1993 to 2011, nearly three hundred Chinese companies have opened businesses in Uganda, creating nearly thirty thousand jobs for Ugandans. The Chinese built the National Stadium, new Government Offices and the Naguru Uganda-China Friendship Hospital. Chinese credit will fund the new US$ 350 million highway from Entebbe International Airport to Kampala. Under-pinning all this investment was the new farm-down agreement with Tullow and a Chinese oil company for oil exploration and extraction.

China was and is Uganda's friend and the Chinese are interested in railways. Perhaps they will find a use for the rusting line from Pakwach to the Kenya border. If they do, what will West Nile produce to send down the line? Perhaps they will extend it west over the Congo border to bring the rich mineral resources of that area down to the sea, or a short way to the north from Pakwach to take the oil from the Rhino Camp field to the same destination?

*

Aid can have unforeseen negative consequences. Food-aid saves lives as was shown in the late 1980s and 1990s, when the appalling pictures of starving Ethiopians prompted Bob Geldof's 1985 Live Aid concert, but most of that food-aid came from the grain surplus stock-piled in Europe and America to ensure that world grain prices remained high. Free food for starving Africans saves lives but it can also put local African food growers out of business.

It is not just food. A Hollywood movie-star hears of African children dying from malaria for want of a mosquito-proof bed-net. She takes out her cheque book and donates thousands of dollars to send bed-nets to Africa. Other rich celebrities join her and soon millions of dollars worth of bed-nets are bought in America and shipped to Africa. African children are saved from mosquitoes, but African bed-net manufacturers go out of business. No-one wants to buy a bed-net when the Aid agency give them out for free.

Every Ugandan town in the 1960s had local tailors who earned a living making school uniforms and clothing for local people. In 2011, the only tailors left were in the most remote corner of West Nile, in Koboko, the only place sufficiently far from Kampala to be beyond the distribution of second-hand clothing recycled from charity shops in the West.

So what giving has been helpful? Moyo points out that in Israel and in India very large sums of hard currency are received from ex-patriate Jews and Indians living in the affluent West. Uganda has an overseas *diaspora* of relatively affluent individuals. Around 150,000 of them live in the UK and Europe and many more in the USA. Just as the overseas communities of Jews and Indians regularly send large sums of money back to Israel and India, so the community of Ugandans overseas are being encouraged to remit funds back to Uganda. Many already do so, making significant contributions to school fees and other costs born by their extended family members still living at home. Some have already been encouraged to contribute as 'alumni' to support the work of their former schools. With the increased ease of money transfer using mobile phones, now used and owned by millions all over East Africa, such money transfers will become more common, bringing significant amounts of hard currency funds into Uganda's economy and helping development.

Uganda earns significant revenue from tourism. We were part of that process, paying to see the Bwindi gorillas and the Murchison Falls lions. Uganda has worked hard to develop the full range of tourist opportunites from those for the very rich to those within the budget of back-packers. There are the high-end offers for those with the money to spend. There are thrills for the adventurous, attracted by the white waters of the Nile and the high peaks of the Ruwenzoris. There are quieter opportunities for those who come to find the rarest birds amongst the Albertine endemics.

Increasingly, visitors come from Europe, America, Japan and all over the world to discover the variety of cultures in Uganda at traditional village level. Across the country, there are communities who have developed cultural experiences to share with visitors. An enterprising women's group at Boomu, on the way to Murchison Park from Masindi, have set up a 'village' of traditional but relatively comfortable huts where visitors can stay. All of these developments provide local employment, offer activities (basket-weaving, pot making, food preparation, cooking, music, dancing) with the local people and accommodation in simple 'bandas' (or grass roofed huts). They aim to bring visitors into friendly contact with local people.

West Nile has little or no obvious tourism potential. There are no mountains, apart from the small isolated peaks of Liru, Wati and Otzi. There are no gorillas, chimpanzees, lions, herds of elephants, no river rapids for white-water adventure or city museums. The bird life is interesting but it is not a 'birding hotspot'. It is a long way from Kampala. Yet West Nile does have some advantages: a remote and exotic location close to Congo and Sudan, good fast tarmac road access from Murchison Park in two hours to Arua and to Kampala in a day, a regular daily air service from Entebbe via Eagle Air and a good range of inexpensive hotel accommodation in Arua town.

It is also an area where 'development' has not yet swept away village life, where five distinct peoples are still proud of their traditions, crafts, music and languages. So is there perhaps a unique opportunity to actually celebrate West Nile's cultural heritage and to share it with visitors? Visitors who do get as far as Arua have described the extreme friendliness of the people. Is there a place for some sort of 'West Nile Heritage Centre' somewhere on church land or school land where visitors could experience these features and bring income into the church or school, just as other communities have developed such opportunities in other parts of Uganda? There seems to be a hunger for cultural experience amongst overseas visitors to Uganda. Uganda has an incredibly hospitable Church community. Just as earlier generations of Western Christians planted the gospel in the minds of Uganda's people, is there an opportunity to plant the gospel in the minds of visitors to Uganda and to share in fellowship with Christians from all over the world?

\*

The second thought-provoking argument about development in Africa and the role of the Christian Church in countries like Uganda, was from an unexpected source. The former UK MP, writer and atheist, Matthew Parris had written in December 2008 in the Times newspaper about what he saw as the enormous contribution that Christian evangelism makes in Africa. For him, this was sharply distinct from the work of secular NGOs, government projects and international aid efforts. 'In Africa', he wrote, 'Christianity changes people's hearts. It brings a spiritual transformation. The rebirth is real. The change is good.'

Parris had gone back to Africa, where he was brought up, to see the work of a small water charity in Malawi. But while he was there, he had to admit that one of his assumptions about the work of the Christian church, that the good works were what really mattered, the healing of the sick, the teaching of the young, was just wrong. It was the faith that made the difference, not just the works, the faith he found in Africans working on the water project and the faith he had found as a child in the lives of missionaries. He had to admit that the Christians were different. Their hearts were changed and it was for the good.

He applies this judgement to 'Africa', not just Malawi, and many would endorse it for Uganda, where the Christian church has helped many to find hope and a purpose in life, particularly young people. Uganda has the highest proportion of young people in her population of any country in the world and it will get higher still as Ugandan women continue to have large families. This provides all parts of Ugandan society, including the Christian Churches, with major challenges and that is why the work of organisations like Scripture Union in schools and colleges is so important.

Discovering that this work, which had taken me to schools all over West Nile in the 1970s, is continuing and flourishing was, for me, very good news. The conference at Goli which we came across was encouraging young people to find a faith of their own, to find a clear purpose in life and gave them firm foundations for living and hope for the future.

The Governors of Ushindi Secondary School have caught this vision for the young people of Uganda. Their school is already being used as an ideal base for residential Christian youth conferences, opportunities for the Christian leaders of tomorrow's Uganda to learn together how to organise meetings, influence young people and bring about positive change. During school holidays, for at least fourteen weeks of the year, the school buildings and facilities can host Scripture Union and Church conferences specifically for young people.

Such gatherings also provide Uganda's young people with opportunities to develop music and drama for worship and to establish links with the world-wide Church. Now that the Madi-West Nile Diocese of the Church of Uganda has developed a link with the Andover Deanery of the Winchester Diocese in UK, there is a wonderful opportunity to access the world-wide Anglican network. Such use of school premises has one other major benefit. It generates significant income for the school and encourages a very business-like approach to school finances.

*

At the height of the Second World War, a young Swiss Christian left home to set up a new community in France. His aim was to help people suffering as a result of the war. He settled in the small village of Taizé and his community became a place of safety for those in need, of any faith or none. They lived simply with no running water and basic food. Each made a life-long commitment to live together under the 'Rule of Taizé' which they have followed ever since. 'Taizé' has also come to mean a distictive way of praising God, a form of worship now used all over the world and right across the Christian denominations.

A recent meeting of young people in Kampala, led by a Taizé brother, discussed the need for greater communion and trust in their country, trust between men and women, trust between young people and adults, trust between different religious groups, what it means to live in communion, in a place of peace. Brother Alois, the Prior of Taizé, has written: 'As we continue the pilgrimage of trust on earth that brings together young people from many countries, we understand more and more deeply this reality: all humanity forms a single family and God lives within every human being without exception.' Thousands of young people still come to Taizé each year to share in worship and fellowship.

There are many parallels between the experience of people in West Nile over the last fifty years and that of the founders of the Taizé community. The experience of suffering and of war, the need to live a simple life, the wish to find ways of praising God using music and words accessible to young people. West Nile is the only area of Uganda where five, at least, differing tribal groups have lived at peace with each other for generations, a Ugandan 'United Nations' of Alur, Lugbara, Madi, Kakwa and Okebu. Each has their own strong cultural and language traditions and exceptional music skills. Traditional craft skills of pot making, basket weaving and even iron working, are still found in the area. West Nile could offer a rich cultural experience to visitors to Uganda of any age. At Ushindi, members of the Christian Church in West Nile already offer a place where the youth of Uganda meet together to praise God, to welcome visitors from all over the world and to commit themselves to their country's future as they sing together:

> Oh, Uganda! May God uphold thee,
> We lay our future in thy hand.
> United, free, for liberty,
> Together we'll always stand.

**Notes**

**Part 1. Into West Nile**
1. Uganda, Kenya and Tanzania formed the East African Federation in the 1960s and agreed an Economic Community, including a common airline, East African Airways. When the Community ceased to exist in 1977, Amin's regime established Uganda Airlines. This was closed on economic grounds by the Museveni government in 2001 and the country now has no national carrier.
2. In the 1960s, British Overseas Aid to Uganda was administered by the Ministry of Overseas Development (ODM). British teachers were recruited by ODM and posted by the Ministry in each East African country to schools where there were appropriate vacancies.
3. The Africa Inland Mission (AIM) is a Protestant Interdenominational Faith Mission founded in 1895 by the American, Peter Cameron Scott. His missionary vision was to see Christ centred churches established from Mombasa on the Kenya coast to Lake Chad in the heart of Africa. In the 1960s, AIM had both American and British missionaries working with the local churches in Kenya, Uganda, Tanzania, Congo and adjacent countries. Today, as AIM International, the mission has over 900 people from the USA and the UK, South Africa, Australia, Canada, many European Countries, South Korea and other countries, all working at the invitation of the African Church in over twenty African countries. Their goal remains to see 'Christ-centred churches among all African people'.
4. The best account of the exploration and colonisation of East Africa is now Thomas Pakenham's *The Scramble for Africa* London: Abacus Edition 1992; pp 27-28 covers the Speke story.
5. Thomas Pakenham, *op. cit.* pp. 413-419
6. The World Heritage site at Kasubi Tombs, five km from central Kampala on the Hoima road, is both a burial place and an active religious centre for the Baganda people. Their Kabaka is the unquestioned symbol of the spiritual, political, and social state of the Buganda nation. As the burial ground for the previous four Kabakas, therefore, the Kasubi Tombs is a place where the Kabaka and others in Buganda's complex cultural hierarchy frequently carry out important centuries-old Ganda rituals. The great reed-thatched houses cover the tombs of four Kabaka's, from Muteesa I (1835-1884) to Muteesa II (1924 – 1969). Sadly, they were burnt down in March 2010 and have not yet been rebuilt.

7. *murram* is the orange laterite subsoil which is used over most of East Africa to make roads by scraping off the top soil and grading and rolling the *murram* to form a flat road surface.
8. Thomas Pakenham, *op. cit.* p. 77
9. Ugandan peoples are divided into the Southern Bantu, the Baganda, Banyoro, Bakiga and many others, the Northern and Eastern Nilotic, the Acholi, Lango and others, and the West Nile Sudanic people, the Lugbara, Madi, Okebu, and Kakwa. The Alur people of south-eastern West Nile are related to the Acholi, and the Kakwa in the north-east are linked to the Sudanic Bari tribes. In general terms, the Bantu tribes are shorter in stature, less black and have more complex language patterns than their northern neighbours.
10. *cassava* (or manioc) is the root-crop originally from South America which was introduced to Uganda at the time of World War II as a famine crop as it can survive when the rains fail. The West Nile people at first disliked this tasteless substitute for their beloved millet, but some was grown and cassava flour is now used mixed with millet to produce *enya*, the boiled millet/cassava staple still eaten by most Lugbara families.
11. There is a good brief biography of Amin in Andrew Roberts' revision of Philip Briggs' *Bradt Uganda Guide* 6th Edition 2010 pp. 22-23.
12. Phares Mutibwa's book *Uganda since Independence* Kampala: Fountain Press 1992 covers the political changes from 1962 to the coming of the NRM in a thorough and very readable way.
13. The Crusader Union was started by Albert Kestin in 1900 when he set up a Bible Class for boys with the aim of 'advancing Christ's kingdom amongst public and private school boys with the promotion of all that leads to Christian manliness'. Since then, 'Crusaders' has developed to include boys and girls from all Christian denominations and none. It has always been a missionary movement to unite and equip leaders to reach non-Christian youth with the exciting and life-changing truths of biblical Christianity. The movement changed its name to 'Urban Saints' in 2007 and now has 800 groups serving about 20,000 young people.
14. Lay preachers in the Methodist Church are called Local Preachers. They take services in their own local 'circuit' of churches and can transfer to any other circuit.
15. 'Confirmation' in the Church of England is the formal acceptance into full membership of the Church, conducted by a Bishop with the laying on of hands.
16. At that time, if you had a science or maths degree it was possible to go into teaching without a formal Education qualification, but we both recognised that not completing a PGCE would limit our future options.
17. Silvanus Wani and John Dronyi were the first two West Nile Ugandans to be ordained in 1942. Both became leaders of the Church of Uganda in West Nile. For an account of the growth of the church, see John Dobson's *Daybreak in West Nile* London: Africa Inland Mission 1964

**Part 2. Mission and School**
1. Margaret Lloyd wrote of the spread of the East African Revival in the West Nile district in *Wedge of Light* privately published in 1979 and distributed by AIM.
2. All Ugandan schools, primary and secondary, had uniforms at that time, usually brightly coloured cotton dresses for the girls and shirts and shorts for the boys, made by local tailors from Jinja cotton.

3. Professor E.B.Castle *Growing up in East Africa* London: Oxford University Press 1966 pp. 255-256
4. David Gill *Men Without Evenings* London: Chatto and Windus 1966 p 38. Gill taught at Nyakasura High School, Fort Portal, Uganda in the early 1960s.
5. Dr Milton Obote *Policy Proposals for Uganda's Educational Needs* Uganda Education Association, Kampala 1969
6. The Acholi poet Okot p'Bitek wrote the *Song of Lawino* in Acholi while at Makerere in 1964. His poems were published in English translation by East African Educational Publishers, Nairobi 1989. These lines are from p. 99
7. The story of the development of Kuluva Hospital and the work of the Williams brothers is told in Dick Anderson's *We were like grasshoppers* Nottingham: Crossway Books 1994 pp. 109-114
8. OICCU is the Oxford Inter-Collegiate Christian Union, the student Christian organisation which arranged the John Stott mission while I was a student at St Catherine's College.
9. CPAS is the Church Pastoral Aid Society, the evangelical Anglican organisation which sponsors parishes and which arranged the holidays for children I helped to lead as a student.

**Part 3 Living and working in Arua**
1. The Rt. Hon. Winston Spencer Churchill MP *My African Journey* Toronto: William Briggs 1909 p.182 (reprinted in the Hardpress Classic Series)
2. John Middleton *The Lugbara of Uganda* Belmont, California: Wadsworth Group 2002 2nd Edition pp. 21-29
3. Weatherhead had a profound effect on Lugbara culture yet they retained a respect and admiration for him as 'a little man but very fierce, and walked among us without guns'. (Middleton *op.cit.* p4.)
4. Stuart Cole and I used to enjoy the occasional game of squash in this court, once we had swept out the cow-dung and avoided the holes in the floor!
5. 'Matilda' on account of her alarming tendency to waltz uncontrollably on wet *murram* roads.
6. Nakivubu Announcment by Dr Milton Obote on 1 May 1970
7. Okot p'Bitek *op. cit.* p. 80

**Part 4. Surviving Idi Amin**
1. Judith Listowel *Amin* Dublin: IUP books 1973 p 70
2. Alan Moorehead *The White Nile* London: Penguin Books 1963 p 302
3. Winston Churchill *op.cit.* pp. 175-177
4. The article was published: Haden, John *Okebu Iron Smelting* The Uganda Journal, **34**, 2 (1970) pp.163-170
5. Manzoor Mogdal *Idi Amin – Lion of Africa* Milton Keynes: Authorhouse, 2010
6. see Iain Grahame *Amin and Uganda* St Albans:Granada Publishing, 1980

**Part 5. Enduring Obote II and the coming of the NRM**
1. There is a good account of this period in Mutibwa *op.cit.* pp. 125-138
2. An account of the Ringili massacre is recorded in the papers of Laura Belle Barr at
www2.wheaton.edu/bgc/archives/trans/481t02.htm

3. Richard Dowden's *Africa – altered states, ordinary miracles* London: Portobello Books, 2008 is a very good account of many of Africa's current challenges including two chapters on Uganda
4. Yoweri Kaguta Museveni *Sowing the Mustard Seed* Oxford: Macmillan Eduction, 1997 This autobiography by Uganda's President has a detailed account of all the NRM fighting but includes very little about the suffering of the Baganda people in the Luwero Triangle
5. Carlos Rodriguez Soto *Tall Grass* Kampala: Fountain Publishers, 2009 gives a very good account of the efforts of this Catholic Priest and others to negotiate with the LRA to bring peace
6. The AIM base in Uganda at this time was at Lubowa just south of Kampala on the Entebbe Road, where the McCulloughs and others provided a guest house, 'Matoke Lodge', for visitors

**Part 6. God does not make blunders**
1. RFU has a website at www.rhinofund.org/
2. Tullow Oil has details of the Uganda exploration and finds to date at www.tullowoil.com/
3. Kizza Besigwe's sibling, Olive Lobusingye, a Kampala surgeon, has written a critique of President Museveni's regime in her *The Correct Line* Milton Keynes: AuthorHouse UK 2010, quoting widely from Museveni's own writing.
4. Dambisa Moyo *Dead Aid* London: Penguin Books 2009

## Acknowledgements

Our book would not have been possible without the help of many friends, particularly Janet Burden who read the first draft and encouraged us, Gordon McCollough who drew the three maps, Trevor Gazard who checked the text and many others in Uganda and elsewhere. The text includes sections of John Ondoma's unpublished 'Cost of Radical Faith'. All the photographs are by John Haden, apart from the images on pages 202, 216 and 230 which are in the public domain. Our wives, Jenny Haden, and Kezzy Ondoma, have supported our efforts and aided our memories with their own recollections, copies of letters and photographs to help us to tell the story. For their patience when our interest in writing about West Nile has got in the way of doing other jobs, for all the times we have shared together and for their love for us and our families, thank you, *a wa di fo*!

## People Index
Ablewhite, Stan 121
Adrabo, Silas 48,66,153-158 293
Amin, Idi (General and President) 21- 23,39,144,166,168,187,201-
203,204-206,280
Anderson, Dr Dick and Joan 132
Aneco, Dison and Esther 47,64,70,79,141,145,154,190, 197,293,300

Avinya, Milcah and Baranaba 172,229-230
Baker, Sir Samuel 19
Barr, Laura Belle 146,219
Binaisa, Godfrey (President) 219
Brown, Colin 198,202
Chawda, Brothers 105,290
Childs, Peter and Margaret, 149,198,211
Churchill, Winston 110,191
Cole, Stuart and May 44,87,91,127
Corker, Lance 148,158
Dow, Andrew (Canon) 56,109,112
Drati, Bishop Enock 269
Gazard, Trevor 149
Grindey, Joy 84,146,211,213,290
Inwood, Richard (Bishop) 55,65,110,121
Kasamba, Canon Lusania 300
Kerunen, Guy 46,143
Kony, Joseph 240,241
Lakwena, Alice 240
Lloyd, Margaret 21,23,41,44,70,146-148,292
Lule, Jusuf (President) 204
Luwum, Janani (Archbishop) 39,211,280
Maclure, Canon Seton and Peggy 33-34,40-43,55-57,81,114,218,230
McCullough, Grace and Gordon 12,56,58,120,124,132,241-243,251,258
Martin, John (Rev) 56,100,110-112.121
Martin, Simon and Claire 230,2251
Moghal, Manzoor 205
Moore, Maureen 211
Moore, Wendy 148,180,199
Murchison, Sir Roderick 19
Museveni, President Yoweri Kaguta 39,207,219,224,225-228,239,280,301
Mutesa II, Kabaka 22,131,170
Nyai, Dick 161,283
Obetia, Bishop Joel 296
Obote, Milton (President) 15,21-23,78,130,131,144,156 218,224,279

Okello, Tito (President) 214
Ondoma, John and Kezzy 37,87-91,215-218,228-232, 234-239,246,248,250,252, 258,260-276,292-300
Orombi, Henry (Archbishop) 88,268
Pasha, Emin 191-192
Peck, Jenny (Haden) 23,27, 128,132,150,164,172,174,176 179,180,184,186,190,193,194 -196,198,201,203,204,232-233,242-246
Peck, Philip and Mary 23
Pope Paul VI 126
Read, David 177,179
Sentamu, John (Archbishop) 213
Speke, John 14
Stephenson, Lewis and Angela 13-14,16-21,41,44,48, 69,86,157,158-160,163-164, 172-175,176-177,186
Turyagyenda, Samuel (Brigadier) 201,207-208,214, 224,259,262,280,301
Vollor, Canon and Mrs 35,44
Walker, Christine 52
Wani, Silvanus (Archbishop) 39-41,55,174,212
Watford, Janet (Burden) 128-129,134
Williams, Dr Peter 23,80,82
Williams, Dr Ted 23,80,82, 108- 110,176,22075, 76,101,109,167,210